T0311382

Biomimetics for Architecture

Learning from Nature

Jan Knippers, Ulrich Schmid,
Thomas Speck (Eds.)

Biomimetics for Architecture

Learning from Nature

Birkhäuser Basel

Preface

Jan Knippers / Thomas Speck

For as long as people have been building, they have taken nature as their example. However, until now the correspondences were mostly of an esthetic nature, and only forms and ornaments were transferred. Only today is it possible—mainly based on the transition to digital methods that has occurred in all scientific disciplines—to accomplish transfers at the functional level and thereby to arrive at a new definition of the relationship between nature, architecture, and technology.
The dialog between the disciplines begins with the quantitative analysis of the functionally important characteristics of biological systems. These are abstracted into models that represent the characteristics of interest and the construction principles they are based on. The models serve as the basis for carrying out an engineering-based simulation of functional morphology and are the starting point for the transfer into technology. Conversely, as part of the process of reverse biomimetics, these simulation results also provide the impetus for further basic research and deepen our understanding of biological systems.
The objective of the projects presented in this book is to investigate the possibilities of biomimetic transfer on the basis of very diverse questions, and thereby to make a contribution to establishing biomimetics as an independent scientific discipline.
The main focus is on the analysis of construction principles in biology and on their transfer to architecture and structural engineering. Using the processes of mutation, recombination, and selection, living creatures can adapt during evolution to continually changing environmental conditions. The efficient use of natural resources is of key importance and provides a huge selection advantage. With the help of genetically controlled self-organization processes, living creatures form hierarchically organized, finely tuned, and highly differentiated materials, materials systems and structures that enable complex and heavily interrelated functions whilst at the same time fulfilling requirements, some of which may be contradictory. Living creatures consist of a small number of mostly lightweight chemical elements and basic molecular components that, as a rule, are derived from the organisms' direct surroundings and are built up under environmental pressure and temperature. In this, biological structures are fundamentally different from most technical constructions. The latter are made up of a large variety of materials and consist of individual components, which most of the time have no or very little cross-linking. They are independent of each other

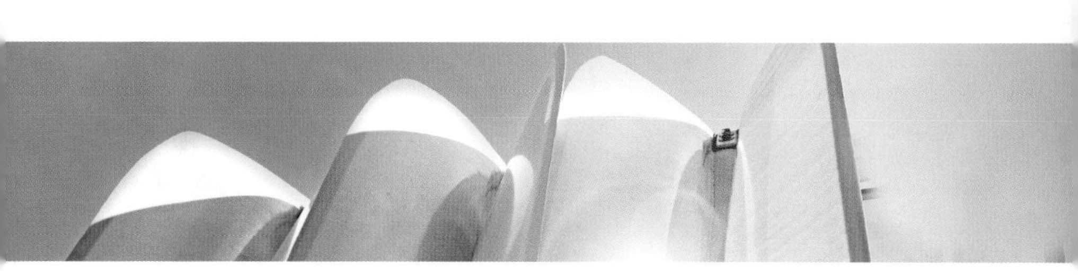

and usually optimized to satisfy just one or a few specific functions. Most of the materials used in building construction are produced using methods with a high energy input (i.e., under high pressure and at high temperatures). Functional principles such as adaptability, multifunctionality, or hierarchical structuring have, up until now, been used only to a very limited extent in technology and particularly in building construction, even though they are ubiquitous in nature.

The starting point of the research activities presented here was the development of Flectofin, a biomimetic facade shading system. The idea for the principle of the opening mechanism came from the violet landing perch of the flower of the bird-of-paradise plant *(Strelitzia reginae)*. Under the weight of birds landing on the perch this bends downwards, thereby releasing the pollen, which becomes attached to the birds' legs. When these birds visit the next bird-of-paradise flower, the pollen is transferred to its stigma, thus ensuring pollination. The elastic change in form of the perch when it opens is of interest for mechanics and is the starting point for the biomimetic transfer. It is performed without any localized joints and, in the case of the bird-of-paradise flower, can be repeated over three thousand times in an identical way without incurring any damage or functional blocks. This joint-free elastic opening-and-closing principle was transferred to the Flectofin biomimetic facade shading system, which, as a result, is low in maintenance and extremely robust, but also as esthetically appealing as the biological example.

This book summarizes the results of the TRR141 trans-regional Collaborative Research Centre "Biological Design and Integrative Structures" that attracted sponsorship from the German Research Foundation in the years 2014 to 2019. This joint effort by architects, engineers, and natural scientists from the Universities of Stuttgart, Freiburg, and Tübingen was inspired by the idea that progress in the arts, the sciences, and technology would in future come about more at the interfaces of the disciplines rather than within the disciplines themselves. This book is a slightly revised and extended version of the volume that was published on the occasion of the *Baubionik—Biologie beflügelt Architektur* exhibition that took place from October 2017 to May 2018 at the Natural History Museum in Stuttgart.

Why biomimetics?

Jan Knippers / Thomas Speck

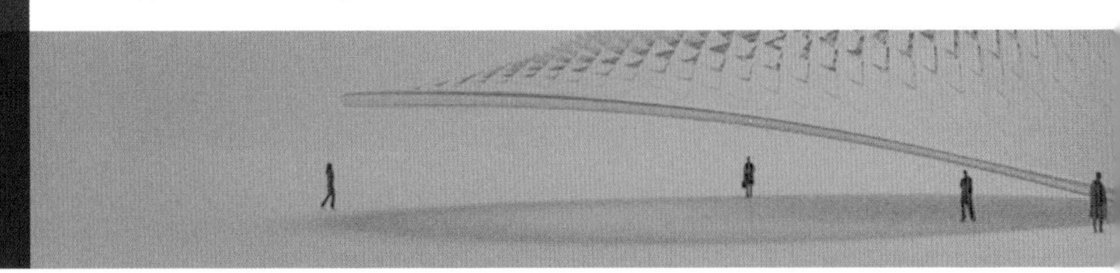

The warming of our planet and the increase in pollutants forces us to fundamentally review our relationship with nature if we do not want to destroy the foundations of life for future generations. In this context, construction and housing are of critical importance because, on the one hand, they are needed to satisfy basic human needs and, on the other, they are responsible for a significant proportion of the consumption of resources and of the emission of pollutants. Worldwide, 40 percent of the consumption of energy, 40 percent of the output of waste, and 30 percent of carbon dioxide emissions are due to global building activity.

If we want to provide adequate housing for the world's rapidly growing population, we have to drastically increase the output of our building activity over the next decades. In this scenario, the collapse of the Earth's ecosystem can only be prevented if we build in different ways, that is to say, more intelligently. This poses some key questions: How can houses be built using locally available and renewable raw materials, and how can these houses be disposed of at the end of their service life without creating waste? How can we live and work in our homes without consuming finite resources for heating and lighting and so on, and without producing waste? How can a building's envelope react to changing climatic conditions in the course of the day and the year, and thereby reduce energy demand? How can homes and offices be adapted to the ever-changing requirements of users so that they can be serviceable for as long as possible? For all of these questions we need solutions that are not technically highly sophisticated and hence prone to failure, but straightforward and robust, and ultimately we need economically viable solutions that can be adjusted to the possibilities and needs of the different countries and societies of our world.

These key requirements of the architecture of the future are fulfilled almost automatically in nature's own constructions. Fundamentally, all plant and animal structures rely on the use of solar energy. Natural constructions consist of few elementary basic components that are part of a closed material cycle. In this process, most of the substances and energies used are available in the immediate vicinity. Making efficient use of scarce resources is an evolutionary advantage. At the end of their lives, all living beings decay into their basic components, which then form the basis of life for other, new living beings, thus completing the circle of life.

Furthermore, natural constructions feature other characteristics that are important in architecture. They are robust;

that is, they can survive unforeseen events without being knocked off balance. When damage occurs, they are capable of repairing themselves. They can adjust to changing mechanical forces and climatic conditions, both during the course of the day, throughout the year, and during their entire lifetime—and beyond—in the course of subsequent generations in the context of evolutionary adaptation.

It is therefore worthwhile for architects and engineers to take a close look at natural constructions.

The step towards digital processes, which has taken place in all areas of science and technology over the last 25 years, has opened up new opportunities for exchange between biologists, architects, and engineers. Digital images of natural constructions, for example those generated using magnetic resonance tomography or (micro-)computer tomography, can be transferred directly to engineers' computer-based simulation models. In turn, these enable biologists—in a process referred to as reverse biomimetics—to gain a deeper insight into the function of biological structures while at the same time serving as the starting point for the implementation of biomimetic building elements with the help of computer-based production methods, such as 3D printing, which nowadays is cost-efficient and widely available.

Even though our technical means are still far from capable of transferring nature's constructions—which are the result of 3.8 billion years of evolution—in all their entirety and complexity into architecture, the study of these may show us new avenues beyond rigid and standardized principles of design and construction. Whether the endeavor will lead to a more sustainable architecture will have to be verified in each individual case.

In biomimetics, a distinction is made between two principal approaches, referred to as the bottom-up process of biomimetics (biology-push) and the top-down process of bionics (technology-pull). In reality, there are many transitions between these approaches, which is also apparent in the development of biomimetic buildings.

In the bottom-up process, biologists' discoveries—fundamental research in biology—are at the beginning of a biomimetic project ⌈1. The interesting biological structures and functions are analyzed quantitatively and investigated using methods that are frequently taken from physics, chemistry, or the engineering and material sciences, thus demonstrating the interdisciplinary character of biomimetics. In this phase of a biomimetic project, in addition to the biologists, there should be engineers, architects, and materials researchers involved for the purpose, among others, of assessing the relevance of the application of the investigated biological structures. The objective of the quantitative analysis of the context between form, structure, and function of the biological example is to understand the principle, that is, to obtain a basic understanding of a function that is of interest for a biomimetic implementation, and of the relevant structures. This provides the basis for the next phase, which is often the critical one for a biomimetic project, involving "the abstraction and detachment from the biological example." This step involves—detached from the actual biological role model—elaborating the concept for the development of the biomimetic product in greater detail. This concept is based on the fundamental physical and chemical principles governing the required function. In this phase of the project in particular, close cooperation between scientists from biology, architecture, and the engineering and materials sciences is very important, and a common language has to be developed for this purpose. During this phase, it is common for numeric simulations to take place, which make it possible to check and, in some instances, improve the quality of the abstractions produced prior to the creation of real demonstrators. This phase is followed by the technical implementation—the construction of demonstrators (in the researchers' laboratories) and prototypes (in the workshops of industry)—in which the biologists (most of the time) have only an advisory role. Once the prototypes have been tested successfully, the biomimetic developments can be deployed in building construction.

By contrast, at the beginning of a top-down process in biomimetics, engineers, materials scientists, architects, or representatives of industry, respectively, will ask a specific question with respect to a certain application ┌2. Initially, this technical question is analyzed in greater detail, and in this phase there will be cooperation between all representatives of the various science disciplines involved in the project. This stage is followed by a search for the best fitting role model in biology. In this project phase, referred to as the screening process, the objective is to find the biological concept generator that provides the best idea for the technical problem. Once promising working principles have been identified in the selected biological structures, they will be characterized quantitatively. At the end of this project phase, the working principle will be understood and—as in the bottom-up process—the next step will be abstraction and detachment from the biological role model. When this phase has been completed successfully, technical implementation and the construction of demonstrators and prototypes will follow. If these tests are successful, the biomimetic products are usable.

The investigations that are part of the abstraction and technical transfer in the bottom-up and top-down processes of biomimetics—for example, scaling from small to large or vice versa, or use of materials with other properties—and, in particular, the numeric simulations can also often be transferred to the biological role model that provided the source idea, thus leading to a better understanding of its structures. This procedure, referred to as reverse biomimetics, can—in addition to the acquisition of knowledge of biology—also be used to further deepen the understanding of the working principle involved, and thereby also additionally improve the processes of abstraction and technological implementation.

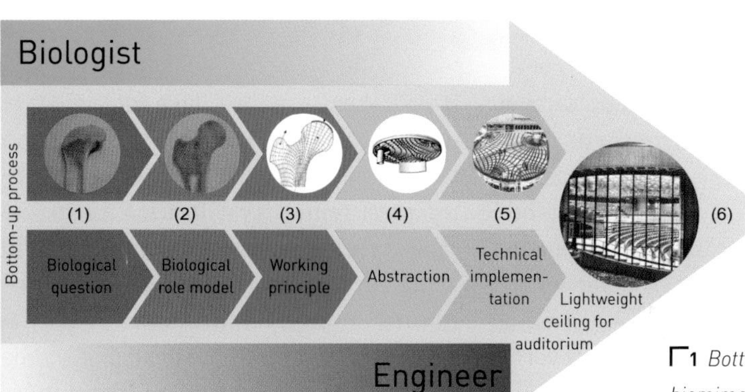

1 Bottom-up process in biomimetics (biology-push) using the example of the development of a biomimetic ceiling structure with reinforcing elements, as in the bone trabecula of the neck of the human femur

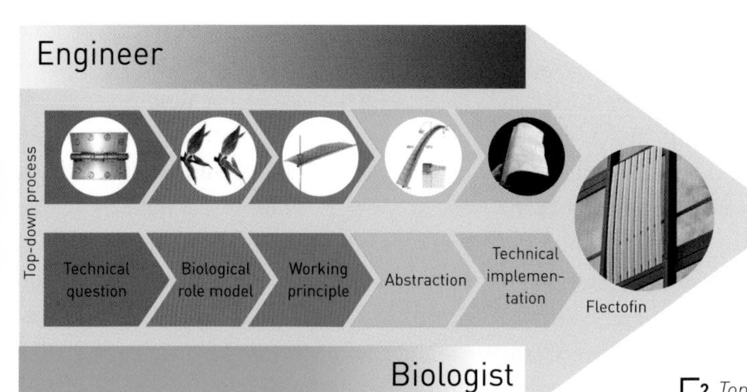

2 Top-down process in biomimetic using the example of the biomimetic Flectofin facade shading device, the development of which was inspired by the flower of the bird-of-paradise plant

EVERYTHING MOVES

Jan Knippers / Thomas Speck

Animals and plants move in order to take in nutrition, perform photosynthesis in the optimal way, protect themselves against danger, and adapt to changing weather conditions. Movement is indispensable for most species of animals and plants in order to ensure the survival of the individual and hence also the species.

Our houses, too, are faced with continually changing requirements. Not only are they subject to changes of light, temperature, sound, and humidity in the course of a day and throughout the year, but the needs of their users are also subject to change, both during the course of a single day and throughout the service life of the building. In spite of this, our houses are static and rigid constructs. The walls of houses are insulated for the coldest winter night in order to prevent the loss of energy in the form of heat. However, this also prevents the utilization of solar energy in the transition periods. How can we control and manage, on an ongoing basis, the entrance of daylight, thermal insulation, and the input of solar energy depending on user requirements and the position of the sun? Floors and walls are designed to bear the maximum expected structural load. However, the loadbearing capacity of the building structure is hardly ever used to its full extent. Would it be possible to create structures that avoid exposure to wind forces by deforming and/or react to higher loads by bracing?

A key objective of our research is to turn rigid and immobile houses into constructs that adapt to continually changing external conditions and internal user requirements through movement and deformation in the same way that biological systems do. Currently, however, architecture is far removed from that ideal. At present, the principles of adaptation and change are applied only in very elementary forms in architecture: roller blinds and facade shading devices, for example, or movable stages and stadium roofs. In most cases, mechanical principles are employed that date back hundreds of years. Typically, rigid elements are connected via rollers, joints, and hinges. These are prone to jamming and blocking, and require constant maintenance. Furthermore, in many cases, only the two extreme positions—open and closed—are structurally stable. All intermediate states must be passed through as quickly as possible in order to avoid instability, and are therefore not usable even if they would be functionally desirable to the users. Such systems are most often activated by external electrical or hydraulic motors that apply forces and movement to the system from the outside.

How much more elegant and movable are the biological systems! Many animals and

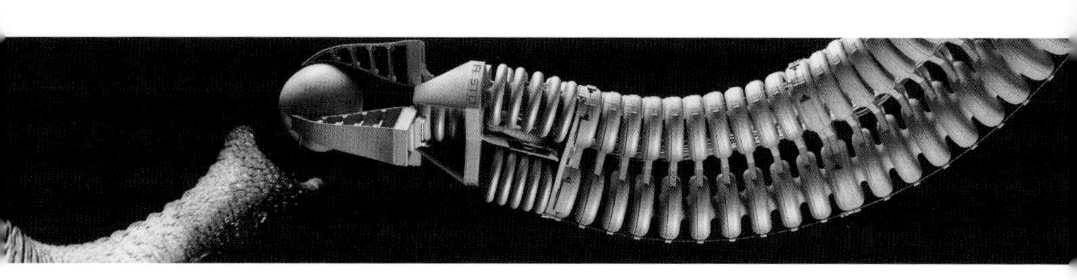

plants have responded to the challenge of movement with elastic deformation of linear or two-dimensional elements. This ensures a high degree of functional reliability even for geometrically complex movement processes. Impressive examples from the world of plants are the opening and closing processes of flowers, in which the petals, densely packed in the flower bud, unfold during flowering and sometimes later close again, or the unfolding of leaves measuring several square meters.
A further source of ideas are the changes that take place in the form of flowers, such as that occurring when pollinators visit a plant (e.g., birds landing on the "perch" of the bird-of-paradise flower p. 7). Another inspiration comes from the principle of movement of carnivorous plants, such as the Venus flytrap or the waterwheel plant p. 32.
In the animal kingdom, the folding principles of insect wings or the proboscises of bugs and mosquitoes are examples of how complex movement patterns can be achieved with differentiating stiffness of the materials and can be made possible with just a single type of material p. 22.
Furthermore, in the case of living beings the actuators (i.e. the drive elements) are frequently integrated into the material structure. Plant movements are often initiated by changes in the liquid pressure in the cells, the so-called hydrostatic or turgor pressure. Furthermore, movements in dead tissue, such as the scales of pinecones, can also be driven by drying and re-humidification processes in the dead material itself. Animals usually use muscle contraction to move. The muscles are connected to rigid elements (bones) via ligaments, and the bones in turn are linked via joints. This construction results in robust and long-lived systems with a minimized input of energy and material.
Even though these are development targets, which also apply to architecture and technology, comparable movable systems that rely on locally adjusted and changeable compliance of the materials and that are driven by integrated actuators are virtually unknown. Therefore, the objective of current investigations is to analyze the known biological principles in the plant and animal kingdom, to understand their working principles, to abstract them, and to transfer them to architecture and technology.

Plants in action

Olga Speck / Marco Caliaro / Anja Mader / Jan Knippers

Materials and structures adapt automatically when their environment changes. A dream? No. In living nature, this goes without saying. In particular, plants that are tied to their location have developed different adaptive mechanisms in the course of evolution and can therefore react to changes in environmental conditions. Often overlooked, but of special fascination, are plant movements, because these are accomplished without joints whose parts glide across each other or rub against each other and are therefore subject to wear. These adaptations and the underlying functional principles and structures are of great interest, both for a deeper understanding of the biological role model of plants and for the development of computer simulations as the basis for a later transfer to technology.

Adaptations to environmental changes

Plants are masters of adaptation

In contrast to animals, plants are firmly tied to their location. They cannot run away from drought, heat, or cold; neither can they hide behind other plants, stones, or animals when there is a storm. For this reason, for plants, long-, medium-, and short-term adaptations to environmental changes are particularly vital to survival. All adaptations that have developed in the course of 3.8 billion years of biological evolution are or were ultimately necessary for the survival of a species. However, plants can also react to environmental changes within years, hours, and even minutes. For example, trees form thicker growth rings and denser wood when they are exposed to high wind loads for long periods of time. Plant stems can lignify over the course of a summer so that they are able to carry their heavy fruit in the autumn. But plants can also wilt within minutes or hours, or rehydrate, depending on the availability of water.

Adaptive buildings

The numerous mechanisms that allow plants to react to changes in environmental conditions are of great interest for a transfer to technology in general and to buildings in particular. Biologists work together with structural engineers and architects in cooperation projects in order to fully understand the selected biological role models and to apply the underlying functional principles to so-called "adaptive buildings." Like plants, buildings are also tied to their location and have to cope with different climate conditions and user requirements; therefore, adaptable elements can be helpful. For example, adaptive building envelopes could control the amount of sunlight entering the building

⌜3 *Shading elements at the Thematic Pavilion, EXPO 2012, Yeosu, Korea. Design of a kinetic facade: SOMA Architecture, Vienna, and Knippers Helbig Advanced Engineering, Stuttgart.*

via the windows in order to prevent the building from heating up too much in the summer. For the development of adaptive facade shading elements, biologists and engineers took inspiration from nature ⌜3 and have developed elastically actuatable systems such as Flectofin ⌜2 and Flectofold ⌜27 (for the terms "to actuate/actuator," **p. 20**). Such structures work completely without joint- or hinge-like connections between several rigid components. Instead, the entire system becomes a single component, which deforms elastically. The omission of joints or hinges with moving parts reduces mechanical complexity, lessens friction, and hence also cuts down on wear and tear. The moving system becomes more robust and less prone to failure. There is almost no need for maintenance and care. In an ideal case, such systems are as flexible as possible during the movement in order to reduce the amount of energy required for the actuation that causes the movement. However, when they are exposed to wind and snow loads, they will become stiff. This adaptive stiffness is also modeled by plants, because the stiffness of plants changes in accordance with water content.

Bauplans of plants

Living plant cells are under pressure

Water is a vital factor for plants. It plays an important role in their metabolism, but it is also critical to the mechanical properties, in particular in herbaceous and non-woody plants. In trees and shrubs, mechanical stiffness and strength are primarily achieved by lignified tissues consisting of dead cells and fibers. Quite the opposite is the case in all non-woody stems, leaves, and flowers. In these, the structure and associated function of the living plant cells of the ground tissue is mainly responsible for the mechanical properties. Every living plant cell consists of a thin cell membrane that encloses the interior of the cell and a rigid external cell wall. The aqueous cell sap inside the cell stretches the surrounding membrane and exerts pressure on the surrounding rigid cell wall ┌4. This internal cell pressure (= turgor) can vary a great deal depending on the available water. Values of between 0.07 and 4 megapascal (= 0.7 and 40 bar) have been measured inside plant cells. As a comparison: the air pressure in a car tire is approximately 2.5 bar; an industrial high-pressure cleaning device works at approximately 100 bar. Technically speaking, each plant cell is therefore a small hydraulic system that can also function as a drive element (= actuator). In plants, the non-lignified cells form the ground tissue (parenchyma). When all cells of the ground tissue work together, it is possible to move entire plant organs.

Hydraulic plant movements

The effects of turgor changes in plant cells can be easily observed in herbaceous plants. When there is a shortage of water, the plant loses moisture through evaporation from the leaves. This loss of water causes the turgor to drop inside each cell. The immediate effect: the herbaceous plant wilts and its leaves and/or stems become limp. When the plant is watered again, the interior cell pressure increases due to the intake of water. Eventually, the interior of the cell is fully refilled, the cell membrane presses against the cell wall, and the plant becomes erect again. Using this "turgor system" enables some plant stems to develop astonishing forces, and

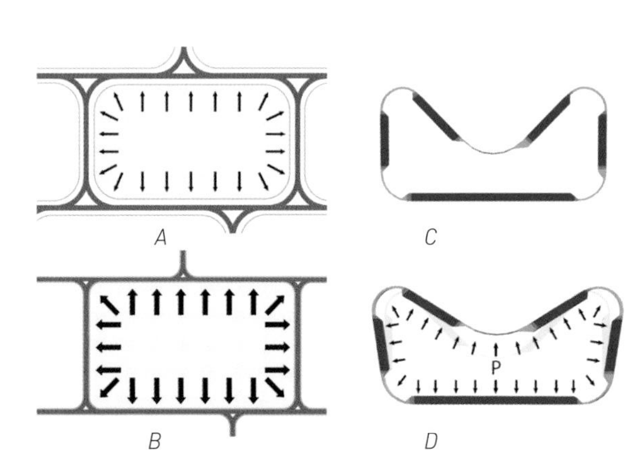

┌4 Schematic drawings of a plant cell (hydraulic) in wilted (A) and in turgescent (B) state. Finite element model of a technical cell (pneumatic) without (C) and with (D) increased internal pressure.

Γ5 *Comparison of "turgor system" and "ring of strengthening tissues" system of plants*

"Turgor system"		"Ring of strengthening tissues" system
Non-lignified ground tissue, few vascular bundles with fibers distributed across the entire cross-section, epidermis	**Structure**	*Distinct ring of lignified fibers and vascular tissues, very little non-lignified ground tissue, epidermis*
Stability achieved by living cells of the ground tissue that are filled more or less with aqueous cell sap and therefore are subjected to varying degrees of internal cell pressure (turgor)	**Mechanics**	*Permanently stable due tolignified dead cells of the ring of vascular and strengthening tissues*
Adaptation to short-term environmental changes, such as drought or sufficient availability of water	**Period**	*Adaptation over weeks and up to months in the course of individual development*
Short-term decrease (wilting) or increase (rehydration due to water intake) of the stiffness of the peduncle	**Effect**	*Long-term increase in stiffness over the lifetime due to increased formation of lignified vascular and strengthening tissue*
*Adaptation to different degrees of water availability can be repeatable (*Gerbera jamesonii *'Nuance') or non-repeatable (*Caladium bicolor *'Candyland').*	**Repeatability**	*The lignification of the tissue is irreversible. In contrast to bones, plants cannot remove or rebuild dead strengthening tissues.*

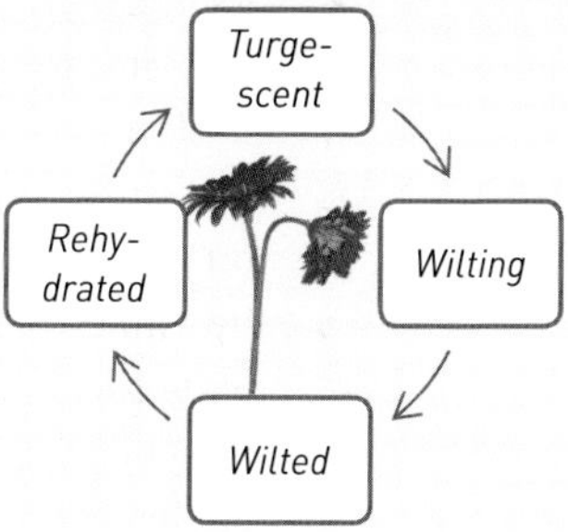

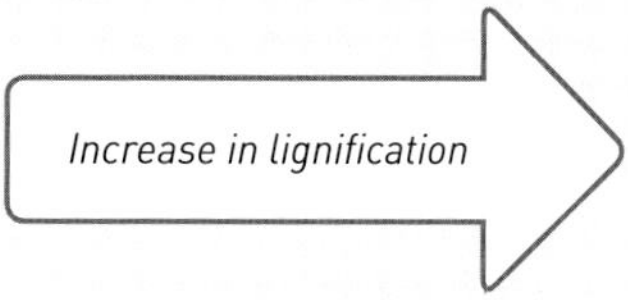

to lift not only their own weight but also heavy flowers and leaves against the force of gravity. Plant stems stabilized by a more or less wide ring of strengthening tissue react very little or not at all with a change of stiffness to a lack of water and remain unchanged stable Γ5.

When looking at thin sections of plant stems under a microscope, we see quite different three-dimensional arrangements of the various tissues, which can be organized both asymmetrically and symmetrically in cross-section. Plant cells with a special mechanical function are the so-called "motor cells" that can be found in the leaves of grasses from the Poaceae and Cyperaceae families, for example. These are particularly large non-lignified cells that are arranged in groups in the area of the epidermis. Opposite these cell groups are lignified tissues that serve as a counter bearing. In combination, they function

⌈6 *Microscopic cross-section of the leaf of blue sedge (Carex flacca) (A) and a schematic illustration of the tissue distribution (B). The lignified tissues shown in red in (B), together with the motor cells, function as a joint without gliding parts. When the turgor in the motor cells increases, the leaf opens; when the turgor drops, the leaf closes.*

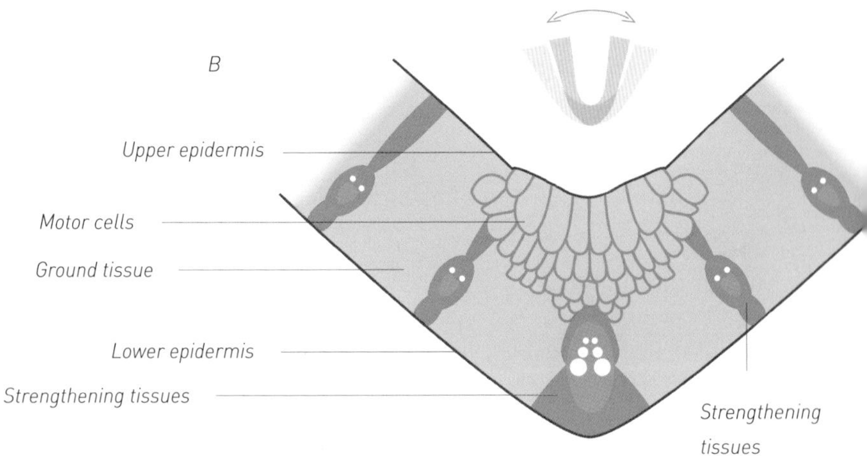

like a jointed connection, except without sliding parts such as those normally found in technical joints and hinges. When the motor cells are fully turgescent, the two halves of the leaf are open; when they are less turgescent, the leaf is closed **⌈6**.

From plant model to computer simulation

The objective of a cooperation project involving biologists, engineers, and architects is the development of buildings or building envelopes that are inspired by biology and can adapt to changing environmental conditions. In the first step, suitable model organisms are selected from a multitude of plants—biological role models that feature movement mechanisms without joints. The selected plant models are then investigated in detail, and data are collected on the external shape (for example, the diameter and length), on the internal structure (such as cell diameters, cell wall thicknesses, the distribution of different cell types), and on the mechanical properties (bending stiffness, damping property). Step by step, the multitude of detailed findings gained from the plant models are reduced to the data needed for a computer model **⌈7**. Then, with the help of computer simulation, it is possible to investigate, in different bauplans, the influence of the turgor on the stiffness of the plants. Also, it is possible to simulate various scenarios in the computer, such as artificial wilting or

Caladium bicolor *'Candyland' Heart of Jesus (petiole)*

Primula veris *'Cabrillo' Cowslip primrose (pedicel)*

Gerbera jamesonii *'Nuance' Barberton daisy (peduncle)*

Dianthus carthusianorum *Carthusian pink (pedicel)*

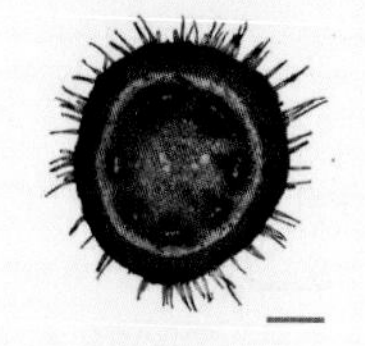

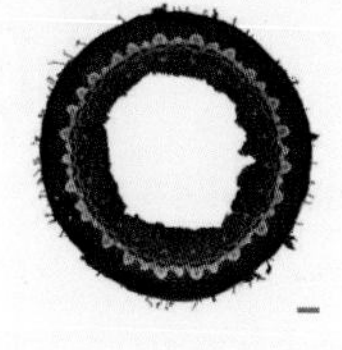

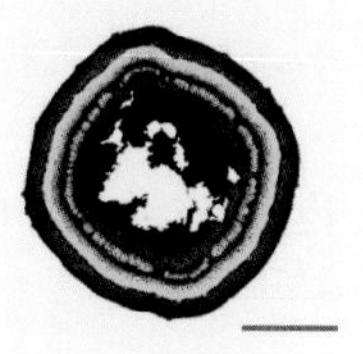

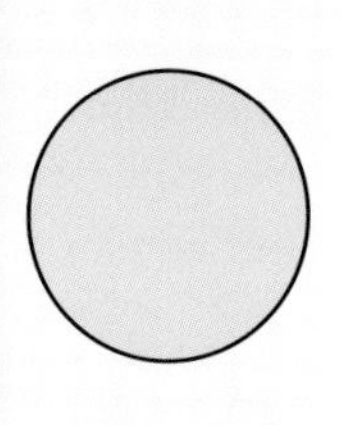

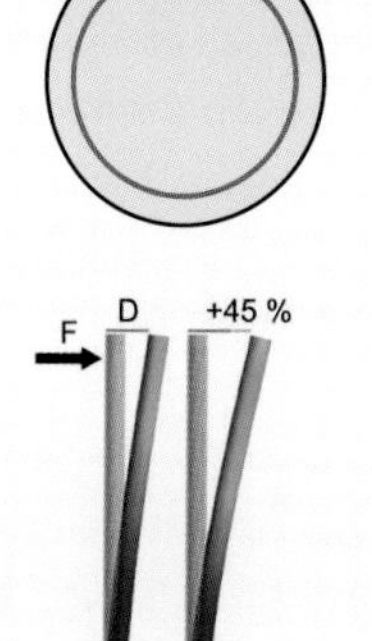

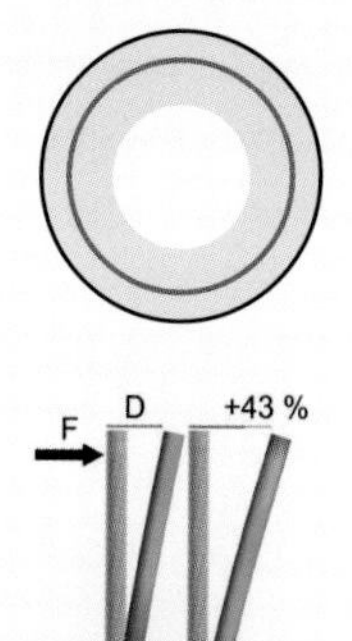

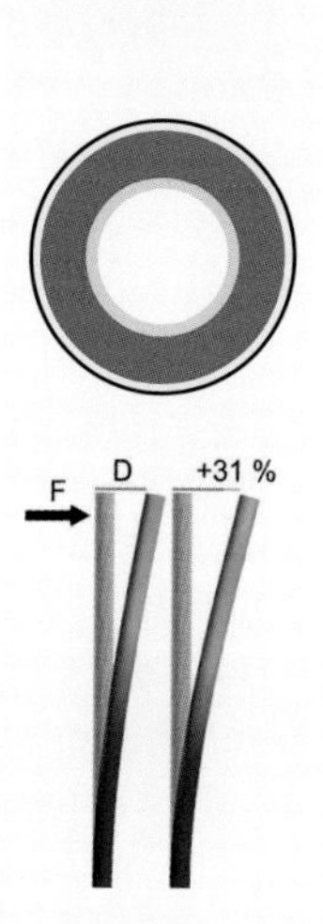

7 *From plant model to computer simulation. Plants have various bauplans, which can be used as a basis for computer models and, ultimately, for implementation in the form of biomimetic products. Top: microscope photographs of stained cross-sections of different plant stems (yellow-orange: lignified tissue; scale bar = 0.5 mm). Middle: schematic models to differentiate between various tissues (black: epidermis; blue: non-lignified ground tissue; red: lignified tissue). Bottom: results of computer simulations. What can be seen is the deformation (D) of the plant stem due to the horizontal force (F) at high turgor (left in each case) and the additional deformation in percent for a turgor reduced by 50% (right in each case). The color gradient from blue to red shows the horizontal deformation (blue: small deformation; red: large deformation).*

artificial watering. Such computer simulations are a basic prerequisite for the later transfer to technical applications and, conversely, can also help us to better understand the biological role model.

The simulations indicate that, with plants having a higher proportion of lignified strengthening tissue, the effect of turgor changes due to changes in the water content is smaller. If the turgor drops, the plants with a ring of strengthening tissues deform less when exposed to the same external force compared with plants consisting mainly of non-lignified, turgor-stabilized tissues. With the help of simulation, it is possible not only to show these relationships in visual form but also to quantify them.

Technical transfer

Pressure-dependent generation of movement

The above-explained plant movements rely on the help of motor cells, which are combined with counter bearings. When the cells take up water and thereby increase their internal pressure and volume, one side of the leaf is actively elongated. This causes the overall structure to bend. In the abstracted model of this functional principle, cells with a flexible exterior wall are applied to a stiffer material ⌜8.

When the cells are filled with compressed air, they behave like balloons: they try to adopt a round cross-section as this maximizes their volume. This means they become wider. As the lower area cannot expand in the same way, bending occurs. Engineers also call such drive elements of mechanical movement actuators. In order to transfer this principle from the plant to technology, the technical actuator must be constructed of cells that—as described above—change their shape depending on the internal pressure. Like the plant cells, these technical cells also have a "cell wall" that is compliant and therefore allows deformation when the internal pressure increases or drops. In the cellular structure, the individual cells are arranged and connected such that they elongate on one side but on the other side remain unchanged in length. Overall, this results in bending of the total structure that consists of the cellular actuator and the rigid plate attached to it ⌜9.

In this scenario, the individual cells of the actuator are laid out such that the external walls tilt outwards as the internal pressure increases ⌜4. By arranging several such cells next to each other in a row, the upper area of the cells becomes wider and causes a bending movement in the opposite direction. In such technical solutions, the internal pressure can be generated in different ways: hydrostatically with water, as in a plant, or pneumatically with air, as in the technical cellular actuator.

Pressure-dependent stiffness

The increase in the internal pressure not only causes deformation of the entire system but also increases its stiffness, and thereby its ability to carry external loads. In plants too, an increase in turgor leads to a stiffening of the tissue, because the entire plant cross-section is mechanically stressed. When developing a technical system that consists of several differently shaped cell layers, it would be possible to utilize both the adaptive stiffness and the generation of movement resulting from internal pressure. The movement then depends on the difference in pressure between the various layers of cells, whereas the stiffness of the system depends on the absolute internal pressure, assuming identical cell wall material.

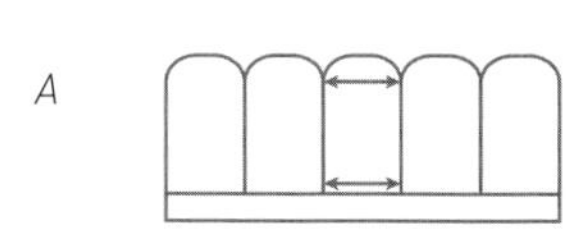

Cells without internal pressure

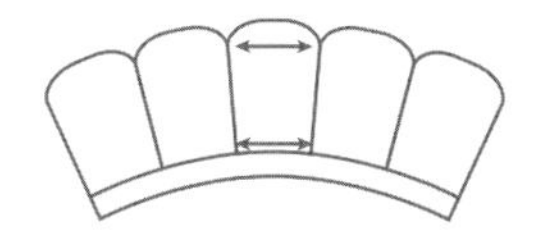

Cells filled with compressed air

⌐8 *Functional principle of a cellular actuator for generating bending. As the cells become wider due to the increase in internal pressure compared with the original state (A), they cause bending of the entire structure (B).*

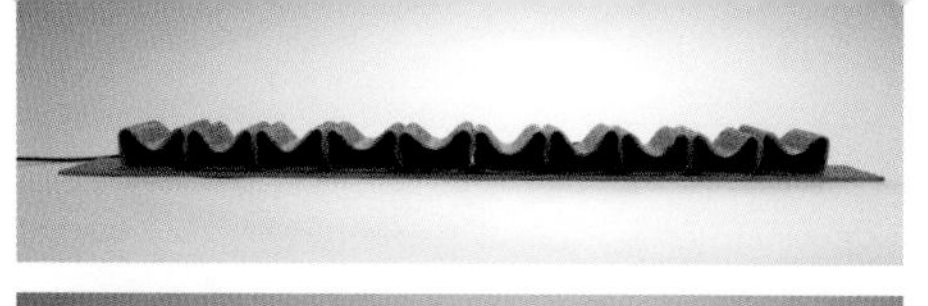

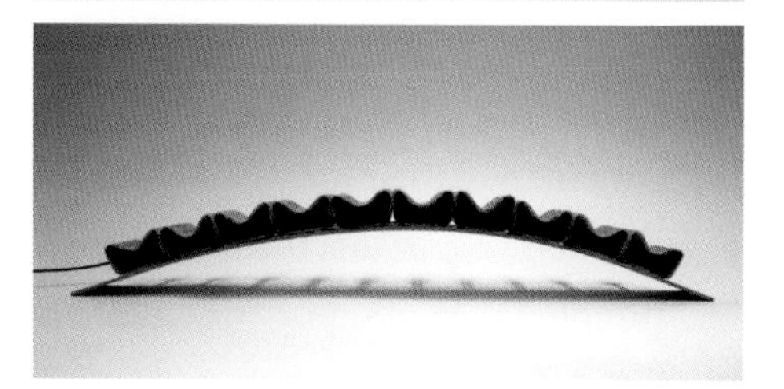

⌐9 *Cellular actuator: the increase in internal pressure causes a widening of the upper side of the cell and thereby the bending of the entire structure.*

Potential technical applications

Current research is focused on actuating compliant facade shading elements such as Flectofin or Flectofold **⌐27** based on the help of adaptive and joint-free drive elements, as in the plant models. It would be easy to integrate the cellular actuator in such a biomimetic element.

The basic principle of such a movable system is the bending of a rod arranged laterally or in the center, which could be generated by the cellular actuator. In the case of the Flectofold, the bending of the central rib leads to a lifting of the wings, whereas in the Flectofin it causes the louvers to fold away laterally **⌐10**.

⌐10 *Integration of a cellular actuator in joint-free facade shading elements, such as the Flectofold (A) and the Flectofin (B).*

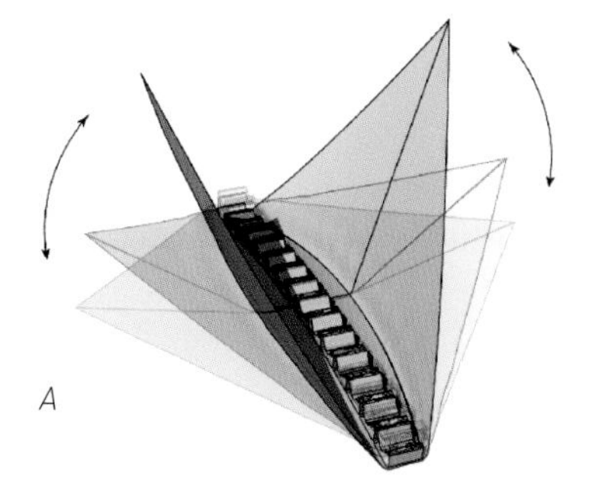

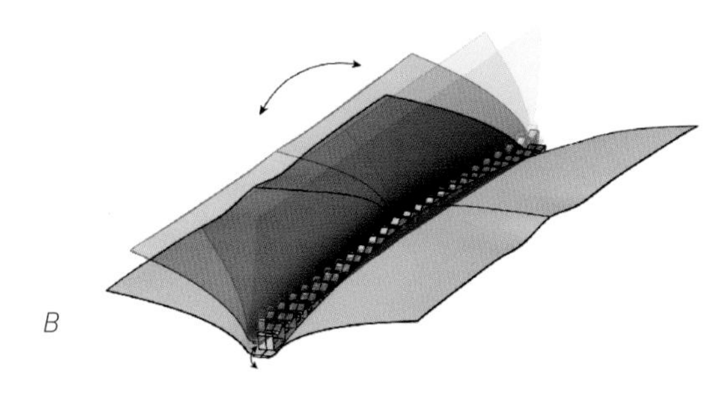

Movement without joints: (how) does it work?

Oliver Betz / Benjamin Eggs / Fabian Henn / Annette Birkhold / Oliver Röhrle

The ability to move actively gives unicellular organisms and animals the possibility to freely change their location. This has many advantages with regard to the search for nutrition and mates, the distribution of genes, and the avoidance of unfavorable environmental conditions. The wide range of movements animals perform includes the fast gallop of horses, the skillful clambering of monkeys, and the impressive maneuvers of flies. Such movements require joints like those familiar to us from arthropods (millipedes, spiders, crabs, and insects) and from vertebrates. However, movement can also be accomplished in quite different ways!

From a biological or engineering perspective, a joint is a movable connection between two or several (rigid) bodies (for instance, bones) that defines their movement in fixed directions in relation to each other. From an evolutionary perspective, however, genuine joints appeared relatively late. Initially movement was achieved without joints but by means of continuously changing the geometry of the structures involved. In engineering, this principle is known as "continuum kinematics." In animals this principle is common, examples being the changes in shape exhibited by earthworms or the wide range of movements of an elephant's trunk ⌈11. Such systems are typically soft to flexible, but can often mechanically stiffen to become more resistant. This is usually achieved through the contraction of muscles. The joint-free mechanisms and principles employed in continuous kinematics are of interest to engineering not only because—in contrast to joint-based systems—they are often simpler. The technical systems based on this feature are also capable of achieving much more complex movements and therefore are better suited to adapt to external constraints and requirements. The principle of the muscular hydrostat, which also governs the complex movements of an elephant's trunk, is only one of several joint-free movement principles. In zoology, the term "hydrostat" refers to incompressible compartments filled with fluid or muscles that, due to a change in pressure, induce a change in movement and stiffness. For example, the human tongue is another example of a muscular hydrostat. Within the tongue, the wide variety of movements is a result of the arrangement of various muscle groups and its orchestrated activation. A common aspect of the elephant's trunk and the tongue is that their movements are often highly complex and therefore require a high level of control. It is difficult to transfer the properties of these biological materials to technical solutions with controllable and hence functional characteristics. Computer simulations can help us gain deeper insights into the function of hydrostats. The big advantage of simulations and computational model is that many dif-

ferent "what if" cases can be performed in a very simple, controllable, and straightforward way by just changing the relevant input parameters. However, realistic computational models of muscular hydrostats are not easy to develop, because this requires in-depth knowledge of the underlying working principles. Below, we outline these principles in more detail. Most joint-free movements are based on muscle activation; however, the resulting movement mechanisms are often governed by the mechanical properties of the passive structures. We provide here a short overview of four joint-free movement mechanisms found in unicellular organisms and animals.

⌈11 *The trunk of the elephant is a muscular hydrostat. This joint-free movement principle was adopted for the construction of a continually movable technical gripper by the FESTO company.*

Amoeboid movement

The term "amoeboid movement" refers to the creeping/flowing form of movement found in many kinds of cells (e.g., in rhizopods) **⌈12A**, which belong to the unicellular organisms, or in the white blood cells of humans (leucocytes). In this movement, the mobile cell produces pseudopodia (false feet), which are extensions of the surface of the gel-like exterior cell plasma. This contains a concentrated network of protein fiber elements. When these filaments extend beneath the cell surface and, at the same time, are foreshortened at their base, the cell moves forward **⌈12B**.

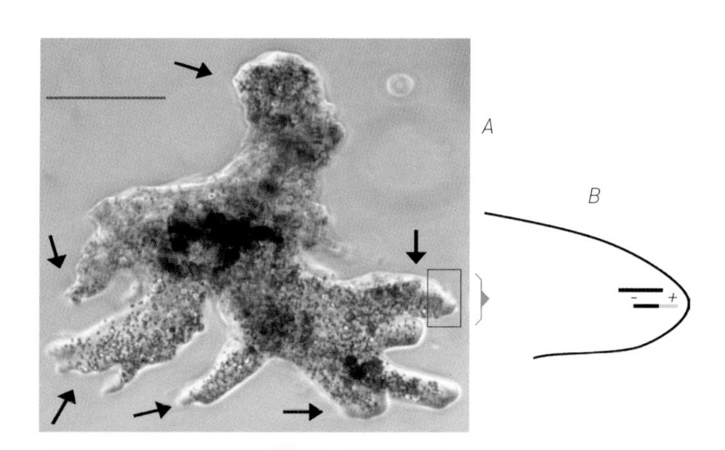

⌈12 *(A) The rhizopod* Amoeba proteus *moves with the help of its* false feet *(arrows). Scale bar: 0.2 mm. (B) The false feet advance by permanently removing filaments at their* minus end *and subsequently adding filaments (shown colored in the image) at their plus end.*

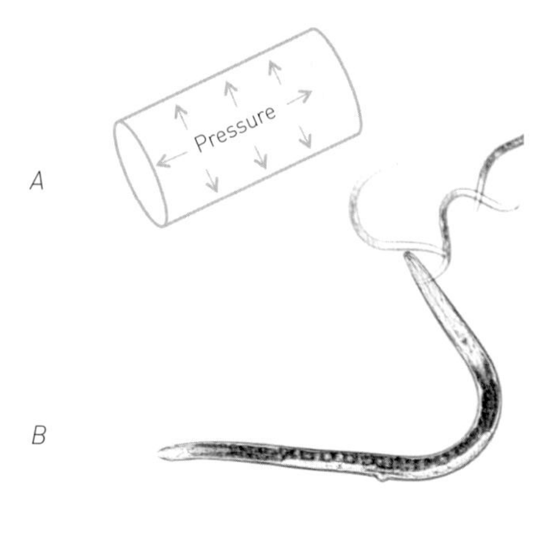

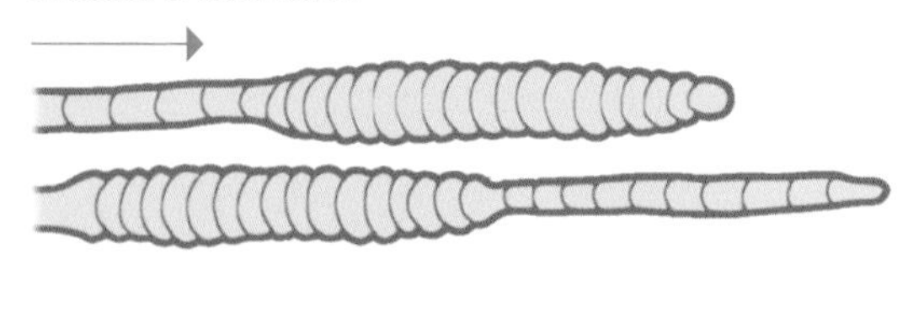

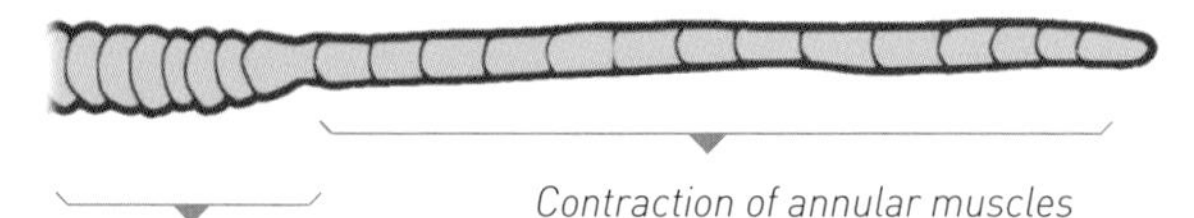

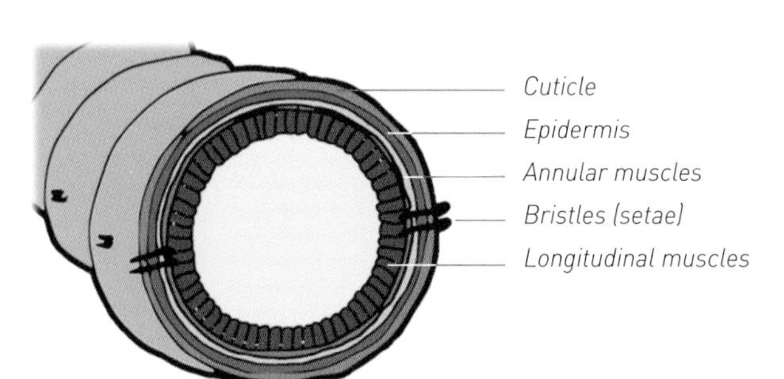

13 *Principle and examples of hydrostatically driven joint-free movements (A) Principle of the dermal muscular tunic, in which the fluid of the body cavity functions as a counter pressure to the body wall (adaptive rigidity) while, at the same time, it changes its position along the longitudinal axis, facilitating changes in the body shape. (B) In its outer body layer, the nematode* Pelodera strongyloides *only has muscles in longitudinal direction; this means that it is only capable of performing snaking movements (mature female and three juveniles in the first larval stage). (C) Schematic of the peristaltic movement of an earthworm. Waves of shortening and lengthening body segments move from the front to the rear of the body. In contrast to the nematodes shown in (B), this is possible because of the subdivision of the body cavity into a series of compartments and because of the presence of annular muscles in the body wall above the layer of longitudinal muscles.*

Movement via hydroskeleton

When muscles are involved in the production of movement, they need counter bearings, normally skeletons. These do not have to involve bones; phylogenetically, the oldest types of skeleton are hydrostatic skeletons. They are based on the principle that a fiber-reinforced and fluid-filled body wall that is limited to the outside and resists tension and pressure is itself pressurized. Because the muscles are integrated in the body wall, this system is termed a dermal muscular tunic. In general, due to muscle contractions and the fact that the fluid cavity cannot be compressed, the pressure increases and is hydraulically transferred to other areas of the body. This causes changes in body shape, which can also be used for locomotion. As a rule, such hydroskeletons are common in invertebrates with soft and flexible bodies, such as earthworms. Here, the muscles responsible for movement are located in the body wall, and the hydrostatic skeleton in the form of the fluid-filled body cavity takes on the role of the skeletal antagonist ⌈13.
These principles have been introduced in biomimetic applications, for example in new drive technologies and in soft robots or parts of robots (e.g., robot arms that must have great freedom of movement). So-called "pneumatic" artificial muscles are hoses consisting of a pressure-proof fabric mesh. By increasing the internal pressure the pneumatic muscles contract. Complex deformations can be achieved through various arrangements of the fabric mesh.

Muscular hydrostats

Muscular hydrostats are cylinder-like structures that predominantly contain muscle tissue (instead of a fluid); the muscle fibers can be arranged in various directions. Such systems are self-stabilizing, yet completely mobile. Examples include the human tongue, the elephant's trunk ⌈11, the muscular foot of the Roman snail, or the tentacles of an octopus. Like the fluid-based hydroskeletons, such as that of the earthworm, muscular hydrostats cannot change their volume. Therefore, the muscles can act as counter bearings and do not necessarily require a rigid or fluid-based skeleton. Muscular hydrostats can perform an impressive variety of movements and, at the same time, adapt their stiffness to the mechanical requirements.
This principle is also often applied in the field of soft robotics. However, instead of the relatively rigid fabric mesh, soft plastics are used in this case, enabling the development of highly specialized surgical tools for interventions inside the body. The combination of various plastics or diverse wall thicknesses makes complex movements possible when the hose is pumped up. For example, the aim of snake robotic microsurgery is to carry out surgical interventions at any place in the heart through a small opening.

A

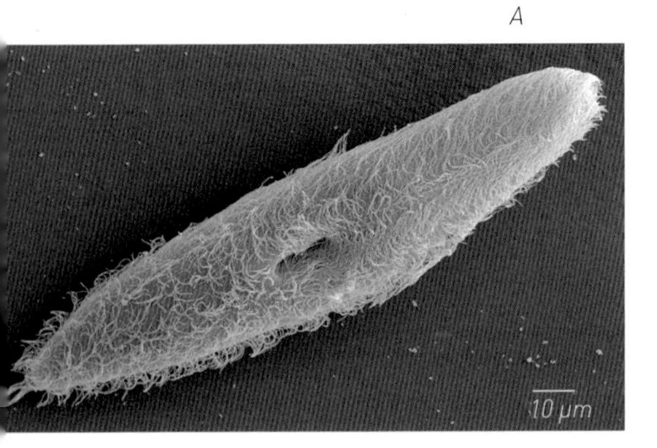

B

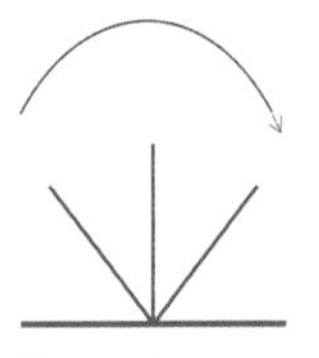

Forward movement

Backward movement

┌14 *(A) Scanning electron micrograph of a Paramecium The surface is densely covered with cilia. (B) Forward and backward movement of a cilium. During the forward movement, the entire shaft remains stiff. During the backward movement, it bends and becomes supple in certain areas.*

Slide-lock mechanisms

Prominent examples of adaptive joint-free structures are the slide-lock mechanisms of cilia and flagella ┌14. The unicellular *Paramecium*, for example, uses this mechanism to move through water freely. This type of joint-free movement is associated with one of the oldest movement mechanisms. It can be found in both uni- and multicellular organisms (such as rotifers) and in sperm cells, which swim towards the egg cell using their flagella. To understand the movement of cilia and flagella, we need to observe their complex and minute structure in cross-section, an aspect that leads us too far away from our main interest in this review. Simpler slide-lock mechanisms we have investigated include the piercing/sucking proboscises of bugs and the ovipositors of parasitoid wasps. These structures do not have any inherent joints and function via remote control (i.e., by means of using muscles in the head or abdomen). Ultimately, the basic working principles employed in these structures are the same as those in cilia and flagella. In such structures, two or several rod-shaped elastic fibers are linked to each other in longitudinal direction with the help of a tongue-and-groove system. These fibers can be moved in relation to each other longitudinally. However, if longitudinal sliding is inhibited or even fully prevented by a mechanical block, the result is—depending on the stiffness of the materials—a relative bending of both fibers. This is similar to the ideas behind bimetals ┌15. Bimetals consist of two layers of different interconnected metals. Changes in temperature, for example, can lead to the bending of the bimetal strip. The reason for bending is due to the fact that the metals are temperature sensitive and each of the metals reacts differently to temperature changes. Bimetals are therefore commonly used as thermometers or temperature switches (e.g., to control the heat in water boilers).

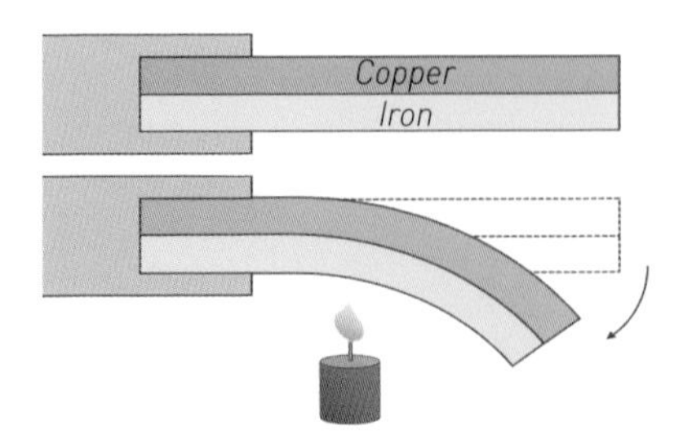

┌15 *Bimetal principle. A metal strip consisting of two layers of different metals changes shape when exposed to temperature changes because the two metals expand at different rates.*

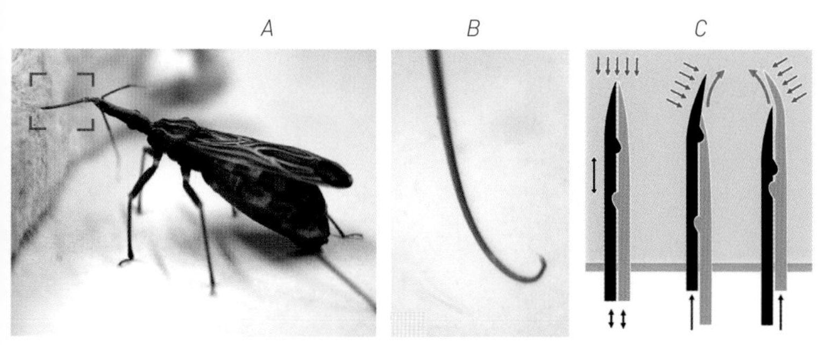

⌜16 *The principle of slide-lock is used by insects to perform bending movements similar to the bimetal mechanism. (A) The assassin bug* Rhodnius prolixus *sucking blood from an anesthetized rat. In this process, the needle-like extended proboscis (frame) is extended forward. (B) Individual image of a video sequence showing the joint-free bending movement of the maxillae, which are connected along their length with the help of a tongue-and-groove system. (C) The bending movements needed for finding a suitable blood vessel (green bent arrows) are generated by the right (light) maxilla moving relative to the left (dark) maxilla in longitudinal direction but are restrained by the mechanical block. In addition, the mechanical resistance of the surrounding medium (red arrows) can reinforce the deflection.*

In insects, the slide-lock principle can be found, for example, in the needle-like extended proboscises of bugs. Blood-sucking assassin bugs native to South America (Reduviidae, subfamily Triatominae) use this movement principle when searching for small blood vessels in tissue after they have pierced the skin of the host (e.g., a human being) with their proboscises ⌜16. In these insects, the two maxillae are extended like needles and interlocked with the help of a tongue-and-groove system. When one of the maxillae is moved forward longitudinally relative to the other, it is subjected at one point to a mechanical block that exists at the end of the tongue-and-groove system. The maxillary bundle moves in one or the other direction depending on which of the two maxillae was moved. In this context, the surrounding medium also plays an important role as the beveled tips of the maxillae are diverted by it. Because of the asymmetrical forces acting on the tip, the movement of the maxillae relative to each other often also leads to an offset resulting in the bending of the entire bundle.

The same principle is employed in the ovipositors of parasitoid wasps (e.g., ichneumonid and chalcid wasps). These wasps lay their eggs in or on other insects (usually during larval or egg stages), upon which the hatched parasitoid larvae later feed. Because the hosts often live hidden in plant tissue, these wasps must first find the host and then locate a suitable place for depositing the eggs, either on the surface of the host or inside it. This is achieved through search movements of the ovipositor ⌜17. In this case, up to four elements can be involved, some of which are independently movable (the valves or valvulae), are connected with each other with the help of a tongue-and-groove system. Depending on which of these elements are shifted (against each other), more diverse bending movements can be achieved, compared to the above-described proboscises of the blood-sucking bugs.

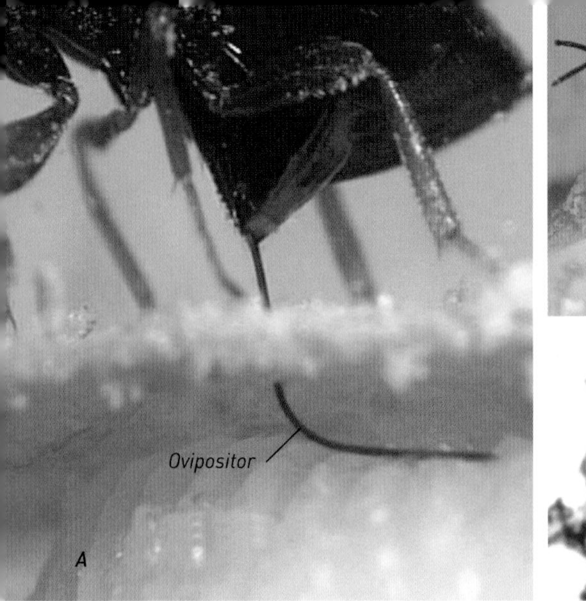

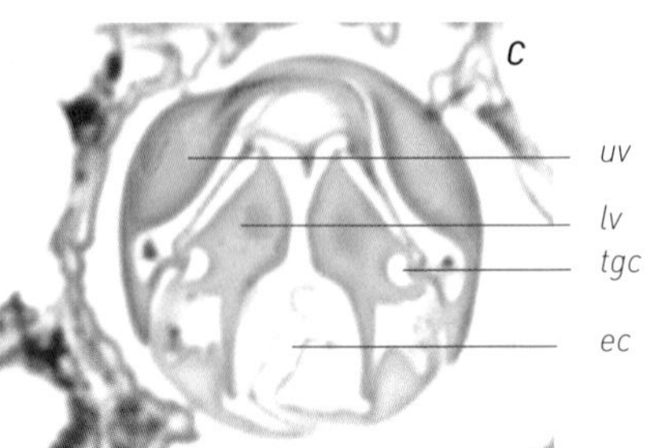

17 *The pteromalid wasp,* Lariophagus distinguendus, *is a parasitoid of the larvae of several beetle species that live in cereal, causing damage. (A–B) A female pteromalid wasp deposits an egg on a larva of the corn weevil* Sitophilus granarius; *the joint-free movements of the ovipositor can be clearly seen. (C) Cross-section through the ovipositor. The upper valve (uv) comprises two asymmetrically overlapping halves, which are grown together at the tip only. They are joined to the two lower valves (lv) via a tongue-and-groove connection (tgc), which makes it possible for the lower units to slide along each other. The lower valves enclose the egg canal (ec).*

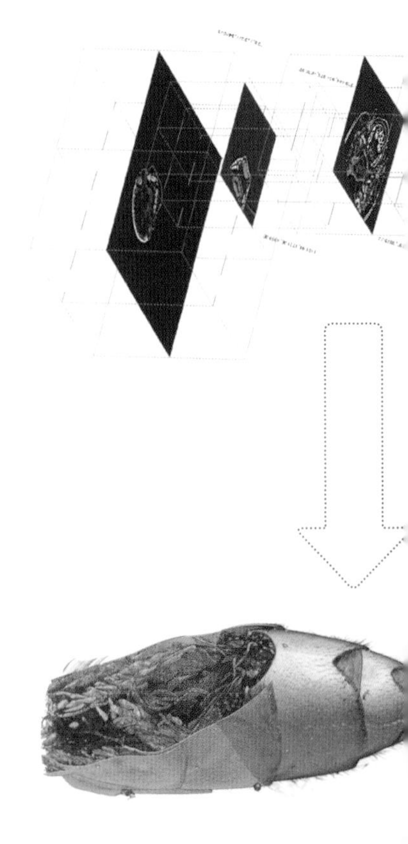

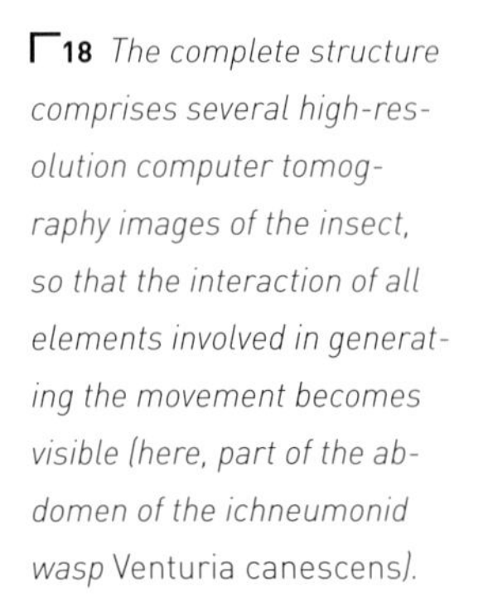

18 *The complete structure comprises several high-resolution computer tomography images of the insect, so that the interaction of all elements involved in generating the movement becomes visible (here, part of the abdomen of the ichneumonid wasp* Venturia canescens*).*

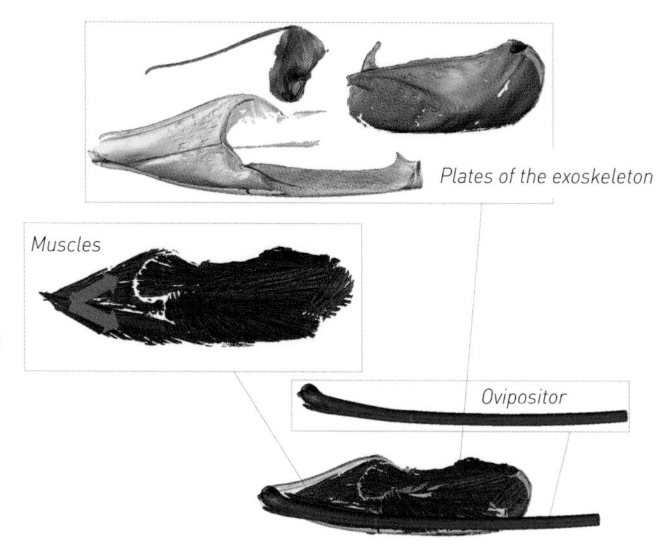

⌈19 *Breakdown of the CT image of an ovipositor of the ichneumonid wasp* Venturia canescens *into the individual structures involved in the movement. These include the parts of the exoskeleton that have been relocated inside and the muscles. The tip of the ovipositor is not shown.*

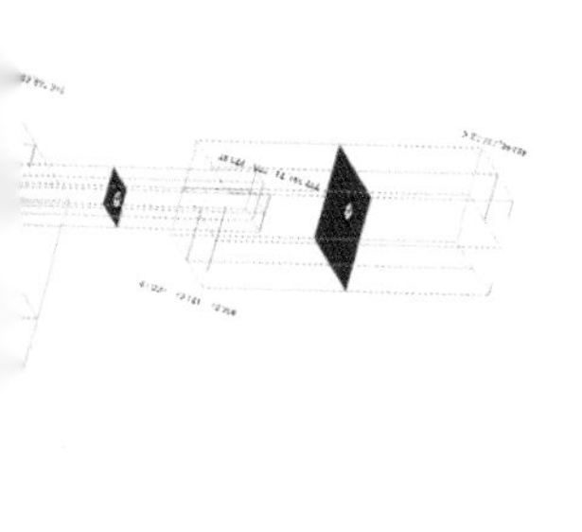

Investigation of the movement principles

In order to understand the movement principles of the proboscises and ovipositors of insects, we have generated three-dimensional images of the structures involved. Since most insects are minute, we employed extremely high-resolution imaging techniques such as synchrotron computer tomography (CT), which is an X-ray technology that can reveal even very small structures. Because of the high resolution, it is not possible to X-ray the whole insect in one take. This means that several high-resolution computer tomography images of different parts of the insect have to be stitched together to form an image of the entire structure **⌈18**.
On that basis we have produced three-dimensional models of the objects investigated. The 3D images or the models can also be taken apart to isolate the individual structures involved in the movement **⌈19**. This method has allowed us to investigate, amongst other things, the individual muscle strands responsible for movement. Moreover, the models can be used within simulations to increase our

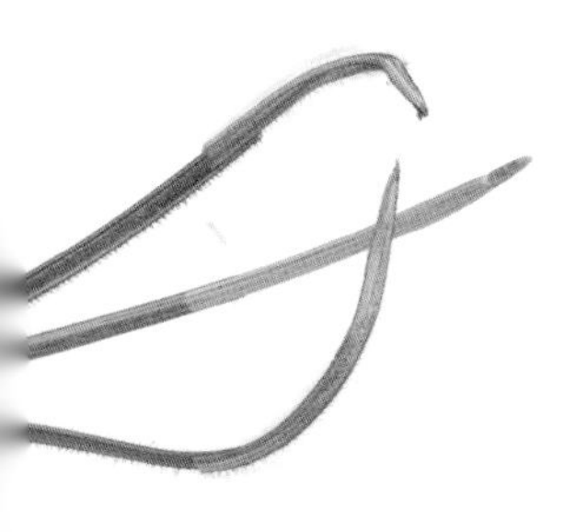

understanding of the mechanisms leading to movement and to predict movements. By using the number and diameter of the individual muscle fibers it is also possible to estimate the strength of the muscle packs. Studies of the points of attachment of the muscles on the plates of the insects' exoskeleton (sometimes relocated to the inside) and on the structures to be moved (such as the ovipositor), enable the determination of the direction of the muscle forces and hence the direction in which the muscle pulls when it contracts. Unfortunately, in spite of the extremely high resolution of the synchrotron CT images, the imaging has its limitations. We cannot detect the smallest details in the 3D data sets. Thus, for investigations of the small-scale mechanisms in even greater detail, for example, the connecting rabbet (or groove) between the different parts of the proboscis, we employed light- and electron-microscopical images ⌈**20A** in order to build models from these structures and to simulate the influence of these small-scale mechanisms on the resulting movement. In this way we can check whether we have correctly interpreted the material properties and the assumed tongue-and-groove structures. Making assumptions with respect to mechanical properties at the microstructure level is a big and often (still) insurmountable challenge. One possible way of gaining more insights into the microstructural properties of the proboscis is to use fluorescence microscopy ⌈**20B**. This imaging method can be used to identify softer and more rigid areas, and to adopt them to build realistic computational models (structural information necessary). With this information it is then possible to produce highly detailed simulations of the movement processes.

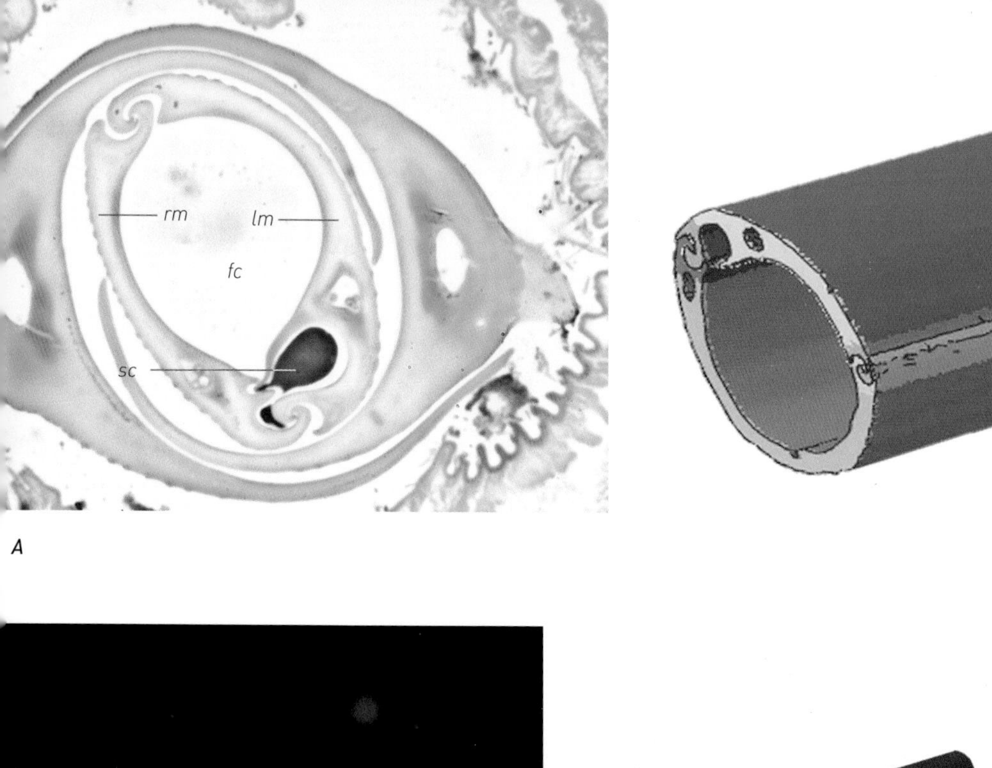

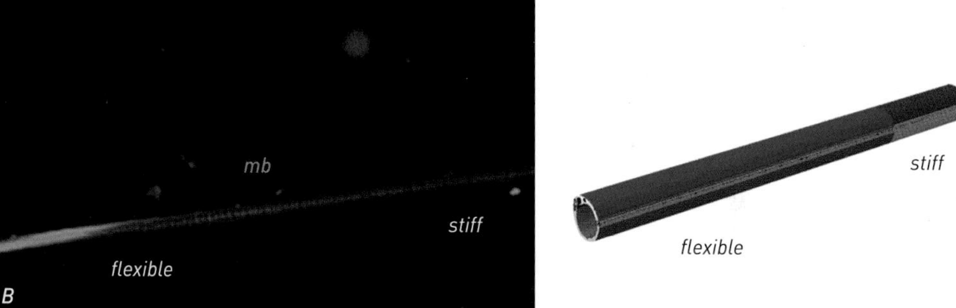

20 *Extension of the model of the proboscis of the assassin bug* Dipetalogaster maxima. *The proboscis consists of the two needle-like extended and connected maxillae (lm = left maxilla, rm = right maxilla) that form the food channel (fc) and the salivary channel (sc). The maxillae connected with each other via a tongue-and-groove system are also called the maxillary bundle (mb). Technical models are continually being refined; this is accomplished using light-microscopy investigations of cross-sections (A) that show structures in detail, and by means of fluorescence microscopy images (B) that can be used to assess mechanical properties.*

No joint ailments: how plants move and inspire technology

Anna Westermeier / Simon Poppinga / Axel Körner / Larissa Born / Renate Sachse / Saman Saffarian / Jan Knippers / Manfred Bischoff / Götz T. Gresser / Thomas Speck

Plants have neither muscles nor "classic" local joints—and yet they can move. In the course of evolution, efficient movement mechanisms and esthetic movement forms have developed. Architects and engineers, in cooperation with biomechanists, are benefiting from this botanical "offering" and drawing inspiration for the development of new types of facade shading systems for modern buildings.

How do plants move?

In spite of the fact that most plants grow roots in the true sense of the word and therefore are tied to a particular location, they nevertheless are able to perform an astonishing range of movements. These range from slow growth movements, for example when a flower opens, through to very fast movements, such as the almost explosive release of seeds by the touch-me-not plant (*Impatiens glandulifera*) ⌜21 or the snapping of the Venus flytrap (*Dionaea muscipula*) ⌜22. Such movements are faster than can be perceived by the human eye. These capabilities are all the more surprising when we consider that plants do not have muscles.

In common technical components, but also in the human body, movements can only be performed with the help of jointed connections between more or less rigid elements. Such joints suffer considerable wear, because they are subject to strong mechanical loads. Typical examples are the troublesome knee joint or worn-out door hinges. By contrast, plants do not have this handicap. They do without local joints and achieve mobility by deforming elastically in the respective areas. For this

purpose, the mechanical properties of the various areas, such as stiffness, are adjusted to the function needed. This causes the stresses resulting from the movement to be spread to the surrounding tissue. In this way, it is possible to avoid peak stresses and to reduce mechanical wear to a large extent.

22 *The carnivorous Venus flytrap (*Dionaea muscipula*). When the trigger hairs that can be seen on the inside of the lobes of the trap are touched, the trap snaps shut and catches its prey.*

Plant movements can be based on different kinds of processes. They can be active, in which case plants use energy to regulate the internal pressure of their cells—the turgor—causing tissue to swell or to shrink. But the movements can also take place completely passively, in the form of swelling or shrinking processes that generate movement when, without consuming energy, water input or water removal takes place (hygroscopically) in dead tissues. A typical passive hygroscopic plant movement can be observed in pine cones (*Pinus* sp.), for example. In these, the scales of the cone open up when it is dry so that the dispersible seeds fall out and can be distributed by the wind. However, when the weather is rainy and damp, the scales of the cones close again, thereby preventing release of the seeds, which are not carried in the air when the weather is wet **23**. Given that water is shifted in the tissues in both the active and passive types of movement, the time taken for the movement is determined by the thickness of the moving organs that the water has to penetrate. But how do plants such as the touch-me-not or Venus flytrap manage to perform incredibly fast movements, which would not be possible simply by shifting water (hydraulics)?

21 *Ripe fruit (seed capsule) and inflorescence of the touch-me-not plant (*Impatiens glandulifera*), which distributes its seeds widely by opening its fruits, which are highly tensioned, with an explosive burst.*

Faster than the human eye

In most cases, the acceleration trick works on this basis: Using hydraulic and often slow movements at a preceding stage, plants build up and store elastic energy in certain structures. As with a bow and arrow, this energy can be released in an instant. This type of movement acceleration can be divided into two categories.
In the first category, the plant structures involved are destroyed when the energy is released. This movement is nonrecurring and irreversible. The term commonly used is "explosion mechanisms." This movement can be clearly observed in the fruits of the touch-me-not ⌈21 or, even more spectacularly, in the fruits of the sandbox tree (*Hura crepitans*). The dried fruit of this tree breaks up into its individual segments with such power that, even though the pieces still measure several centimeters, they reach speeds of up to 70 meters per second and can therefore be dangerous to humans.

In the second category, the energy is released by a change in shape of the respective part of the plant. In this case the structure is not destroyed, but a rapid, reversible change from one geometric state to another takes place. A special instance of this is so-called "snap-buckling," in which shell-type structures snap over from one state of curvature to another. In architectural structures this process is normally referred to as uncontrollable stability failure. Snap-buckling can be well observed when the Venus flytrap snaps shut ⌈22. In the open, un-tripped state, seen from the outside, both lobes of the trap are curved outwards (concave). As soon as the trigger hairs on the inside of the trap are touched several times, this curvature is rapidly reversed through a hydraulic process so that the lobes in the closed state are curved inwards (convex). The same snap-buckling mechanism can be found in reflective slap bracelets and in the popular children's toy called the jumping disc ⌈24. By this mechanical "trick,"

the Venus flytrap closes within fractions of a second, not giving its prey, such as flies, any chance to escape. Then the prey is digested within the closed trap, leaving only the chitin of the fly's exoskeleton, and the nutrients are absorbed via the leaf surface. As a result, the trap grows and thereby reopens, and is again ready to catch prey.

24 *A similar mechanism to that used by the Venus flytrap can be found in jumping disc toys. When the disc is inverted, it can trigger at any moment and jump away, owing to the release of energy stored by way of pre-tensioning.*

23 *Many plant movements, such as the opening and closing of the seed scales of pine cones (*genus Pinus*), are driven by the drying out and swelling of the tissue.*

25 *The waterwheel plant (*Aldrovanda vesiculosa*) is a small carnivorous plant that grows underwater. An individual whorl with eight snap traps can be seen at the top. At the bottom is a shoot of the entire plant with many such whorls. Scale bar line: 1 cm.*

Source of ideas: waterwheel plant

The carnivorous waterwheel plant *(Aldrovanda vesiculosa)* is the little sister of the Venus flytrap and lives underwater. Both derive from a shared ancestor, whose identity is unknown (to date no fossils have been found). The waterwheel plant lives in still waters that are poor in nutrients, but it has died out in many of its natural locations because the habitats have been destroyed by human activity. The traps are four to 7 millimeters long and arranged like the spokes of a wheel around the central stem, hence the name "waterwheel" ⌈25. The traps function like those of the Venus flytrap, although the curvature of their lobes does not change when they snap shut ⌈26. The two lobes are connected by a midrib, which is straight when the plant is ready to trap its prey. However, as soon as the trigger hairs on the inside of the trap are touched, the midrib will bend, probably because cells along the midrib actively reduce their internal pressure. This causes the lobes to snap shut within a few milliseconds. By this motion principle the waterwheel catches small prey such as crustaceans, which are then digested within the closed traps. Given that even a minimal curvature of the midrib is sufficient to generate a comparatively big movement of the lobes, this phenomenon is called kinematic amplification, which means amplification of movement.

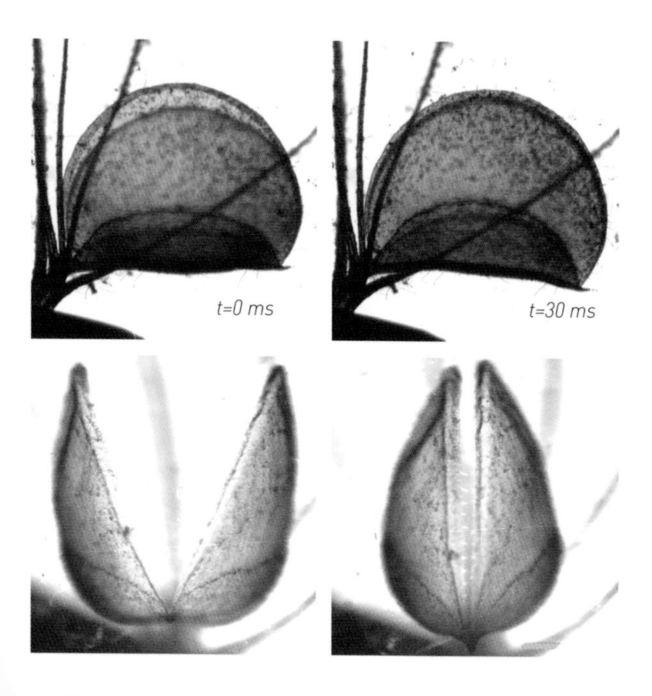

⌈26 *A snap trap of the waterwheel in open and closed state. At the top, the trap is seen from the side (on the left open, on the right closed). At the bottom, the view is from the front. The midrib connecting both lobes of the trap is straight when in the open state. When it bends, the trap snaps shut.*

⌜27 *Demonstrator of the biomimetic facade shading device that was inspired by the waterwheel and, because of the flexible folds that are important for its movement, was named Flectofold. The demonstrator exhibited here illustrates the function of the Flectofold, including how even curved facades can be shaded by the device.*

Technical implementation

These joint-free movements that are not activated by muscles have been the source of many ideas for engineers and architects developing new kinds of movable technical structures. In particular, the fascinating trapping movement of the carnivorous waterwheel has inspired architects, with the help of biologists, structural engineers, and material scientists, to develop a new kind of facade shading device, the Flectofold ⌜**27**.

From the plant to the computer model

In order to transfer plant movements, such as those of the waterwheel, to architectural applications, the first step is to identify and characterize those properties of the snap trap that enable this movement. Then they have to be abstracted in such a way that a similar movement can be generated with technical materials (such as fiber-reinforced plastics). For this process, the plant movement is first simulated as a geometric computer model. In this way it is possible to analyze the mechanical properties underlying the movement and vary them as needed. In the case of the waterwheel, looking at the snap trap of the plant itself, one can see that the transition between the lobe and the midrib is shaped like a curved line. This connection can be abstracted using curved fold lines. Such

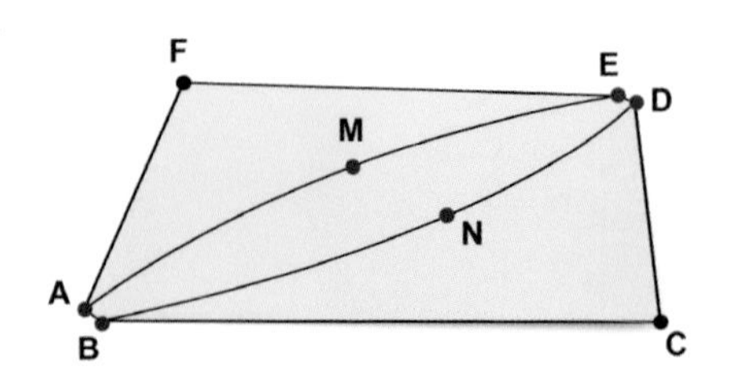

curved fold lines (or curved-line foldings) are similar to the folding used in origami ┌28. This method has long been known in both product design and architecture, although it has mostly been applied to rigid objects. How this method for moving elements can be used has as yet not been widely researched.

In one such abstracted geometrical model, the snap trap was transferred to a flat element in which two shading flaps are connected with a lens-shaped midrib via curved fold lines. The radius of these fold lines can now be varied, and a kinematic model can be used to determine the influence of the radius on the movement. This kinematic model is used to investigate how the movement takes place when various parameters are changed. However, this type of model can only be used to explore geometric parameters. The required forces or the stresses created in the elements cannot be investigated. When the midrib is bent into a curved shape, the two adjoining lobes fold along this curve. The analyses show that, with a larger radius, that is to say, with less curvature in the fold lines, significantly less bending is needed to generate a closing movement; in other words, the geometric amplification is greater.

After that, the movements and also the required forces and stresses can be investigated in greater detail—not in reality, but using a kinetic model on the computer ┌29. In this simulation, which is referred to as a nonlinear finite element analysis, real material properties are assigned to the model. This makes it possible to compare how the variations generated affect the actuation energy required for executing the movement, and how they affect the stresses in the building components. In the case of the Flectofold computer model that was inspired by the waterwheel, certain material properties and thicknesses are assigned to the different areas, using glass fiber reinforced plastic, for example. Furthermore, the fold line, which, in the geometric and kinematic models, was a simple line, is in some zones modelled as hinge zone with a certain width. This model is important in order to understand what material properties and thicknesses have to be retained in those specific zones in order to ensure that the movement principle functions. It is also possible to investigate how the radius and width of the folding zone affect the required energy and the stresses in the different zones. It is also important to find out how the elements behave when external forces act on them.

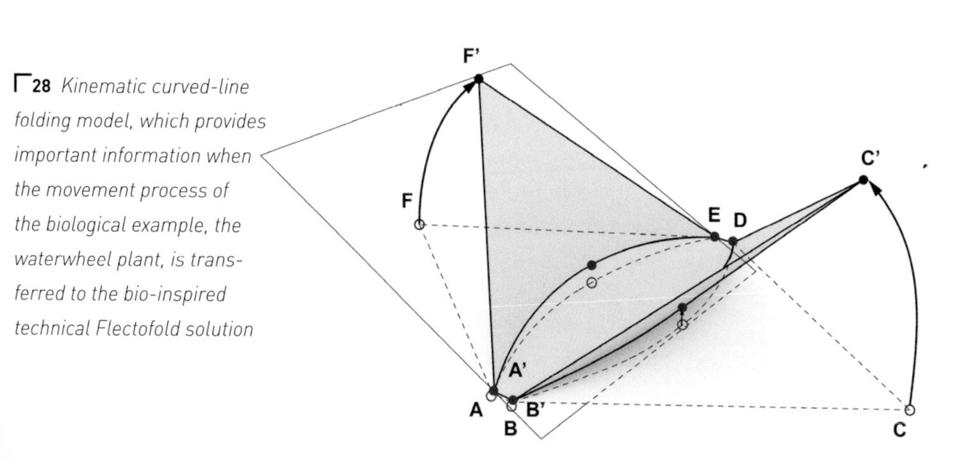

┌**28** *Kinematic curved-line folding model, which provides important information when the movement process of the biological example, the waterwheel plant, is transferred to the bio-inspired technical Flectofold solution*

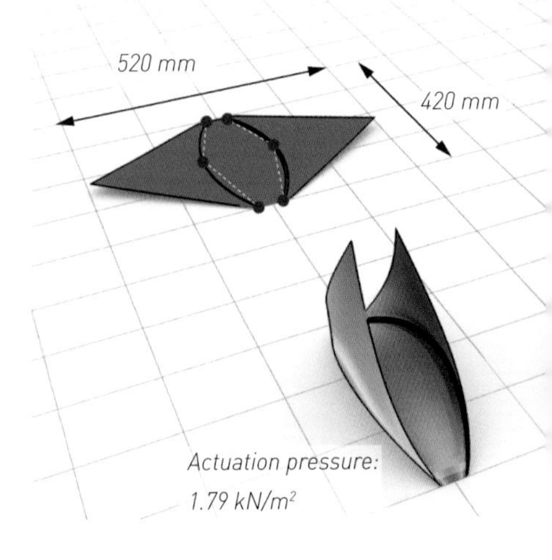

For example, shading systems must be able to withstand strong and gusty winds. As an important result of the investigations and calculations, we can state that, with a larger radius of the curved fold lines, reduced bending of the midrib needs to be generated, but more force is needed to close the louver flaps. A smaller radius also results in better performance with respect to external loads (wind or snow) because the more pronounced curvature in the surfaces has a positive effect on the loadbearing performance.

The next step is from the computer back to reality. All information gained to date on the required material properties, the movement process, and the mechanical behavior is now used to transfer the computer-based model to real, built prototypes.

How to build a prototype?

How does one integrate flexible areas that play a critical role in plant movements into a technical component, for example for a facade shading device? An example of a joint that allows movement of its two connecting parts solely through changes in the geometry of the material, which is the same in both parts, is the hinge joint of a lunchbox lid. Here, flexibility is achieved through a difference in the thickness of the material in the area of the joint. By contrast, plants resolve the challenge of a hinged structure through their material properties rather than through extreme differences in thickness, which constitute a weak mechanical point (as evidenced by the typical failure of lunchbox lids' joints). The inner structure of a waterwheel (and of plants in general) resembles that of a fiber-reinforced composite. Stiff fibers are embedded in an elastic matrix in a certain direction, and depending on the orientation and density of the fibers, it is easier or more difficult to deform the tissue when force is applied.

Fiber-reinforced compound materials are used in many technical areas. For example, wind turbine blades consist of glass fibers that are bonded with a plastic matrix. Of course, these are very thick-walled components, which therefore are extremely rigid. In addition, the fiber orientation in the component plays an important role. In the case of rigid components that can withstand strong forces, the high-performance fibers are oriented along the main force vector in the component. This means that the fibers are always exposed to tension, and the component is very strong and rigid. If the high-performance fibers (for instance, carbon or glass fibers) are embedded in a plastic matrix and the component is exposed to forces that apply not along but across the direction of the fibers, then the occurring tensile forces have to be resisted by the matrix only, that is to say, the plastic. However, as this is usually significantly less strong than the fiber, cracks in the component are likely to occur.

In contrast to a rigid wind turbine blade, the facade shading device inspired by the waterwheel plant—the Flectofold—is in-

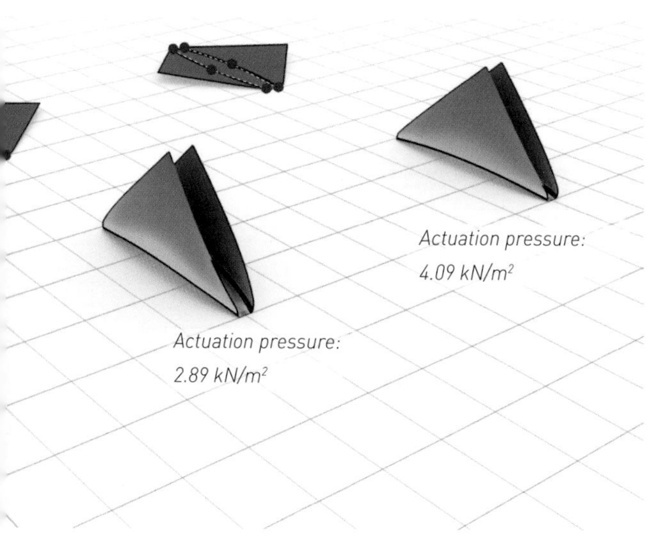

29 *Kinetic model of the Flectofold, which is used for studies on geometric variations and for simulating the distribution of stresses during the movement process.*

tended to be flexible in specific defined areas (such as at the transition from the midrib to the flaps). This characteristic enables the folding mechanism of the shading device **30**. Given that the component is relatively thin throughout, it already has a certain "basic flexibility." In addition, the fibers in the particularly flexible area of the component are oriented so that they are exposed to compression rather than tension. They are placed at a 45-degree angle to the line along which the Flectofold is folded. By orienting the fibers diversely in the various areas of the component, three areas with different rigidities are created. The flaps of the Flectofold are the most rigid parts. This prevents them from deforming when exposed to wind and snow loads. The lens-shaped midrib is of medium rigidity, so that it can be bent in order to initiate the movement of the flaps. The bending zones that connect the midrib and the flaps have the least rigidity, and are in fact very elastic and easily deformable. Depending on the degree of curvature, it is thus possible to generate the required degree of shading in a continuous motion. Another advantage is this: because the individual Flectofold elements can be arranged independently, it is possible to provide shading to buildings with an unusual geometry where conventional blinds would not work.

The Flectofold combines the efficient, joint-free movement and the esthetics of the plant that has inspired its design, the waterwheel. Taking into account the enormous variety of shapes and movements in flora and fauna, we can look forward to seeing how much technology will be inspired by and benefit from this incredible richness.

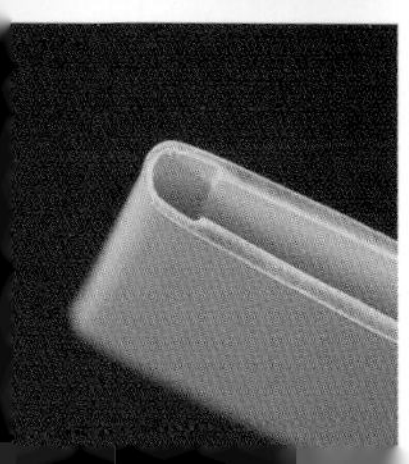

30 *Bending zone of the Flectofold, which, like an extended hinge, facilitates the movements of the laterally placed flaps. It is even thinner than the laterally placed flaps and very flexible due to the special arrangement of the fibers.*

From pure research to biomimetic products: the Flectofold facade shading device

Saman Saffarian / Larissa Born / Axel Körner / Anja Mader / Anna S. Westermeier / Simon Poppinga / Markus Milwich / Götz T. Gresser / Thomas Speck and Jan Knippers

Biology can provide exciting ideas for the development or improvement of technical products. As a rule, the underlying principles are first investigated using a feasibility demonstrator, which does not represent a finished technical product but nevertheless, on the whole, is intended to "function" like the finished product. However, there is a long way to go from this first prototype to a product that is ready to use or to a convincing building method. In this process, numerous ideas that at first seem interesting and promising have to be abandoned. Many aspects must be investigated in parallel, and plausible solutions need to be found, not only in terms of reliable and durable functionality, but also in terms of commercial viability and resource-efficient manufacture. In addition, it is important that an innovative product is accepted in the market. In the case of architecture, this means—above all—that the product is esthetically appealing, because without that aspect, there will not be much interest even if the product functions well.

For the elastic Flectofold facade shading device, initial prototypes could be built and tested relatively quickly. It turned out that even complex movement processes of very small plant structures—such as the snap traps of the carnivorous waterwheel plant *(Aldrovanda vesiculosa)* that served as example for the Flectofold—can be transferred ("scaled-up") to large-scale fiber-reinforced composite elements. The abstraction of the kinetic principle (curved-line folding) of *Aldrovanda vesiculosa* and its parameterization and simulation has been described in the chapter titled, "No joint ailments: how plants move and inspire technology."

However, these first fully functional prototypes also highlighted the challenges of the continuing development. On the one hand, the fiber-reinforced composite structure must be rigid enough to withstand impacting loads, in particular wind loads, but it must also be flexible enough to be actuated by small forces. From this perspective, mechanisms with embedded (integrated) joint zones are preferable to those with homogeneous rigidity. By incorporating flexible regions (the joint zones) as well as stiffer regions (the flaps) that can resist the wind it is possible to manufacture folding structures that can be actuated by low forces.

Material composition and production of the laminate

The integrated joint zone presents special challenges for the development of the material. In particular, there is the need to be able to perform numerous bending cycles without damage (in order to avoid material fatigue). Conflicting requirements have to be dealt with in relation to the overall structure as well as the joint zone: although a wide joint zone reduces material stress that could lead to damage, it also results in geometric instability in the movement when the ratio of rigidity to width is below a certain value.

Initially, smaller Flectofolds with a middle rib measuring 420 millimeters in length between the two lateral flaps and a 520-millimeter lateral span were produced using a vacuum infusion process. The Flectofold laminate consisted of glass fiber mats, epoxy resin, and a PVC cover film **31A**.

However, the material composition used for the laminate production in these first prototypes **31A** proved to be unsuitable for larger Flectofolds. The weight of the wings increased in proportion to their size, which meant that the material in the joint zone had to be reinforced in order to ensure adequate structural capacity. Owing to the increase in the thickness of the material, the rigidity of the laminate increased disproportionately in the joint area, which led to material failure. Based on a large number of fatigue tests using small material samples in which both the orientation and the arrangement of the glass fiber mats, as well as the functionality of layers of other materials, was investigated, the second generation of larger Flectofolds was produced. These had an 850-millimeter-long middle rib and a lateral span width of 720 millimeters. They consist of pre-impregnated glass fiber mats (prepregs) and an elastomer film **31B**, which were laminated at higher temperatures.

31 *Laminate structure of the Flectofold produced in a vacuum infusion process (length/width 420/520 mm) (A) and hot-laminate process (length/width 850/720 mm) (B).*

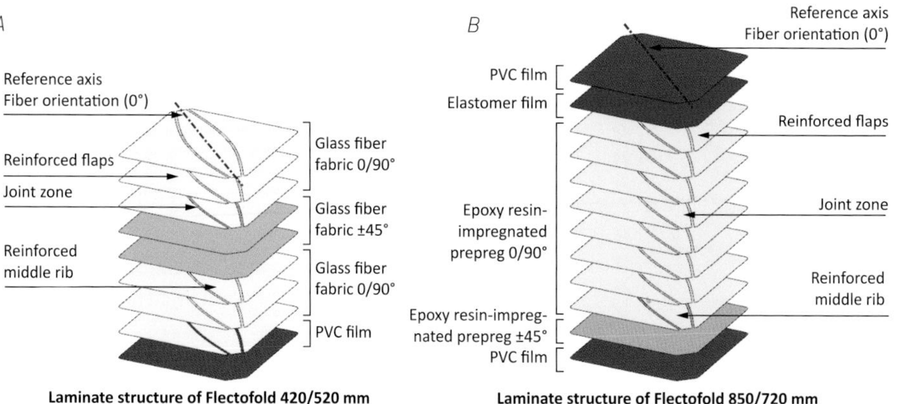

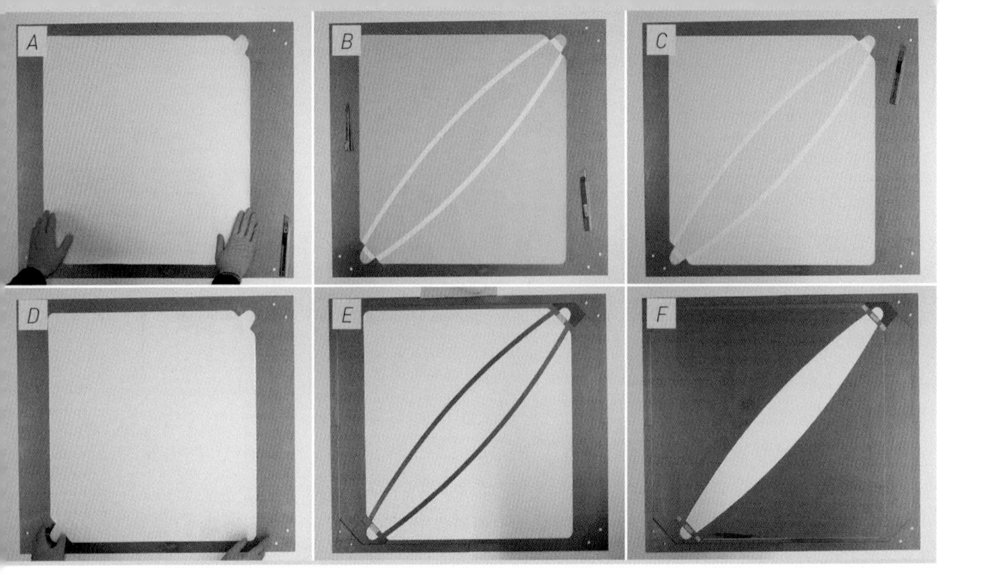

┌32 *Different material layers of the laminate are stacked on a flat metal plate. (A) Laying the flexible 45° middle layer of epoxy resin-impregnated glass fiber prepreg, (B) laying the stiffening 90° layers of epoxy resin-impregnated glass fiber prepreg, (C) epoxy resin-impregnated glass fiber prepreg without protective film, (D) laying the PVC covering film, (E) placing the metal inlays for the joint zones, (F) placing the metal templates to compensate for the difference in thickness of the wings and the middle rib.*

As shown in ┌31, the different layers are stacked on a flat metal mold—a simple steel plate—and are then laminated together in a hot press ┌32, 33. The folding lines, which act as joint zones, are produced directly by using metal inlays during the pressing process. Apart from the finishing of the final contour, no subsequent processing is required. Owing to the short cycle time of the hot-press process, this is also suitable for cost-efficient serial production of larger numbers of Flectofolds.

The Flectofolds produced in this way were tested in test rigs with up to two 2,000 load cycles in order to investigate the wear when exposed to long-term use ┌34. In addition, the demonstrators were tested for their combustibility (building standard), which is important for the approval of the product for use in buildings.

┌33 *Process of hot-laminating the layers of materials*

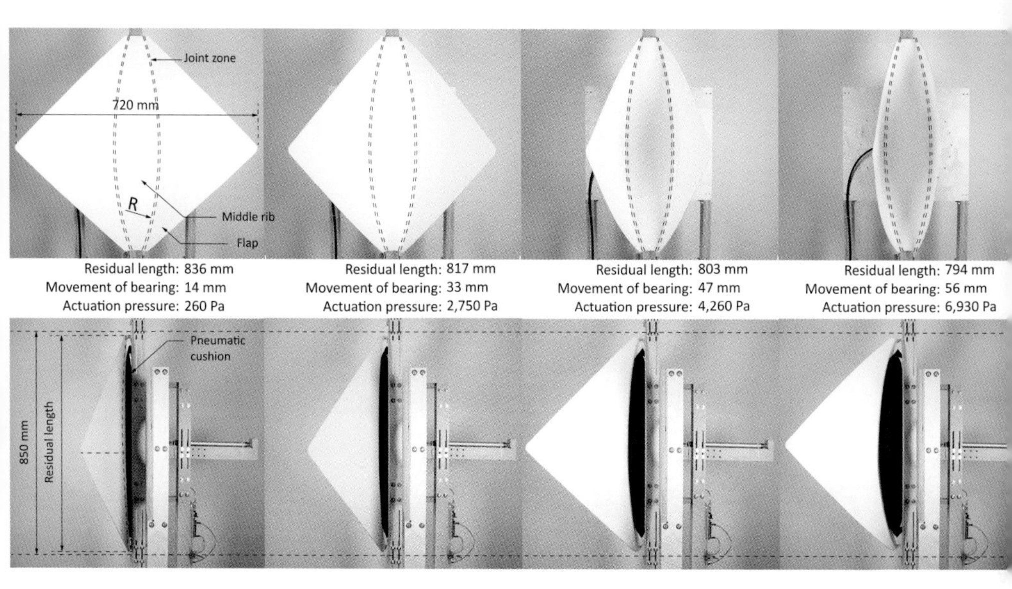

⌈34 *Flectofold test rig and performance test for wear.*

Adaptability of the geometry and design methods

An important aspect for the technical application of the Flectofold is the development of design methods that cover geometric adaptability and applicability to irregularly shaped freeform facades. As part of this process, the Flectofold mechanism was tested for its suitability for synclastic or anticlastic surface geometry. In a first step, an algorithm was developed that subdivides a given building surface with double curvature into many smaller polygons of a similar size. In a second step, the division has to be adapted such that the Flectofold modules fold in the right direction (i.e., the folding direction is defined by a certain anticlastic curvature). Then the anticlastic, four-sided flat elements can be transferred to the Flectofold geometry with the curved folds **⌈35**.

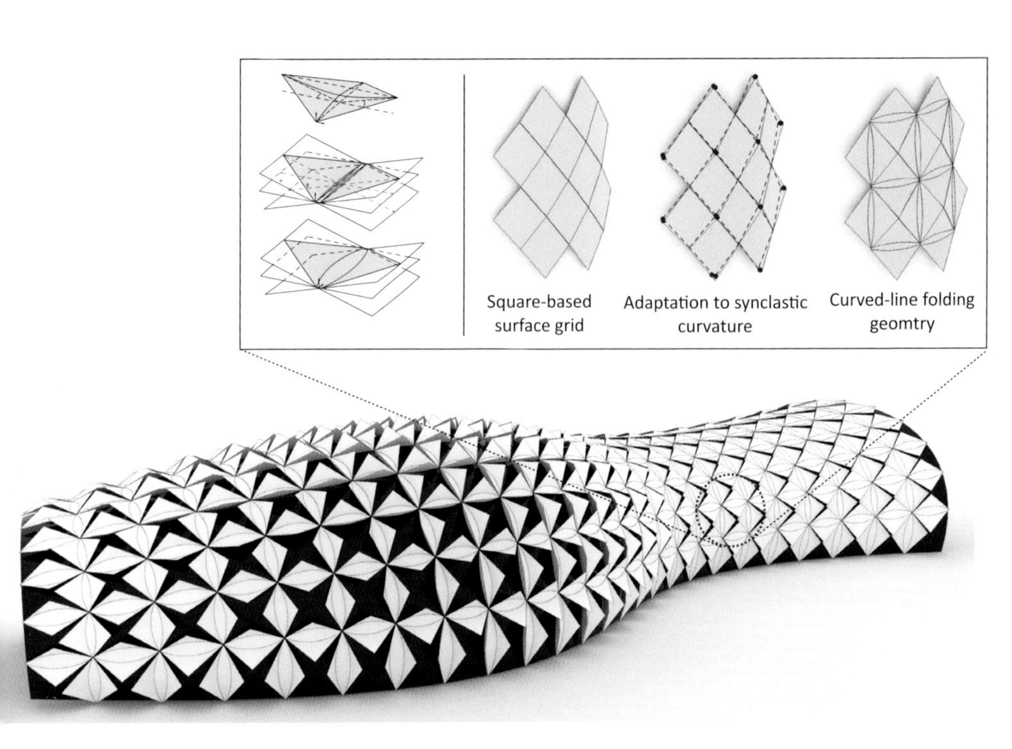

⌐35 *Checking the adaptability of the Flectofold modules to complex geometries with a double curvature.*

Control and actuation

For the large demonstrator in the Rosenstein Museum that shows the adaptability of the facade shading device to a curved surface, a 6-meter-by-6-meter anticlastic curved surface was covered with 36 Flectofold modules with a dimension of 1,100 millimeters (length of middle rib)/1,220 millimeters (lateral span width) **⌐37–39**. Every Flectofold module has an air cushion behind the middle rib that acts as a pneumatic actuator which, under pressure (0.04 to 0.06 bar; compare the pressure in a bicycle tire of approximately 3.5 bar), elastically bends the stiffer middle rib and thereby initiates the folding movement.

In order to check the elastic bending of the middle ribs exactly and individually, a precise pneumatic control system **⌐36** was developed that makes it possible to carry out a dynamic pressure adjustment without time delay. For this purpose, proportional pressure control valves were used that can transform an input voltage signal in the range of 0 to 10 volts to an output pressure of 0 to 2 bar. The voltage is controlled via a custom-designed circuit board on which the 36 digital potentiometers are fitted. Each Flectofold is connected with one potentiometer, which transmits an adjustable voltage signal to the associated precisely calibrated pressure valve. A microcontroller was used to communicate with the main control software, and input data were sent to the individual potentiometers via a digital communication protocol. The wireless, web-based communication with the control software was enabled with the help of another microcontroller. At the exhibition

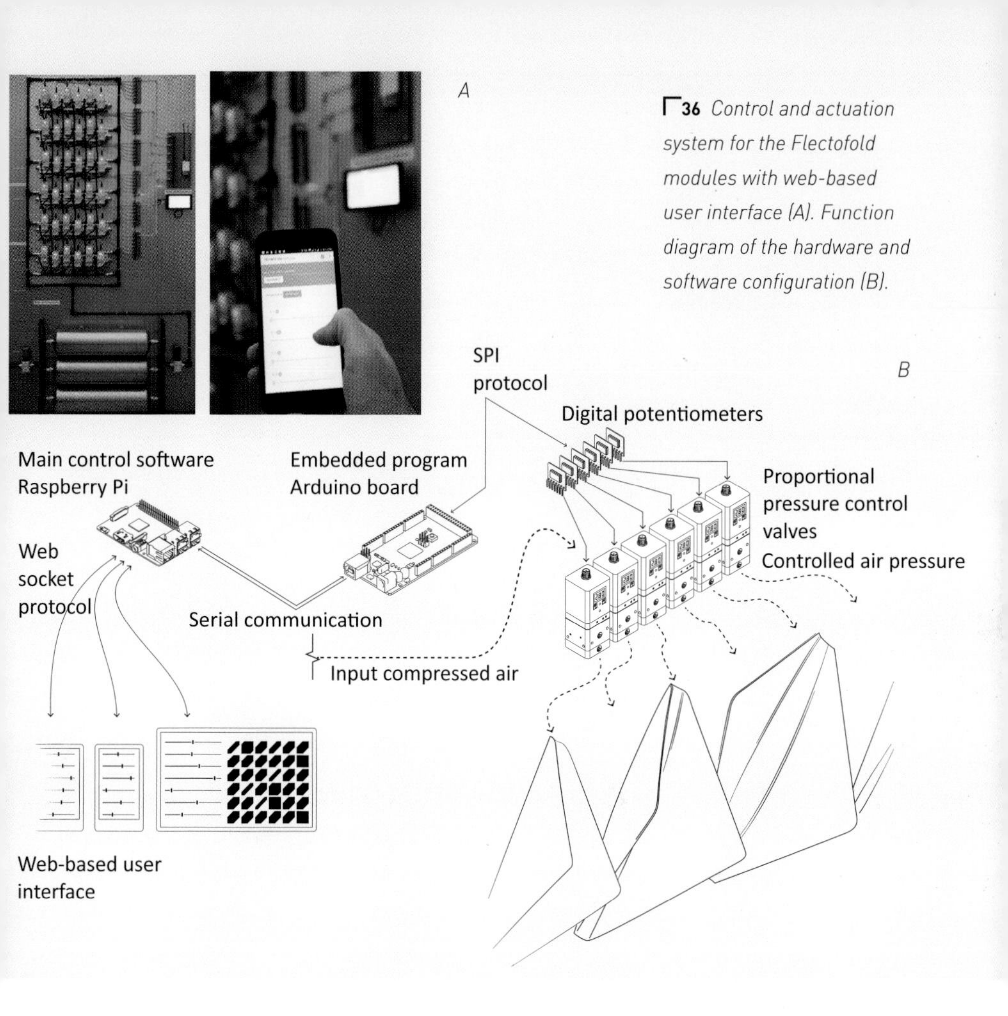

⌐36 *Control and actuation system for the Flectofold modules with web-based user interface (A). Function diagram of the hardware and software configuration (B).*

in the museum, a continuous flow of compressed air was provided by a compressor installed about 50 meters away from the large demonstrator and the control unit. Locating the compressor away from the actuators eliminated undesirable compressor noise in the exhibition hall. In order to ensure that the storage capacity for compressed air was adequate and capable of maintaining constant pressure levels, as well as preventing sudden drops in the supply of compressed air when several components were used at the same time, three interconnected compressed air containers were installed close to the demonstration area.

With this system it was possible to achieve accurate calibration of the actuation pressure for each individual Flectofold module. The resulting movements of the Flectofolds were compared with the input pressure by the program, which made it possible to define the pressure at which the individual Flectofold modules are completely closed.

The demonstrator in the Rosenstein Museum was designed for active web-based control by users, which meant that individual Flectofold modules could be actuated via mobile devices such as smartphones or tablets. However, in principle it is also possible, without any problems, to link the movement to sensor data such as light, noise, movement, and so on.

37 *Frontal view of a large Flectofold demonstrator for the special exhibition* Baubionik—Biologie beflügelt Architektur *at the Schloss Rosenstein Natural History Museum*

38 *Rear view of the large Flectofold demonstrator*

39 *Front view of the large Flectofold demonstrator*

Summary

Large demonstrators, such as the Flectofold with 36 modules in the Rosenstein Museum, represent an important intermediary step between pure research and building practice. Beyond the pure research into the materials, the construction of such a demonstrator required an exemplary resolution of all aspects of construction and control technology. The demonstrator also serves to indicate where there is further need for research and development. And it illustrates the architectural potential of this novel technology, making an important contribution to the public communication of pure research. The objective is to create building shading devices that can adapt to changing environmental conditions but are also robust and economically viable.

A

40 *Visualization of a possible application scenario of the Flectofold for shading free-form architecture in a hot and arid climate zone, where such a system is most useful.*
(A) exterior
(B) detail
(C) interior

C

LIGHTWEIGHT VERSATILITY: STRUCTURE INSTEAD OF MASS

Jan Knippers / Thomas Speck

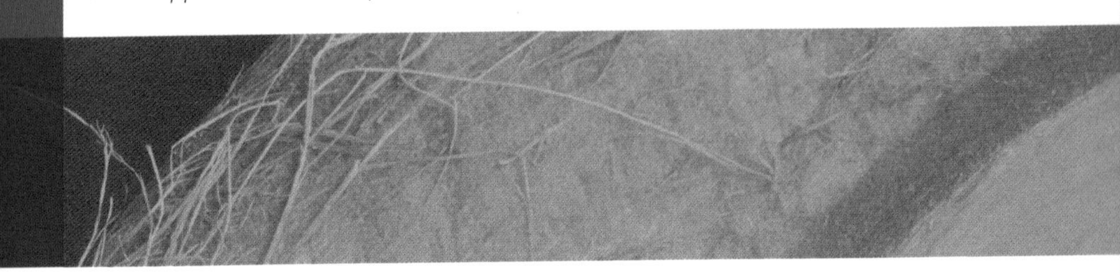

We build our houses out of masonry, concrete, and steel. We use these materials because their properties are easy to characterize and we can rely on our structural calculations for them. When it comes to timber, these calculations become more complicated for engineers. Its strength in the direction of the fibers is quite different from that across the fibers and, moreover, depends on the moisture content. These complicated mechanical properties are one of the main reasons why timber still plays a less important role in modern construction even though, indisputably, its use is ecologically advantageous. The ability to easily and reliably calculate and predict the structural properties of building materials is key to their development and application. This is the reason we prefer building materials with as uniform a structure as possible, and hence easily describable properties.

In nature, these criteria are completely irrelevant. In the course of evolution, materials and structures have developed in which the orientation, layering, and packing density of fibers, the grading of cavities or the placement of intermediate layers is hugely varied and occurs in the smallest of spaces. A hierarchical structure across several orders of magnitude, from the level of the organism down to the level of molecules, is typical. Every structural element consists of smaller elements that are built up of similar basic components. These elements not only determine the mechanical properties of the structure but also transport nutrients and water, act as catalysts for chemical reactions, detect signaling substances, and are able to carry out a wide range of "self-X functions," such as self-organization, self-adaption, self-healing, and self-cleaning. This results in highly complex material systems and structures that are adapted to fulfill a wide range of requirements due to their finely tuned chemical and physical properties. On the one hand, the shell of the coconut has to ensure that the fruit is not destroyed when it falls from the tree. On the other hand, it has to survive many months of drifting in seawater without damage and, once washed up on the beach, allow for germination p. 60. Our native plants have to endure not only winter storms but also intermittent frost periods and, increasingly, longer dry periods p. 74. The exoskeleton of the sea urchin has to fend off predators and be able to withstand mechanical impacts in the reef p. 54.

Comparable construction principles are hardly known in architecture and construction technology. Until very recently, we did not have the calculation methods

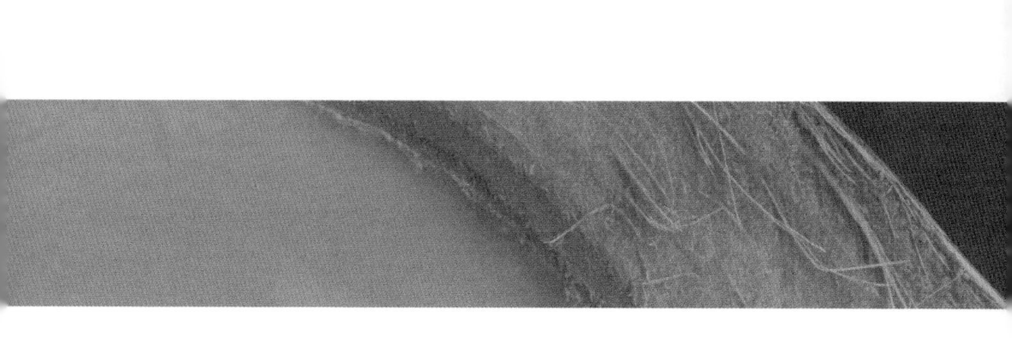

or the production facilities to enable us to implement the main characteristics of natural constructions in the technical realm (i.e., the small-scale adaptation of material properties and the geometric differentiation of building components at varying orders of magnitude). This has changed fundamentally in recent years due to the introduction of computer-based production methods. For example, research is being carried out all over the world to find out how 3D printing, which was originally developed for model building, can be utilized at a large scale for building construction. These considerations focus on concrete, which is applied in layers using computer-controlled nozzles. In this process, it is possible to finely control the composition of the different materials that make up the building components. Sand and graded stone ensure strength, whereas hollow clay or glass spheres increase thermal insulation and reduce weight p. 84. Adding these components in layers using several nozzles makes it possible to carry out very specific and small-scale adaptations of the properties of the concrete similar to those occurring in biology—in bones or other mineral structures, for example sea urchin spines.

But how can we transfer other properties of natural structures to technology, such as the impact damping of coconut shells and tree bark or the resistance to intermittent frost periods of many native plants? The investigation of biological concept generators can provide valuable insights and stimulate the development of effective new materials that fulfill several, sometimes contradictory, requirements at the same time, thereby following the basic principle of all biological constructions: the careful use of resources. This could prompt us to modify Darwin's well-known adage "survival of the fittest" into "survival of the cheapest." It is obvious that it is a huge evolutionary advantage for living organisms if they can form effective compound materials and structures with the minimum input of metabolic energy and material resources.

Reliably withstanding high loads

Stefanie Schmier / Georg Bold / Gerald Buck / Katharina Klang / Christoph Lauer / Nicu Toader / Oliver Gericke / Walter Haase / Immanuel Schäfer / Siegfried Schmauder / Werner Sobek / Klaus G. Nickel / Thomas Speck

When forces—for example tensile or compressive forces—act on an object, the result is a mechanical load. These forces can be either constant (static), alternating, or jerky (dynamic). Such forces act on buildings as well as on animals and plants on a daily basis. Architects and material scientists can learn from animals and plants, and transfer concepts that have proved successful in the course of evolution to buildings or parts of buildings. This is of particular interest in situations with impact from extreme forces. For example, one of these tried-and-tested strategies of nature is to sacrifice part of the whole when a load becomes too much, in order to ensure survival. To date, this is virtually unknown in architecture.

Examples from nature

Sea urchin—controlled failure

Sea urchins must surely be considered one of the most successful groups of animals in the history of evolution. They have been living on this planet for more than 500 million years and today can be found in nearly all marine habitats, whether tropical or Arctic, in shallow or deep waters. In our latitudes, people's most common experience of sea urchins is the pain sustained from contact with the pointed spines. The thin spines of the animal penetrate the foot without any difficulty and break off in the process. Given their brittleness, they are very difficult to remove and, furthermore, they can even contain poison. But sea urchins are much more than a nuisance on the beach. When looked at more closely, they are a miracle of nature and serve as a source of inspiration for bionic applications.

At first, when looking at the creature, we notice its esthetic, highly symmetrical pentagonal structure ⌈**41**. After a closer inspection, the animals reveal some astonishing capabilities. They have self-sharpening teeth, they can use their suction pads to find a hold on slippery ground underwater, and their spines are true all-purpose tools, used for moving about as well as for getting a firm hold on reefs and in rock crevices, and of course for defending against enemies, such as predator fish or people.
However, not all sea urchins feature thin and brittle spines. The imperial sea urchin (*Phyllacanthus imperialis*) and the slate pencil urchin (*Heterocentrotus mammillatus*) have finger-thick spines that are up to 10 centimeters long and offer great mechanical stability ⌈**42**. In order to ensure that the animals are not squashed by the weight of their own spines and can move

easily in water, the spines are highly porous. The pores within their construction material, which is magnesium calcite (a carbonate mineral with an $MgCO_3$ component varying between 2 and 15 mol%), are minute and can only be detected under a microscope. This creates a network of cavities in the spines.

Lightweight construction with great stability is the objective of many engineers, and it seems to have been achieved optimally by these two species of sea urchins. However, an engineer would never use this substance to design a construction material because, owing to its crystalline structure and good fissility, calcite breaks easily and, furthermore, is not very hard. One would suspect, therefore, that the spine is brittle and crumbles easily when impacted by even very small forces. Paradoxically, though, the opposite is the case. In spite of their lightweight construction, the sea urchin spines considered here prove to be strong and extremely tough; a lot of energy is required to break them. These properties are vital for the animals' survival, because the strength of the spines protects them against predators.

41 *Skeleton of a regular sea urchin. The form of the skeleton is rounded and flattened and clearly shows the pentagonal symmetry.*

42 *The slate pencil urchin (*Heterocentrotus mammillatus*, top) and the imperial sea urchin (*Phyllacanthus imperialis*, bottom) have strong spines measuring up to 10 cm in length.*

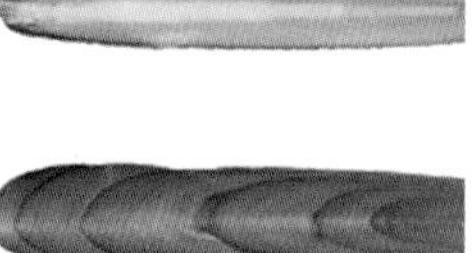

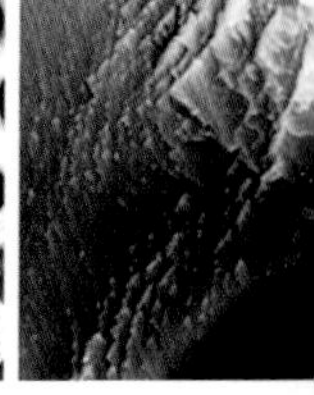

⌐43 Selected hierarchy levels of the sea urchin spines investigated.

⌐44 In the longitudinal section (on the right) the structure of the spine of the slate pencil urchin can be seen. The red growth layers are stacked into each other like a Russian doll (left). The porous structure of the spine and the denser growth layers can easily be observed in the cross-section (far right). Furthermore, one can see that the porosity increases towards the center of the spine.

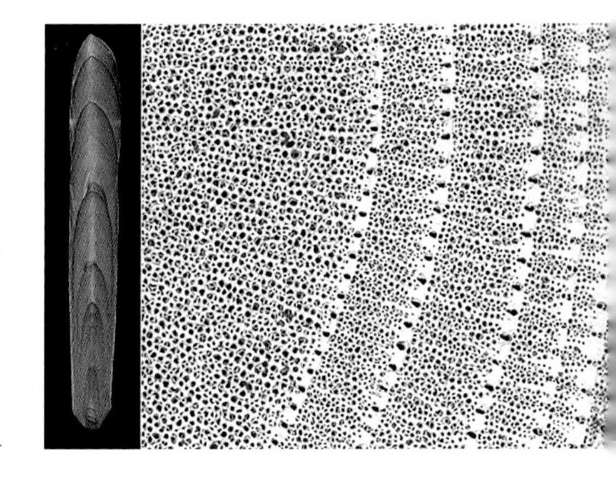

Even though the spines of the slate pencil urchin and the imperial sea urchin behave differently under compression, neither break up completely after the first crack occurs. Instead, small fragments keep breaking off from the upper spine segments, whereas the lower part of the spine remains undamaged for a long time and can therefore continue to support loads. This behavior is not typical of brittle materials: imagine a cup that emerges largely undamaged from the impact of hitting the floor.

The secret of this mechanical reaction lies in the hierarchical structure of the spines ⌐43. A hierarchical structure is a structure that extends across several orders of magnitude and has special configurations at each level, from the molecule to the entire entity, which contributes to outstanding mechanical properties. Such a makeup is typical for natural structures, whether these are sea urchin spines, human bones, or coconut shells.

Slate pencil urchin spines are built using the same schematic pattern as a Russian doll, with the red growth layers symbolized by the dolls that fit into each other ⌐44. These solid layers help to disperse forces. This means that the spine segment breaks off in steps from one growth layer to the next.

By contrast, the spines of the imperial sea urchin have a tube-like structure, which becomes increasingly less porous from the inside to the outside ⌐45. When com-

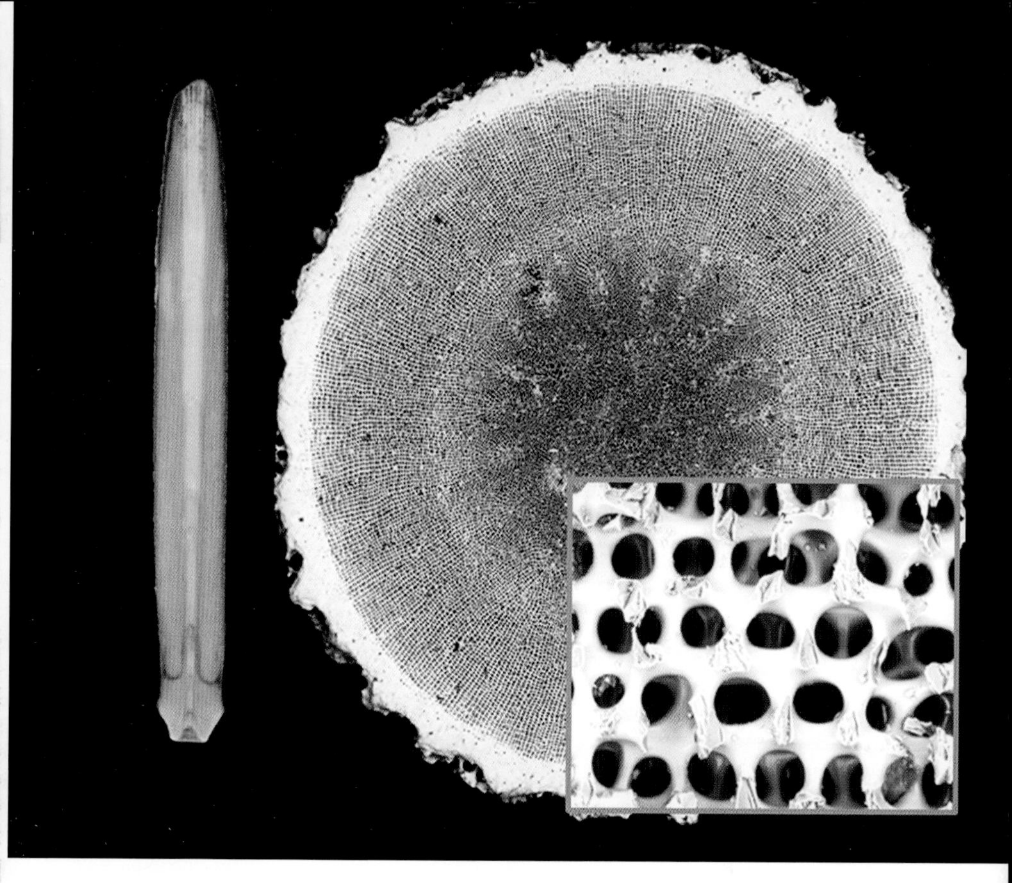

⌜45 *The tube-like structure can easily be detected in the longitudinal section (left) and in the cross-section of the spine of the imperial sea urchin. The porous architecture of the spines can be seen in the enlarged detail at the bottom right.*

pressed, the dense outer layer breaks first and the foam-like inner layer serves as a buffer, just like the crumple zone of a car. At the microscopic level too, the two types of spine have mechanisms that inhibit the propagation of cracks and thereby mostly prevent any direct failure.
In this way, in spite of the many weaknesses of the basic material, calcite, the spines of the slate pencil urchin and imperial sea urchin succeed in building a mechanically astonishingly strong structure, from which man can learn a lot for architectural building components.

⌈46 *Giant redwood tree in the Sequoia National Forest, California (USA)*

Tree bark as shock absorber

The outer layer of trees, the bark, in which we include cortex (phloem) for our purposes here, fulfills many tasks: transport of metabolic products and protection against desiccation, against high temperatures in the case of forest fires, against insect attack and germs, as well as against mechanical damage. This means that the bark, as a barrier to the outside, is the most important protective layer of a tree. Good protection is needed, above all, for the cambium. The cambium is the growth zone of the tree, a paper-thin seam of just a few layers of cells directly between the bark (phloem) and the wood. It ensures that the tree can form wood on the inside and that the bark on the outside is continually renewed. If the cambium is too badly damaged, the whole tree will die. Heavy damage to the bark can be caused by abrasion (a kind of mechanical impact), for example when the stems of two trees rub against each other during a storm, or when large fragments of rock hit the stem during a rockfall or mudslide. Depending on their native habitat and the protective functions developed there in the course of evolution, trees often have distinctly different barks, for example with respect to their thickness or structure. The bark of a tree that is native to an area not subject to regular forest fires does not have to protect the cambium against high temperatures, while the bark of a tree growing in a flat landscape does not have to protect the cambium against rockfalls, such as those that occur in mountainous areas.

⌈47 *A piece of the bark of a giant redwood tree removed by sawing. The thick, fibrous bark consists of several interwoven layers.*

Therefore, if we want to find out how the bark of trees protects the cambium against the impact of rock fragments, we are well advised to look at the bark of trees growing in mountainous regions with regular rockfall events, such as the Sierra Nevada of California (USA). That region is home to the giant redwood tree (*Sequoiadendron giganteum*) ⌈46. However, quite a few of these trees can also be admired in Baden-Württemberg, for example, where they have been popular in public parks since the middle of the 19th century. Giant redwood trees can reach an age of more than 3,000 thousand years, and grow to a height of almost 100 meters. Once they reach that stage, their trunk is a considerable size, particularly near the ground (the trunk diameter can be up to 17 meters), and their bark can become almost a meter thick in the lower area of the trunk. Quite a long while ago, researchers found out that the bark of the giant redwood tree offers excellent protection for the cambium against high temperatures that occur during the frequent forest fires in the Sierra Nevada. It is equally as effective as a shock absorber, protecting the tree against the impact of rock fragments. There are three main reasons for this. For one, the bark of the giant redwood tree impresses with its sheer thickness ⌈47. Where there is a lot of (bark) material, it is easier to dampen any impact. But the

48 *Coconut palms (*Cocos nucifera*) in the Dominican Republic. The fruits grow high up in the crown of the palm tree.*

49 *Coconut as we know it from the supermarket. The two outer layers of the pericarp (exocarp and mesocarp) have been removed. The three germination pores, where the seedling can grow out of the fruit, can be seen in the endocarp.*

outstanding mechanical protection function is the result of the combination with other two properties.
The bark of the giant redwood tree is very rich in fibers. Long, strong fibers permeate the bark along the trunk. This can be seen very clearly in pieces of the bark that have been shed. In contrast to many other types of tree, where the bark comes off in small pieces or falls off in thin fragments, the long fibers of the giant redwood tree ensure that its bark becomes detached in long pieces with frayed ends. These fibers of the bark can divert impact and distribute the load of it to a larger volume of bark, so that the impact does not directly penetrate through to the sensitive cambium.
The third reason for the outstanding impact protection lies in the loose and yet well-interwoven layering of the bark. Interwoven layers of denser and less dense plies of bark fibers ensure that impact is even better distributed to adjoining bark volumes than would be possible without this layering.
In summary, these three properties have the effect that, even though the bark of the giant redwood tree will yield considerably to any impact, it distributes the energy of any such impact to a large volume of bark. This means the impact cannot really seriously damage the cambium itself.
These properties suggest that researchers and engineers can learn from the structure of giant redwood tree bark. With this knowledge, it may be possible to develop buildings and building components that are better protected against impact, such as that caused by rockfall or accidents involving trucks or derailed trains.

┌50 *Coconut cut in half, showing the fruit before the two outer layers have been removed. The seed is protected by the three layers of the pericarp.*

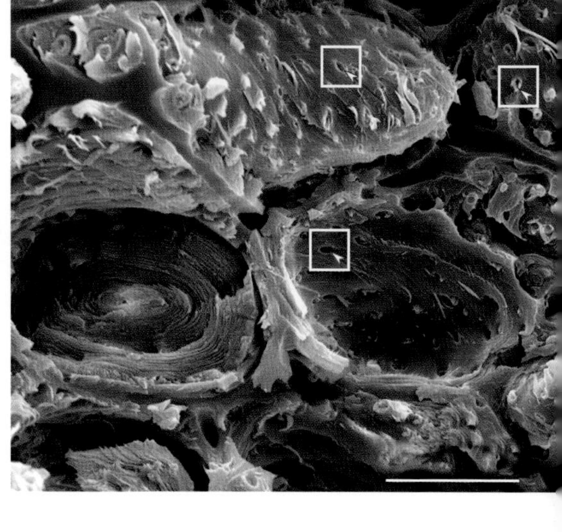

┌51 *Scanning electron microscopy image showing details of the coconut endocarp; the thicker walls of the sclereids are easy to see. The cells themselves are dead. The structures that look like small dots (marked by three arrows) are the connections between the cells. Scale bar: 0.02 mm.*

Shock absorption in coconuts

In nature, the fruit fulfils an important function because it is the means by which the seeds of the plant are dispersed. Under favorable environmental conditions and following successful dispersal, seeds can grow into seedlings and from there into a new generation of plants. To ensure that the seeds remain undamaged until germination, many types of fruit form protective layers. These shield the seeds against external influences, such as those from UV irradiation, germs, heat, dryness, or mechanical damage.

The fruit of the coconut palm (*Cocos nucifera*) is actually a drupe and not a nut, despite the colloquial term "coconut." The reason for this is that its pericarp consists of three layers and only the innermost layer is lignified **┌50**. In the case of a nut, all layers would be fused and lignified, such as is the case in hazelnuts (*Corylus avellana*). The outermost layer of the coconut is the leathery exocarp, which is followed by the fibrous mesocarp and the innermost layer, the hard and tough endocarp. These three layers surround the seed on the inside. For the purpose of export, the two outer layers of the pericarp, the exocarp and mesocarp, are removed. The seed with the coconut meat and coconut milk, which contain the actual nutrients for the seedling, is then surrounded only by the lignified endocarp. This is why coconuts in the supermarket look different from those still hanging on the palm **┌48–50**.

The tropical coconut palm grows on riverbanks and in coastal regions. The coconuts hang in the crown of the palm and, when ripe, fall to the ground or into the water from a height of up to 30 meters. The fruit, which is capable of floating in salt water for several months, often washes up on foreign beaches far away from the mother plant. Provided it is not then eaten by animals (such as monkeys, elephants, or the crabs referred to as "robber crabs") or found and eaten by humans, germination can take place.

What are the mechanical loads the coconut is exposed to? The first mechanical challenge occurs when the coconut falls off the palm tree and needs to survive this drop without damage. When a coconut falls from a clear height of 30 meters, it reaches a speed of over 80 kilometers per hour. Another critical situation occurs when the floating coconut is thrust against rocks in the surge of the sea or on the beach. During these events, the pericarp must not break open—otherwise fungal spores and bacteria, or other germs, can penetrate to the seed and prevent germination. And finally, the white, nutrient-rich coconut meat (botanical term: endosperm) within the seed attracts predators, which means the pericarp must also protect against sharp teeth and claws.

The three-layered pericarp of the coconut is well equipped for such loads. The leathery exocarp, which also controls evaporation and prevents the ingress of salt water when the fruit floats in the sea, holds the fibrous layer of the mesocarp together. These two layers absorb a large proportion of any impact (or, in other words, the kinetic energy resulting from the impact) by compacting the tissue, which after that can relax again. As is the case with the bark of the giant redwood tree, this is made possible by (visco-)elastic and plastic deformation. In these events, the hard and tough endocarp ensures that the seed is not also squashed, which could damage the embryo on the inside. This hard shell further reduces the remaining force of the impact, although small cracks in the endocarp can result. These cracks do not present a problem for the seed as long as they do not completely penetrate the endocarp. This problem is avoided by the structure of this hard and tough layer, which consists mostly of so-called sclereids. These heavily lignified cells are densely packed and connected with each other; as a result, it is very difficult to break them apart ⌜51.

In addition, the endocarp also contains vascular bundles, the transport channels of the plant used to deliver water and nutrients. In contrast to the compact sclereid cell matrix, these are hollow "ducts." They run in parallel to the outer surface of the endocarp. Since cracks tend to develop along these less dense areas, they are less likely to penetrate directly to the seed and cause damage. Instead, the cracks proceed within the hard layer until they come to a stop without penetrating the whole endocarp. In this way, a slightly damaged endocarp still remains closed and continues to provide an intact protection layer around the seed.

However, the pericarp must not be completely impenetrable since the seedling has to break through the protective cover during germination. For this purpose, there are three germination pores on the side of the hard endocarp on which the fruit was suspended from the palm tree. In these areas the endocarp is significantly thinner, allowing the coconut palm to grow through it.

Implementation in technology

These three examples are enough to demonstrate: nature supplies a rich reservoir of clever structures and mechanisms that can face up to extreme mechanical forces and hence withstand high loads. Materials with such properties that are suitable for technical applications are much in demand, and the question is obvious: why do we not analyze these biological systems that have been tried and tested over millions of years and transfer them to technical applications, for example as lightweight or fire protection materials in building construction?
Such a transfer to technology would appear particularly logical when one considers issues such as the conservation of resources or safety. However, in reality, there are considerable difficulties when we try to implement in technical products what we have learned from nature. Usually the biggest challenge in biomimetics is not to understand the actual mechanism used in nature but to abstract it and successfully transfer it to technical applications.

From the sea urchin to the multifunctional material: numeric simulation as a link between nature and technology

Thanks to modern technology, the different materials and structures of the biological role models can be shown in computer models and their interplay can be simulated. Likewise, it is possible in these simulations to replace the natural materials with advanced technical substances that have properties which are tailor-made for their intended application. Substituting the natural materials with technical ones is indispensable for a successful transfer. Simulations enable another abstraction that is necessary in order to be able to produce a technically usable structure in the first place and to test its usability: with the help of simulations, test runs can be performed at significantly reduced cost compared with building models that are then tested experimentally.
To carry out simulations, we need digital images of the biological structures, such as the outer and inner composition of the sea urchin spines. Examples of these are high-resolution X-ray images, which are produced with the help of computer tomography. In this way it is possible to gain an insight into the interior of the sea urchin spine without destroying it. Such images can then be used to produce a three-dimensional virtual model of the sea urchin spine and its inner structure ⌜52. With these structural models, which are created in the computer and represent the actual inner structure as precisely as possible, it is possible, for example, to simulate compression tests and to examine the resulting loads. To represent

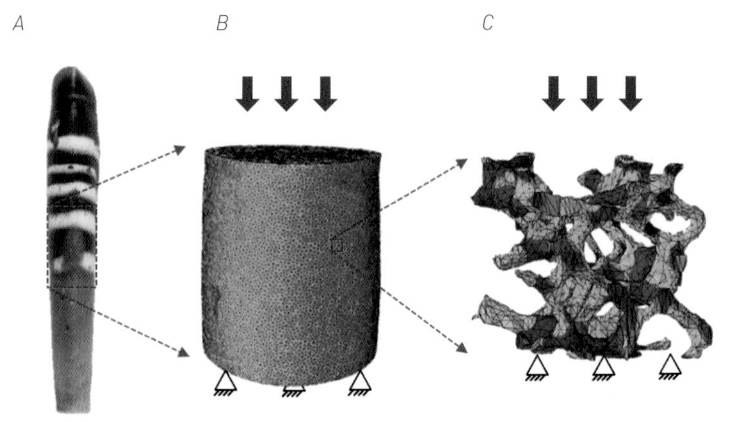

52 *Piece of a slate pencil urchin spine (A, area marked red) has been converted into a computer model with the help of X-ray images. This model was used to simulate compression tests on the computer (B). In order to obtain a better impression of the behavior of the structure (e.g., the network of cavities) under compression, additional smaller areas from the sea urchin spine were used for the simulation of compression tests (C). The red arrows indicate the impact of forces; the triangles underneath symbolize the points of support (of the model). Based on the different colors, it is possible to read off different values for stress. Red and green areas are subject to higher stresses, whereas blue and turquoise areas are hardly stressed at all.*

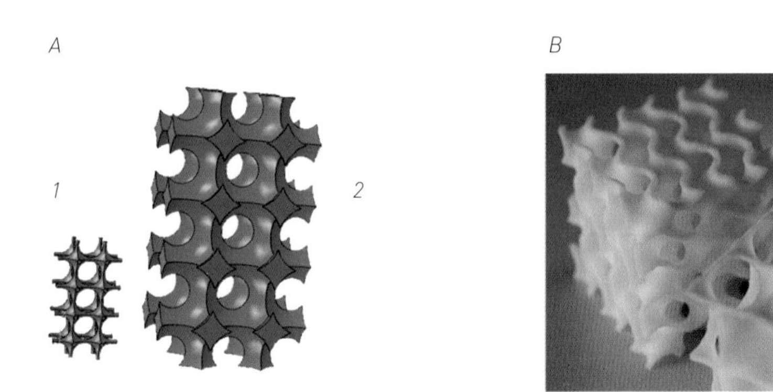

53 *Simplified models of the microstructure of a sea urchin spine produced using parameterized modeling (A). In the model on the right (2) the material between the pores is thicker compared with the model on the left (1), with the pore volume remaining the same. 3D-printed lightweight structures made of plastic using the example of the sea urchin spine (B).*

the hierarchical structure of the biological sample is a big challenge when producing computer models. Simplifications, for example by omitting some of the smaller structure levels, can help to accelerate the simulations and may even be necessary to enable virtual test series in the computer. This means that only the most important construction principles of the microstructure of the sea urchin spine are adopted for simulation. Nevertheless, these are (frequently) sufficient for a transfer of the desired function into technical solutions. These models can be used to investigate, on the computer, the influence of various structures on the stability of the sea urchin spine, for example the pore size or the thickness of the growth layers. These simplified models can be printed using 3D printers. Thus, the computer models can be taken out of the virtual environment and used for real tests or as demonstration examples for architecture ┌**53**.
This procedure is also used to produce models of other examples from nature, such as the coconut and the giant redwood tree bark. The plan is, in a future step, to transfer the results of the individual computer simulations—of the stability of the sea urchin spine or regarding the damping properties of the tree bark, for example—to a unified model. The idea behind this is to combine the different properties—the low weight and favorable fracture behavior of the sea urchin spine and the outstanding damping properties of the tree bark—and to transfer these for technical use.

From the sea urchin spine to the ceramic demonstrator

The freeze-casting technique

The understanding we gain in the abovementioned processes is then technically applied in initial prototypes called "demonstrators." One of the production methods for producing demonstrators to replicate the structure of sea urchin spines is called freeze-casting ┌**54**. This is based on the directional freezing of a ceramic/water mixture and, during a continuing freezing process, forms a directional pore structure that can become very similar to that of the sea urchin spine.
To produce ceramics with the help of the freeze-casting technique, a suspension is produced with ceramic micropowder. In this suspension the ceramic particles, which measure up to one micrometer, are kept floating in the water and prevented from sinking down. This mixture is also called "ceramic slurry" ┌**54A**. Then heat is withdrawn from the slurry from a defined direction, which leads to its direction of freezing. This causes directional ice crystals to form, which accumulate and compact the ceramic particles in their interstitial spaces ┌**54B**. When vacuum is applied to the frozen sample combined with a slow increase of temperature, the water is removed through sublimation ┌**54C** (sublimation = transition from ice to water vapor without liquid phase). The remaining solidified ceramic powder, which is the negative imprint of the structure of the former ice crystals, is hardened by a sintering process ┌**54D**.
By using various adjustment screws in the manufacturing process, it is possible to influence the size of the pores, the pore geometry, and the internal cross-linking.

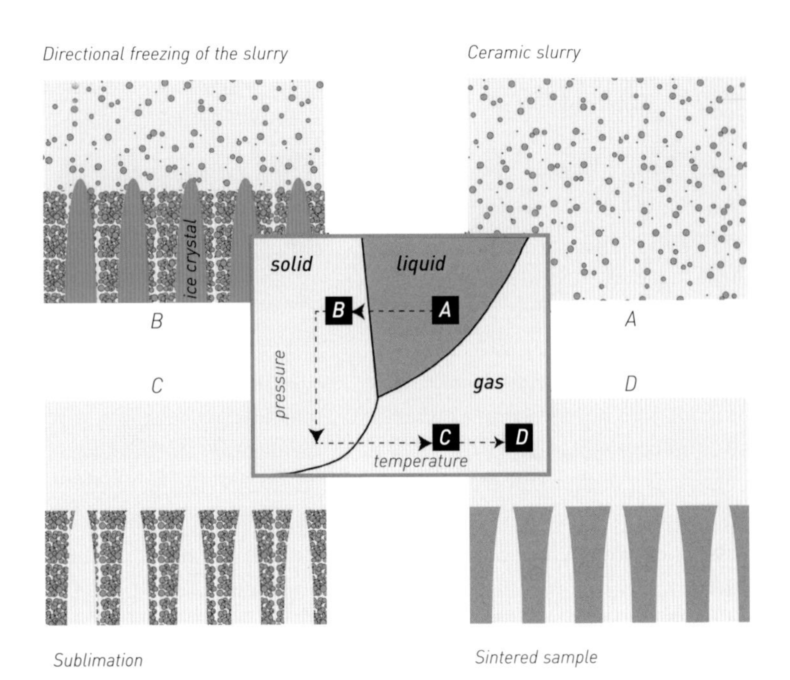

54 *Schematic illustration of the freeze-casting technique*

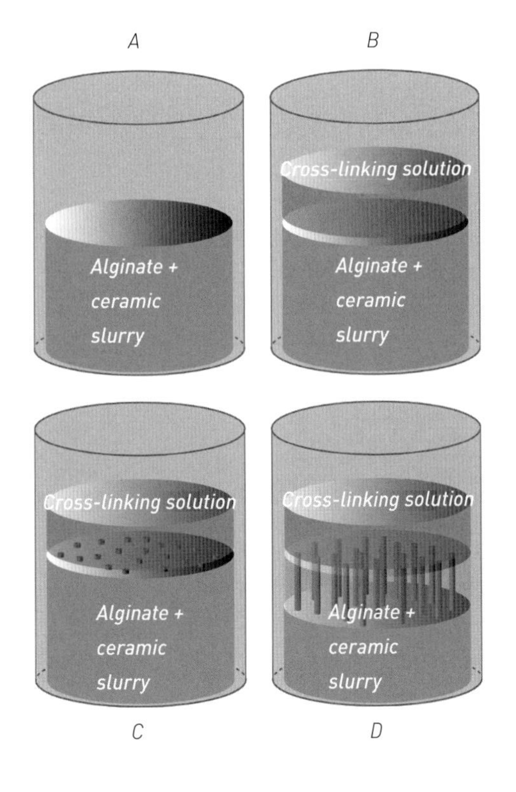

55 *Schematic illustration of the production process using ionotropic gelation method*

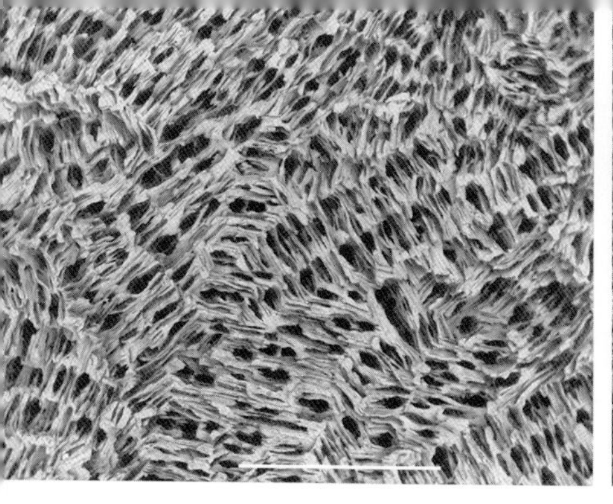

A B

┌**56** *Structures created during the freeze-casting process: chaotic pore structure with lamellar to column-like appearance in top view (A), dendritic growth structure in side view (B). Scale bar: 1 mm.*

Some ways of influencing the design of the pore structure are, for example, by controlling the speed of freezing, the choice of the solvent, or the inclusion of various additives.

The ionotropic gelation method

The ionotropic gelation method is a second technique for producing directional structures ┌**55**.

In the first step, sodium alginate (product of a brown alga) is dissolved in water and mixed with a stable ceramic suspension ┌**55A**. This solution, referred to as "mixed sol," is filled into a production container and overlaid with a cross-linking solution (e.g., calcium chloride $CaCl_2$) ┌**55B**. The cross-linking solution triggers a structuring process of the alginate in which the calcium (as complex) binds with the alginate ┌**55C**, and this causes the formation of small, continuous directional tubes (capillaries) ┌**55D**. Once the structuring process has been completed, the gelatinous body is solidified and dried. In the last step, as in freeze-casting, the ceramic gel body is heated to a high temperature (sintered), which causes the organic component to burn off, leaving a ceramic object with capillary pore structures.

┌**57** *Minute tube-shaped (capillary) structures that can be produced using ionotropic gelation method; cross-section (A) and longitudinal section (B). Scale bar: 1 mm.*

A B

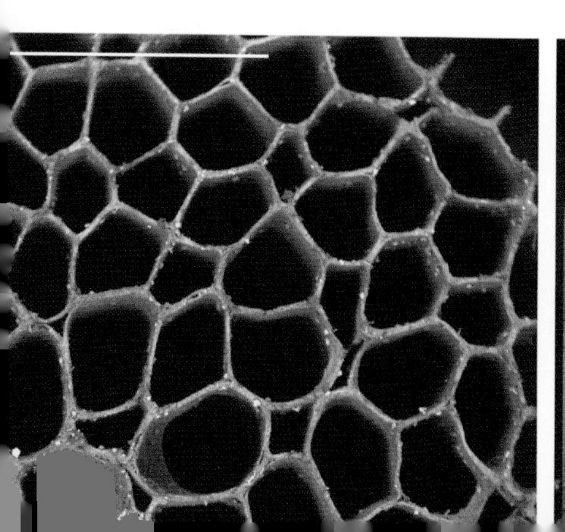

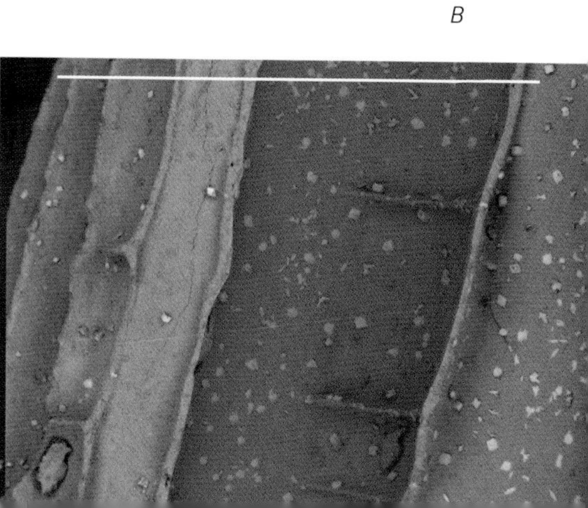

Initial mechanical tests with the capillary structures produced using ionotropic gel formation show a similar fracture behavior to that of the sea urchin spines. This shows that, in principle, a transfer of the fracture behavior of structures to technical materials is possible. However, in order to obtain the observed properties of the natural examples, it is necessary to carry out further investigation.
Whereas the structures produced using the freeze-casting method quite closely resemble the inner structure of the sea urchin spine ⌜56, the structures produced in ionotropic gelation method, which are made up of thin tubes called capillaries, are more comparable to the vascular structures in the wood of trees or in the endocarp of the coconut ⌜57. In terms of their linear orientation, they resemble the fibers in the bark of the giant redwood tree. With this approach it is intended to investigate the influence of the pore geometry on the mechanical properties; furthermore, a contiguous capillary structure offers the opportunity to provide good permeability in a material. By combining the two production methods, it would be possible to develop a lightweight building material that has outstanding mechanical properties and is also permeable in a defined direction.

Graded concrete

Concrete is produced from a mixture of cement, water, aggregates (such as sand), admixtures and additives. This mixture is initially fluid, and then cures to become a solid "artificial stone." These days, concrete is such a common building material that we would be hard pressed to imagine how large-scale building could be done without it. But this is precisely what could happen if we do not soon make radical changes in the way we generally use resources.
But before we tackle these questions, we would like to take a quick look back at the history of this "material of the century." It is believed that concrete was already being used in the construction of the Egyptian pyramids, 5,000 years ago. These structures consisted mainly of blocks that could weigh up to 15 metric tons. A hypothesis by material scientist Joseph Davidovits suggests that at least some of these blocks were not broken from a quarry and then transported to the construction site. Instead, it is possible that the Egyptians produced the blocks directly at the intended site using limestone concrete. According to Davidovits, the Egyptians may have used very soft calcareous sandstone with a high content of the clay mineral kaolinite for these concrete products. The calcareous sandstone was quarried, heated, and subsequently processed with alkaline water to produce a watery slurry. On the building site of the pyramids, this slurry was cast into formwork and thereby given its shape. Once the blocks of a series had cured, the formwork for the next higher row could be built and filled with concrete. In this way, the blocks fit perfectly on top of each other and, to this day, ensure the structural integrity of the pyramids. Under the name "*opus caementicium*," the Romans used a different form of the building material under consideration. This very long-lived Roman concrete was produced from three components: aggregates such as fine gravel or coarse sand, a binder (quicklime, volcanic ash, and pulverized stone) and water. This material was used all over the Roman Empire to build aqueducts and

roads, but also unique buildings. A famous example is the Pantheon in Rome, a temple built of concrete, the dome-shaped roof of which has an astonishing diameter of 43 meters. Up until the end of the 19th century, this well-preserved building was the largest free-spanning construction ever built. It is used as a church to this day.

Following the fall of the Roman Empire, the knowledge of how to produce concrete was lost and was not rediscovered until well over 1,400 years later.

The age of modern concrete began in the 19th century, when, in 1824, Joseph Aspdin developed a new binding agent for the production of concrete, the so-called Portland cement. Shortly thereafter, this was followed, in 1849, by Joseph Monier's idea of embedding metal within concrete components in order to reinforce them. From that point on, the use of concrete spread rapidly throughout the world. With this material of the century it was possible to build roads, bridges, factories, houses, and later also tower blocks more quickly and cheaply, and also more durably.

The triumph of concrete continues to this day. Currently, the worldwide annual consumption of concrete is one cubic meter per citizen. This should be considered in the light of the accelerating growth of the world population on the one hand and, on the other, the increasing scarcity of the raw materials needed for the production of concrete. These raw materials include natural aggregates such as sand and graded stone, cement consisting of limestone, marl, slate, iron ore, clay, and fly ash, and, not least, large quantities of water and energy. Even sand is scarce because only certain kinds of sand are suitable for making concrete; for instance, desert sand is not suitable because the sand grains have become rounded from being blown about by the wind.

When we consider that, today, the construction industry in central Europe is responsible for 60 percent of the annual consumption of resources and 50 percent of all waste produced, it becomes clear how much responsibility for the preservation of our planet rests on the shoulders of architects and structural engineers, and how important the choice of material is.

One approach for drastically reducing the consumption of resources and the production of waste is to build with lightweight components that are fully decomposable and recyclable. An important step in this direction is the manufacture of building components with graded material properties. When a material property—for example, the proportion of lightweight aggregates—is not the same in all parts of the component but consistently changes in at least one direction, this is referred to as a gradient ⌜58. This makes it possible to adapt the material properties of a component at every point to the respective requirements (e.g., bearing large loads). The result is an extremely efficient mono-material, and a recyclable building component with minimal mass.

At the end of the 20th century, the principle of functionally graded concrete was formulated for the first time by Werner Sobek, and since then it has been continually developed at the Institute for Lightweight Structures and Conceptual Design (ILEK) of Stuttgart University. A team of structural engineers and architects researches the design, the material properties, and the production methods of functionally graded concrete components. In addition to conventional calculation methods, the design and construction of such components also requires other

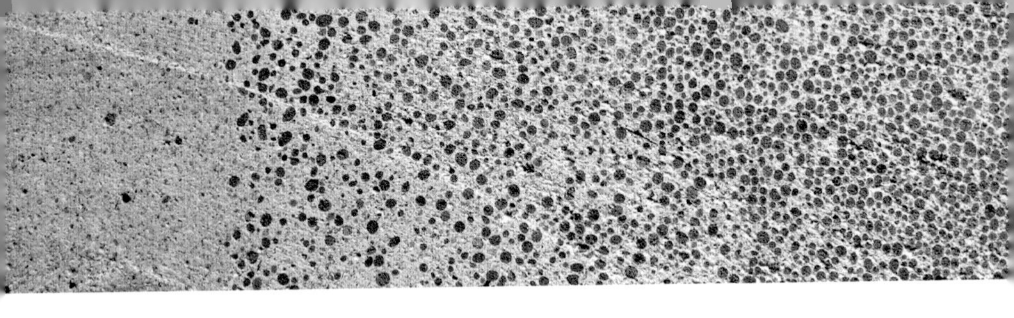

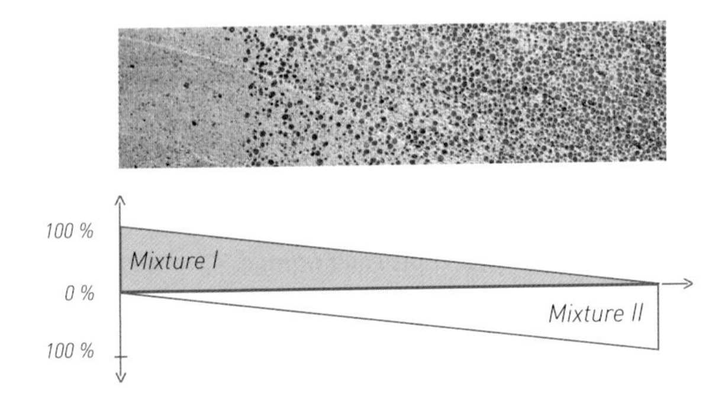

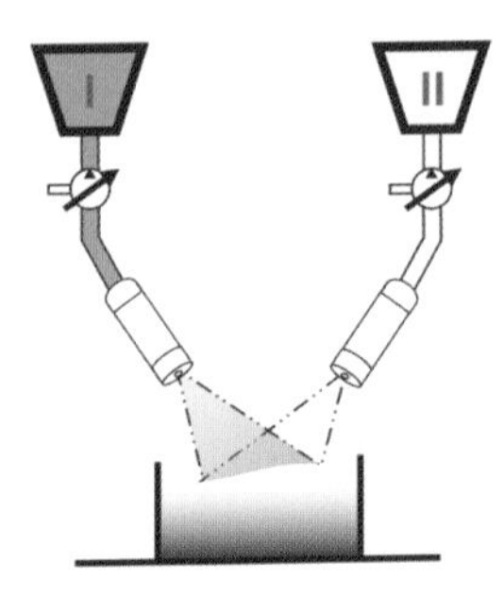

58 *A density gradient is produced within a concrete component using a spray-mist process in which the ratio of two mixtures is varied in the production process.*

less well-known analytical methods, such as the theory of foams. Besides the transfer of loads, such components can also perform other functions, such as thermal insulation, increased fire resistance, or moisture transport. In this way, functionally graded concrete makes it possible to integrate systems of a building that are usually separate, such as the loadbearing structure, the envelope, and building services, and with that can lead to a new esthetic expression of the built environment.

In nature too, there are many examples of material gradients. These can be drawn upon as inspiration for the design of graded building components. Again, the internal structure of sea urchin spines, for example, is a potential source of inspiration. These spines have some very interesting characteristics: low weight, the ability to absorb large quantities of energy, and the hierarchical structure of their skeleton p. 55. As described earlier, the spine of the sea urchin consists of a magnesium calcite skeleton, the porosity of which varies between 10 percent and 80 percent. Based on the internal structure of the sea ur-

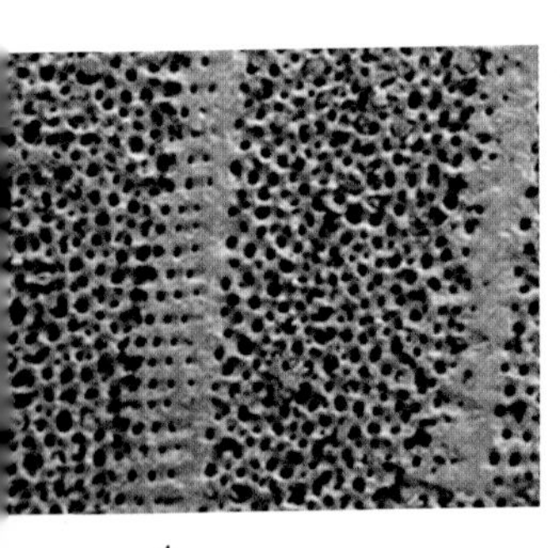
A

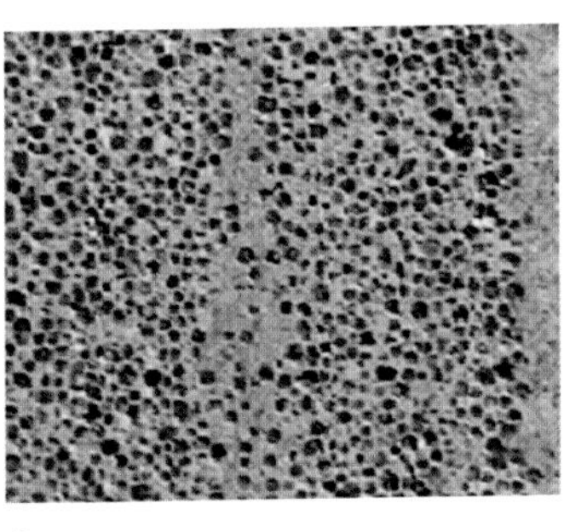
B

59 *Change of density in the spine of a mature slate pencil urchin (A) and in a graded concrete sample (B)*

chin spines, concrete samples with graded porosity were produced at the ILEK and investigated for their resistance to compression ⌈59. Not only was the weight of these concrete samples 35 percent less than that of samples made of normal concrete, but they were also capable of absorbing ten times more energy than concrete samples consisting of non-graded material.

Functionally graded multifunctional concrete components therefore offer huge potential for radically reducing the consumption of materials in construction and, at the same time, facilitate decomposable and recyclable components. As such, functionally graded concrete offers an interesting solution to the ecological and social problems resulting from scarcity of resources and overpopulation.

Scaling—the challenge of enlarging

The key step in working with biomimetics is the abstraction of the biological role model in order to transfer functional principles from the world of animals and plants to technical products. An important part of the abstraction process is to consider the relationship of size between the biological role model and the technical transfer product. As already mentioned, many of the biological structures that are important for a certain function measure just a few micrometers. By comparison, the size of concrete grains is in the order of a few millimeters to centimeters, that is to say, larger by a factor of 1,000 to 10,000. This means that a transfer at a ratio of 1:1 is technically impossible. Furthermore, the simple magnification of natural structures results in poorer mechanical properties.

This can be best explained using an example. Let us consider the dragon bamboo (*Dendrocalamus giganteus*). It reaches a maximum height of 40 meters with a diameter of 35 centimeters at its base. If it were to grow to the height of the Stuttgart television tower (216 meters), the diameter would of course have to become larger. At the ratio of 1:1 (i.e., when all dimensions are increased linearly) this would correspond to a diameter of 1.89 meters. However, since the volume would increase disproportionately, the enlarged bamboo would buckle under its own weight. Theoretically, it would not be stable and capable of at least supporting its own weight unless it had a base diameter of 4.4 meters ⌈60. Just this simple example, in which the exposure to wind—the dominant load to be resisted by plants—has not been taken into account, makes it obvious that it is imperative not to lose sight of the physical boundary conditions. However, since it is not possible to take all physical boundary conditions into account with simple formulae, a theory suggested by the Swedish mathematician and engineer Waloddi Weibull has been established in the material sciences. This theory deals with the mechanical properties of so-called "brittle" materials—materials that break easily, such as glass, ceramic, and porcelain. The failure of a building component made of brittle material is determined by statistically present defects in the material (for example, air bubbles in a glass pane). When scaling the building component to double its size (i.e., twice the length, width, and height), its volume increases eightfold. With the increase in volume,

the probability of defects also increases, which makes the component more prone to failure.
In the animal kingdom, we can also find some examples of "scaling," in which similar structures occur with the same function but in different sizes. One such example is the thigh bone of mammals. It supports the weight of the body in all mammals. Scientific investigations of thigh bones of mammals of different sizes indicate that the mechanical properties do not follow the Weibull theory. Instead, they all fail at a similar exposure to load compared to their size. Most likely this is the case because the bones vary not only in their size but also in their internal structure (e.g., in the arrangement of the bone trabeculae).

There is another example of scaling in the spine of the slate pencil urchin **⌈61**. The growth of the spine leaves behind characteristic growth layers, which can be seen in the cross-section as reddish lines. At one time, when the sea urchin was smaller, each of these lines was the outer layer of the spine. In this way, this structure is similar to the growth rings of trees, even though the growth lines of the sea urchins probably do not occur annually. The extent to which this example of scaling from the animal world can be transferred to technology is an issue of current research. We should therefore sit tight and maintain our curiosity!

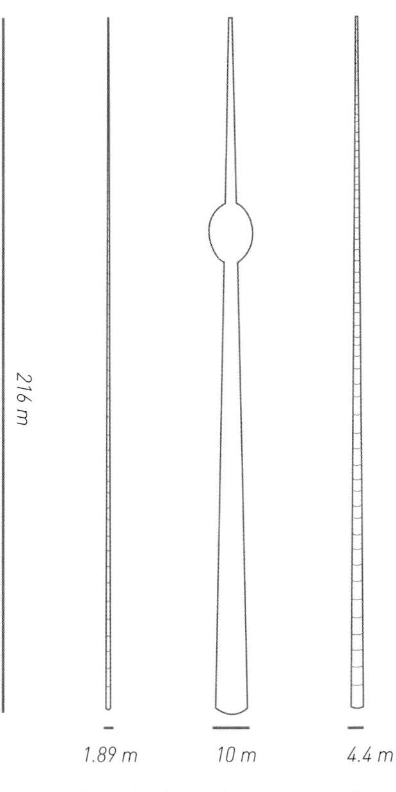

60 *The problem of scaling: Plant stems are well known for their lightweight construction. The dragon bamboo (*Dendrocalamus giganteus*) can reach a height of 40 m, with a diameter of 35 cm at its base. However, if it were to be enlarged to the height of the Stuttgart television tower, it would have to be built comparatively thicker than in the original in order to prevent the structure from buckling under its own weight.*

61 *A large and a small spine of the slate pencil urchin. The red lines are growth lines. It can easily be seen that, three growth phases ago, the larger spine was the same size as the smaller one.*

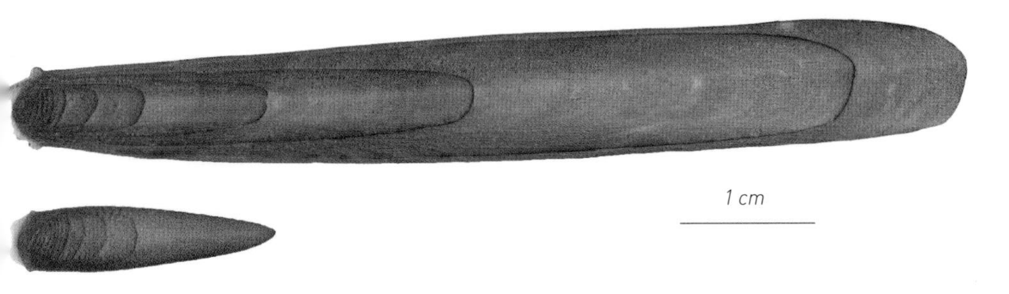

Freezing: the right way

Rena T. Schott / Lukas Eurich / Arndt Wagner / Anita Roth-Nebelsick / Wolfgang Ehlers

Plants growing in areas with cold winters use numerous strategies to cope with low temperatures and alternating freezing and thawing events. In one of these strategies, the plants die off and survive the winter with underground storage organs or seeds. However, numerous species do not discard the parts aboveground. Rather, dense forests exist in areas with very cold winters, and we are familiar with the image of trees deeply covered in snow. Frost-resistant trees and shrubs can even be evergreen, such as most conifers, boxwood, and rhododendron ┌62. Similarly, various types of bamboo and many other grasses are "frost-resistant." The same applies to some climbing plants such as ivy, and even to various herbaceous plants such as the winter aconite and the popular snowdrop. Even though these are deciduous, they appear very early in the season and flower at a time when snowfall and frost are still very likely.

Avoiding frost damage—can we learn from plants?

Many hardy plants cope well with temperatures below freezing and also survive fluctuations in temperature that cause alternating frost and thaw periods in quick succession. By contrast, buildings and roads very frequently suffer from frost damage. One of the problems is that water expands during freezing, which can cause damage through frost bursting. Furthermore, ice attracts liquid water, which means a body of ice that is in contact with a reservoir of water that is still liquid can grow in size. This process can lead to potholes in roads, for example, unless appropriate countermeasures are taken. Such phenomena also affect natural rock formations and are an important part of the weathering process. It follows that there is significant potential for frost events to damage building materials too.

Is it possible to derive technically interesting ideas for the improvement of the frost resistance of technical building materials from the adaptive performance of hardy plants? For this purpose, we have to first understand what happens in plants during a frosty period. A plant can actually freeze inside without suffering damage. How exactly does this happen? And can we gain any knowledge and inspiration from that for technical implementation?

⌜62 *Various frost-hardy plants in winter. Top left: boxwood* (Buxus sempervirens). *Bottom left: ivy* (Hedera helix). *Top right: rhododendron* (Rhododendron). *Bottom right: winter jasmine* (Jasminum nufiflorum).

Initial discoveries—"ice lenses" in plants

In 1869, the French researcher Édouard Ernest Prillieux investigated herbaceous plants, the greater celandine (*Chelidonium majus)*, and a type of comfrey *(Symphytum)*, all of which flower in spring and are capable of withstanding light frost. These plants became limp when exposed to frost at night but fully recovered when the temperature rose again the following morning. Prillieux microscopically examined the frozen plants and found that large ice lenses (mostly three) were forming in cavities within the leaf stalks (petioles) near the inner wall of the stem surface**⌜63**. Almost 140 years later, this phenomenon was

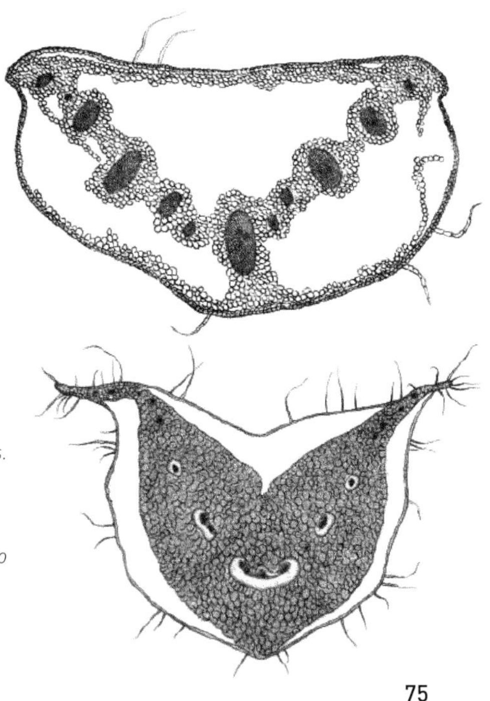

⌜63 *Deformations of the living tissue in the leaf stalks of greater celandine* (Chelidonium majus, top) *and a type of comfrey* (Symphytum, bottom) *in cross-section in historic images by Prillieux (1869). The deformations are caused by the formation of extracellular ice bodies. The gray matter represents the tissue that has shrunk a great deal due to the withdrawal of water.*

Ice forms in a cavity

Water is attracted

Ice has formed a large cavity

Ice melts; meltwater is absorbed

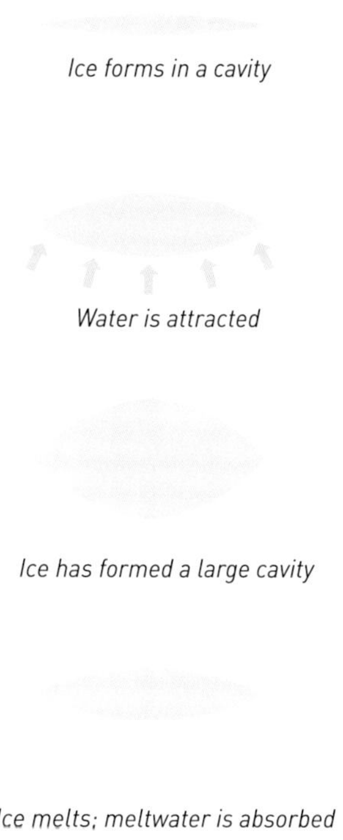

64 *Schematic illustration of the formation of an extracellular ice body*

examined in more detail using modern methods. For this purpose, a cryo-scanning electron microscope was used, which is suitable for studying frozen samples. This time, the same response to frost was also discovered in other plants, for example the white clover (*Trifolium repens) and the California poppy (Eschscholzia californica).* This means that these plants can initiate the formation of ice bodies in anatomically predetermined areas where this clearly does not cause a problem for the plant.
This process is called extracellular ice formation. It has now been documented in a wide range of organs and tissues of many frost-hardy plants. Ice forms in special intercellular spaces in buds, leaves, and leaf stalks, and in the water-conducting elements of roots. This extracellular ice does not cause damage. However, the formation of ice crystals inside cells is dangerous, and must be avoided at all costs as it can lead to the death of the cell. For this reason, to avoid such damage, the extracellular ice formation is an important factor. Not only does it not cause damage, but it even has an advantage, as demonstrated by the example of the white clover.

Extracellular ice bodies—their creation and function

When it is not frozen, the leaf stalk of the white clover has a narrow gap in the tissue directly beneath the epidermis (the "skin") of the leaf stalk. When the temperature drops, water in this narrow gap will freeze earlier than the content of the living cells because these contain dissolved substances. As with the use of de-icing salt, this causes the freezing point to drop, which means that the cell content does not start freezing at 0 °C. When the first layer of ice forms in the gap, it will withdraw water from the living cells that have not yet frozen. This means that the intercellular ice body grows at the expense of the

⌐65 *White clover* (Trifolium repens) *in fresh (A) and frozen condition (B) in a test refrigerator, and the respective cross-sections of the leaf stalks in fresh (C) and frozen condition (D). The ice has primarily formed at the edge outside the cells between epidermis and bark tissue. Scale bar: 0.2 mm.*

water content of the living stalk cells, and expands accordingly **⌐64**. In this process, the living cell layers become dehydrated (i.e., water is drawn off). In this way, the ice body acts as a kind of drying agent. Owing to the loss of water, the concentration of dissolved substances in the cells increases significantly as they remain in the cells. The process ends when the hygroscopic effect of the ice is balanced by the increasing capacity of the cells to hold water, which is caused by the increasing concentration of dissolved substances. At this stage, the living cells contain less water and a high concentration of dissolved substances, which firstly significantly lowers the freezing point and secondly means that, in the case of freezing at even lower

66 *Branch of the dwarf birch* (Betula nana) *in cross-section in fresh (A) and frozen condition (B). Extracellular ice bodies can be seen in (B) in the bark (white arrows).*

temperatures, no dangerous ice crystals can form. Instead, the cell is then "fritted"—it freezes without the formation of crystals—and can thaw again without having sustained damage from the freezing. The dehydration of the living cells is akin to a wilting process **65**. As the temperature rises, the extracellular ice bodies thaw, the cells absorb the meltwater, and the plant slowly straightens up again at approximately 5 °C. The process is completely reversible and can be repeated any number of times.

It follows that extracellular ice formation is extremely useful and protects living cells against the dangerous formation of ice crystals inside them. Using an ice body outside the cells as a drying agent is literally ingenious. This process is used not only by the white clover examined by us, but by all frost-hardy species hitherto examined for this phenomenon. In ligneous plants, for example, extracellular ice collects not only in the body of the wood but also in the intercellular spaces of the bark layer **66**. Spore-producing plants (cryptogams) also have this ability. For example, in the frost-hardy winter horsetail, ice forms in the extensive duct system that runs longitudinally through the plant axes **67**.

However, low temperatures can have a damaging effect in other ways, and the unusually extensive loss of water represents a significant stress resulting from dryness. The cell membranes are particularly sensitive, and need special protection for this situation. As a matter of fact, even frost-hardy plants cannot survive frost events without acclimatization; in other words, they have to become "accustomed" to lower temperatures in a step-by-step process. This means that the plant adjusts to winter as temperatures slowly fall. During the acclimatization period, physiological changes take place. For example, the composition of the cell membranes changes during this phase. Therefore, unexpected night frost events during warm periods can cause damage even to frost-hardy plants.

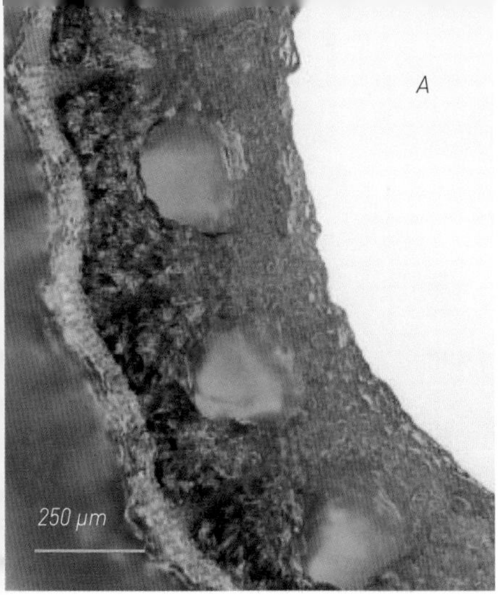

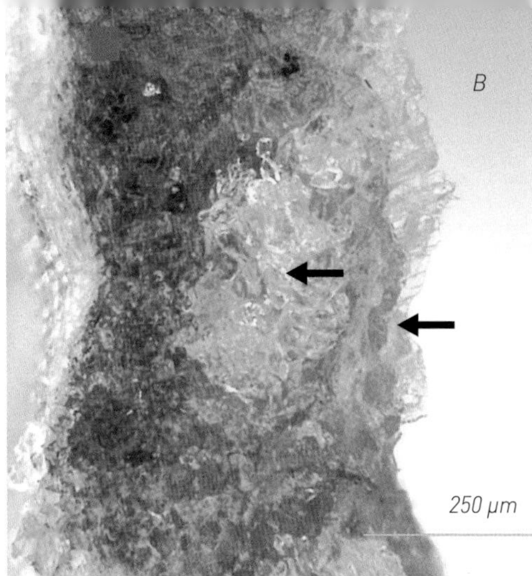

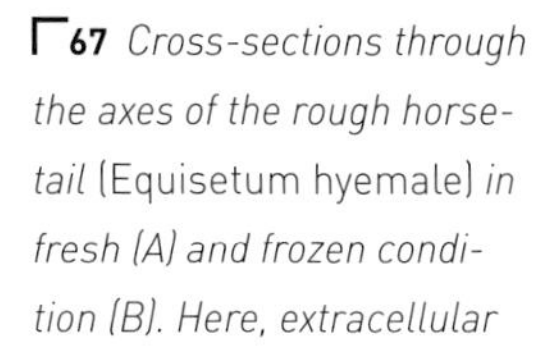

67 *Cross-sections through the axes of the rough horsetail* (Equisetum hyemale) *in fresh (A) and frozen condition (B). Here, extracellular ice has formed in the canals that run along the plant axis (upper black arrow) and at the edge of the pith cavity (lower black arrow).*

Perennials in particular are subject to recurring changes and adaptations. In addition to the restructuring of the cell membranes, other protective measures also exist. Depending on the type of plant, special proteins are formed that work like antifreeze substances, moving the formation of ice to far below the freezing point (supercooling). This ability is particularly prominent in living cells in wood. Furthermore, prior to freezing, the water content of the respective part of the plant plays a role. If the frost period lasts too long, the plant may dry out due to the loss of water from the cells. In winter, container plants also face the risk of their roots freezing, because these do not have such a protection mechanism; normally, roots are protected from deep frost by earth and snow. In spite of these adaptations, however, each type of plant can only cope with temperatures below zero to a point that is specific to the species. If the weather becomes significantly colder, more parts of the plant will freeze or the plant will freeze completely and, depending on the temperature, parts or all of the plant will die.

The principal processes of protection against frost damage using focused ice accumulation are primarily physical in nature. In view of the fact that, like many building materials, plant tissue is a porous material, it should be possible to examine and illustrate the processes physically with appropriate models, thereby using them as sources of ideas for frost protection of technical materials.

A physical model

How can such observations from nature be recorded and translated into a physical model? Engineers try to "translate" the processes that take place within the plant into a model (i.e., to abstract them). This theoretical model is described with the help of mathematical equations and can be used for an analytical investigation of the processes. These can then be simulated using a computer. If this is successful and it is possible to illustrate the relevant processes for the problem in question using such an application-oriented model, this can contribute to greater knowledge—also in biology—and may even enable relevant predictions.

When building an application-oriented model, it is not necessary to take into account all properties and mechanisms of a frost-resistant plant. Instead, it is important to focus on those that are critical to the phenomenon investigated and its technical implementation. In the case under consideration here, these are—in particular—the characteristics that contribute to the plant being frost resistant (i.e., characteristics that ensure the plant does not die when exposed to cold temperatures in winter). A categorical distinction is made between the structural properties of the plant that are part of its blueprint and its physiological properties. In view of the fact that it is usually very difficult to transfer the physiological properties of plants to building materials, we are looking here particularly at the mechanisms influenced by their structure. The physiological properties are therefore not taken into account in building the selected model.

The approach to building the model is one of the key steps, since this has to capture the extremely complex real system of the plant (nature) and establish an idealized, simplified concept of the model with an appropriate mathematical description that can be used for technical implementation.

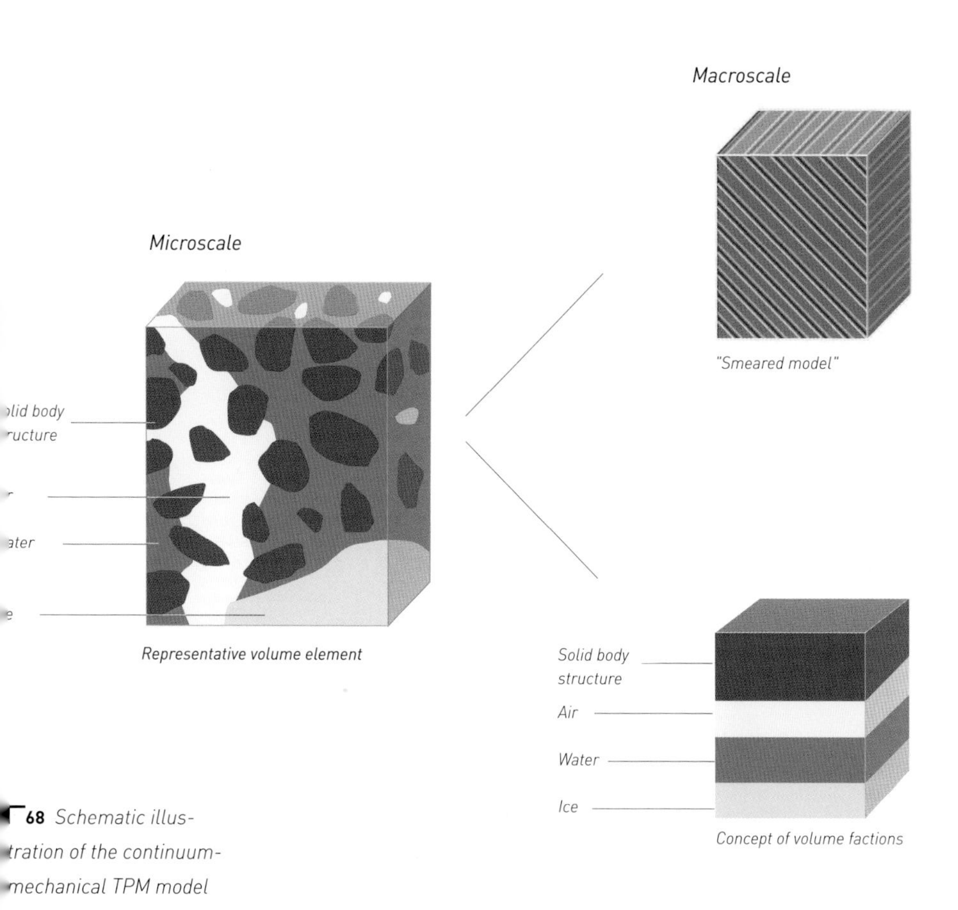

68 *Schematic illustration of the continuum-mechanical TPM model*

Simulations: performance of virtual experiments

Even a simplified consideration of frost processes in plant tissue is still highly complex, which means that the task cannot be successfully tackled using just pen and paper. As a rule, the equations of the model are made accessible to a numeric solution process by way of approximation so that these can be solved by a computer. When these calculations are carried out with the help of a computer, simulating the behavior of the system, the results of the idealized model can be compared with the real system. Such a comparison can then be used to check and calibrate the model. Once the model has been calibrated and, ideally, provides an identical solution for the material to that of the real system, it is also possible to carry out virtual experiments that will not take place in the laboratory but on a computer. This is of particular interest in situations where the experiments are difficult to implement technically, very time-consuming, or very expensive.

What does such a plant model actually look like? The model approach used for frost-resistant plants is based on the "theory of porous media" (TPM), a continuum mechanics theory for multiphase materials in which the material is described not at the microscopic scale but in the sense of a macroscopic observation. For frost-resistant plants, this means

⌐69 *Water supply and water flow in a leaf. Blue: areas with low water permeability. Turquoise: areas with medium water permeability. Green: areas with high water permeability, which corresponds to the location of the vascular bundles. The red arrows indicate the seepage velocity of the water.*

that, microscopically, the material consists of different components. Examples are the loadbearing structure of the solid body, which mostly consists of the lignified part, as well as air inclusions and water contained in the pores. This pore water can freeze at temperatures below 0 °C, in which case the water is still retained in the pores in the form of ice. In the macroscopic observation it is assumed that, at the beginning of the simulation, these localized components, that is to say, the water/ice in the pores, are "smeared" across the entire volume of the porous body; that is the step of homogenization. This means that, in the macroscopic TPM model, each component is initially present everywhere at the same time. The proportion of the component is established by the proportion of the volume taken up by this component. In ⌐68 the model approach for plant-based materials is shown schematically.
It is possible to produce balance equations for each of these components. These are conservation equations of the physical variables of mass, momentum, angular momentum, and energy. These conservation equations also include what are

known as production terms, which can describe mutual interactions and exchange processes. For example, in an enclosed volume, the total quantity of water is retained even though this may be present in liquid form or as ice.
Another step is the completion of the model using material-specific equations. They describe the special behavior of the material and the processes taking place therein, for example the freezing of the water within the plant or the water permeability in a leaf; ┌69 shows an example of the flow processes involved in the water supply of a leaf.

From understanding to transfer

In order to be able to achieve the big objective of transferring functions of the biological examples to bio-inspired technical products, it is essential that biologists and engineers cooperate. For the case described here, the biologists can supply an understanding of the structure of the plants and the processes taking place within them. On this basis, engineers try, in close cooperation with the biologists, to develop a model based on physical laws that can be described with mathematical methods and solved numerically.
In this way it is possible to precisely analyze and understand the processes taking place and their structural prerequisites. However, until the objective is achieved and the knowledge gained can be utilized for technical purposes, many unanswered questions remain, which are of interest both for biology and for the application. For example, there are questions around the role of tissue structures with different porosity (permeability) and the arrangement of the pore spaces, and also the question of why the ice forms preferentially at certain places. Researchers and developers will not run out of questions of interest anytime soon!

Nature as source of ideas for modern manufacturing methods

Frederik Wulle / Daria Kovaleva / Pascal Mindermann / Hans Christof / Karl-Heinz Wurst / Armin Lechler / Alexander Verl / Werner Sobek / Walter Haase / Götz T. Gresser

Nature creates efficient, complex structures using the smallest possible amount of material. The construction principles employed and the intelligent use of materials regarding their specific properties can be transferred to modern production methods. The objective is to produce functional low-weight building components that consume as few resources as possible ⌈70. In this chapter we show how this bionic transfer takes place by continuing the development of production methods, such as fiber technology (pultrusion, fiber deposition), 3D printing, the manufacture of concrete components, and a combination of these three methods.

Sources of ideas for the lightweight construction of tomorrow

In nature, we can detect not only adaptations that are specific to each species, but also general morphological principles. This includes an arrangement of materials in a biological structure that takes account of the loads acting on the structure. In technology, it is common to use homogeneous materials; this means that the density is constant throughout the component. In nature, however, this is almost never the case. Instead, material accumulation and porosity can be found at all orders of size. A famous example of this is the human femur bone ⌈71. On its inside it has a matrix structure that adapts continually to the loads acting on it. In places where the bone is subject to heavy loads, special cells, called osteoblasts, ensure that the bone is reinforced, whereas opponent cells, the osteoclasts, break down tissue in places with low imposed loads. In this process, the orientation of the rods in a certain direction results in increased strength. In other biological structures, such effects can also be generated with highly resilient fibers. These fibers are aligned along the direction of tension and are firmly embedded in the base material, called the matrix. In the stems of bamboo plants, the fiber bundles can withstand high tensile forces, whilst the ground tissue, which is also lignified and in which the fiber bundles are embedded, can very well absorb compressive loads. In addition to their outstanding mechanical properties with respect to tension and compression caused by bending and the attenuation of vibration, bamboo stems also perform other functions, such as the transport of water and of photosynthesis products and, in the case of some types of bamboo with green stems, also photosynthesis itself. In summary, bamboo stems are extremely high-performing, multifunctional compound structures ⌈72.

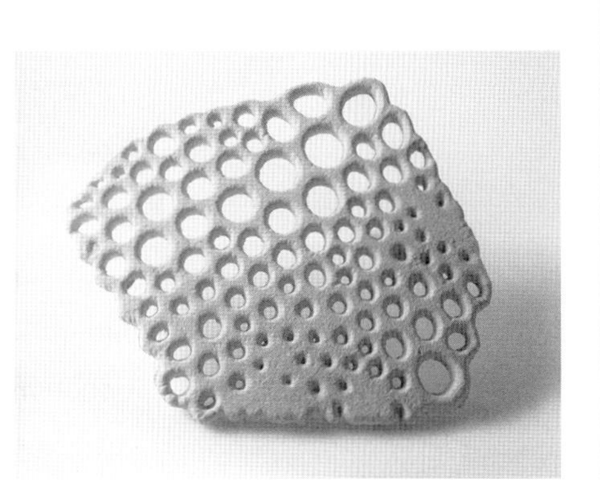

70 *Functionally graded concrete shell segment, manufactured using a special sand casting process*

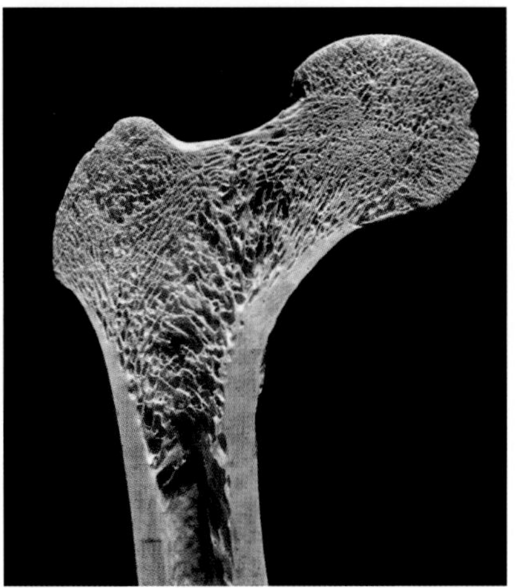

71 *The load-optimized structure of the human thighbone.*

The objective of our biomimetic project is to adapt existing production technologies—such as fiber reinforcement in 3D printing, the production of fiber or of functionally graded concrete components (i.e., concrete with variations in the distribution of density p. 70)—to the biological role models and thereby to continue the development of the respective technology. If this is successful, it would be possible to enormously improve efficiency. Examples are the porous concrete structures in buildings, which can be used to reduce concrete usage by up to 60 percent!

72 *Three examples of complex pultruded profiles (i.e., manufactured using the pultrusion process). Pipe structures compared with technical plant stem.*

Production technology I—Pultrusion

In nature, many structures feature fiber reinforcements or have a fiber-based construction, starting with muscles, in which sarcomeres ensure that we can move our limbs, through to trees, whose special resistance to wind and other mechanical load impact is based on the fact that the cell walls of the wood essentially consist of two components: cellulose and lignin. The microfibers made of cellulose are extremely resistant to tensile forces. The second component, the lignin, forms the essential part of the matrix in which the cellulose fibers are embedded. On the one hand, it ensures that the fibers all stay in their place and, on the other hand, it is responsible for the cell walls' resistance to pressure. This compound material structure in the cell walls of wood fibers and water-conducting cells (tracheids) ensures that trees can not only support their own

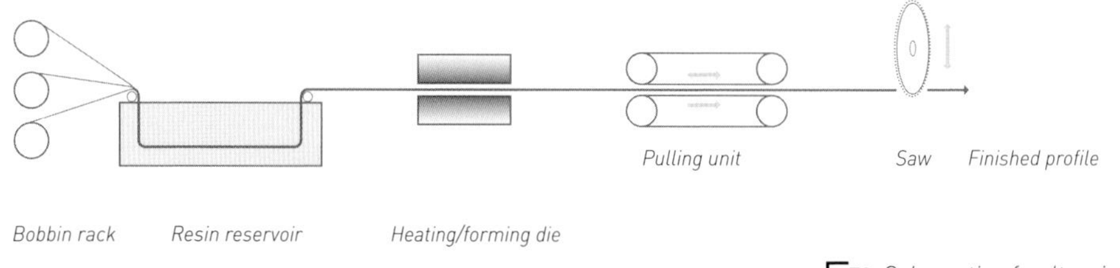

73 *Schematic of pultrusion*

weight but also withstand much greater introduced loads, such as those resulting from bending when exposed to wind during storms. The fact that a combination of fibers with the surrounding matrix produces a strong building substance was recognized early on by human beings, who benefited from nature's examples, for instance in the construction of adobe huts with straw-fiber reinforcement.

To this day, this principle has been used with ever better materials to create more and more lightweight, strong substances. For example, today, the high tensile strength of glass fibers or carbon fibers is exploited in numerous technical applications for the production of high-performance components, such as in the aerospace, automotive, and construction industry. In addition to the production of complex components, which sometimes requires very complex form tools, pultrusion is used to produce profiles from compound fiber materials as an economic alternative to profiles made of steel or other substances.

Pultrusion (a portmanteau word combining "pull" and "extrusion") is the only process suitable for the continuous production of compound fiber profiles at an industrial scale. In this process, reinforcement fibers and a matrix material are pulled together into a heated tool. The matrix material consists of either synthetic resins that, under the influence of heat, become non-meltable plastics, or meltable plastics that subsequently can be deformed again. In the form tool, the fibers are brought into the desired shape and are retained in this shape through the reaction of the synthetic resin **73**. In this way, it is possible to produce profiles in any desired length. In its basic construction, the structure of these technical profiles resembles the wall structure of a wood-fiber cell, with tensile stress-resistant fibers that are embedded in a compression-resistant matrix. Such profiles are capable of withstanding very high tensile stresses because all fibers are aligned along the axis of the profile.

When using special synthetic resins, it is also possible to activate the curing through irradiation with light instead of using a heated form tool. For this purpose, a special, non-visible part of light in the shortwave ultraviolet (UV) range is used. This energy-rich UV radiation, which we must protect ourselves against in summer to avoid sunburn, is used in technical applications to excite the molecules in synthetic resin to form long chains. This creates a fully cured, mechanically strong plastic **75**. This process can also be employed to produce structures with very complex shapes, which can be used in a wide range of applications (e.g., items of furniture).

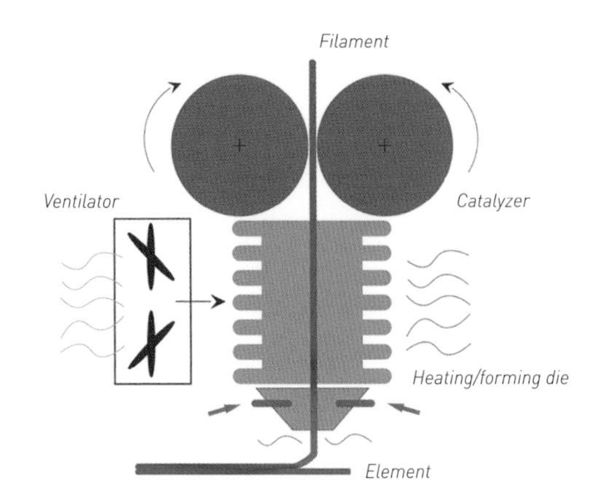

74 *The fused deposition modeling process is a layer process that builds up components from a locally melted plastic filament. Using a feeding mechanism, the filament is transported into the print head, where it is heated until it melts. Then the liquid or viscous plastic is extruded through a nozzle. The print head deposits strands in a horizontal nozzle movement. Moving vertically in steps, the print head applies layer upon layer to create the component. As the filaments can no longer be transported when they are heated too early, a cooling device is used to ensure that the heating component does not heat too early. The movement of the print head is determined using a computer-based model with a schedule for each layer.*

Production technology II—Fiber-reinforced fused deposition modeling (FDM)

What every engineer probably dreams of: the production of components in any shape. Conventional production methods such as casting, milling, or turning are subject to certain boundary conditions and therefore cannot be used for the production of items such as a hollow sphere or very complex, angled components. Through the development of additive manufacturing, also referred to as 3D printing, much greater design freedom has been made possible. By contrast to subtractive processes, no raw material is removed during additive manufacturing; instead, material is applied or added. This method of manufacturing is usually based on a 3D computer model of the desired end product. The model is used later to create a schedule, also called "NC program," for the control of the print head in the 3D printer. A real component is thus created in the 3D printer by applying and connecting material additively in layers. In addition to the original area of application of additive manufacturing—the creation of prototypes in automotive and mechanical engineering—more complex 3D printers are also increasingly used for industrial applications. For example, rare spare parts for machines, or tooth fillings, are already being produced using additive manufacturing. Even components of the aircraft turbines of the new Airbus A350 are produced with additive manufacturing. In medical technology research is being carried out on the printing of organs or organic tissue.

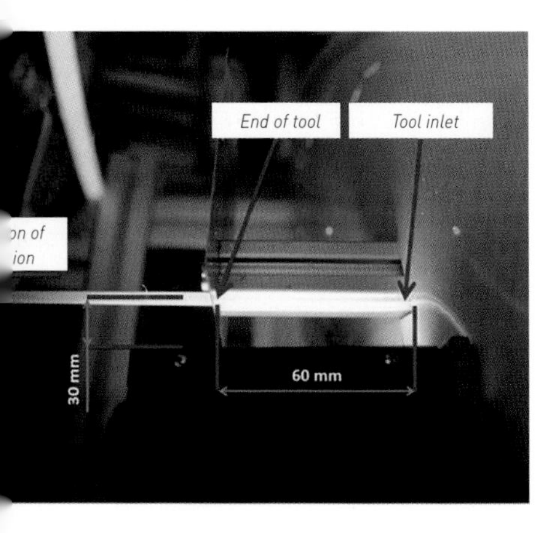

75 *UV pultrusion with glass fibers*

Today, many different additive manufacturing processes exist that are differentiated in terms of their source substance (liquid, powdery, solid), the material (plastic, metal, ceramic, etc.), and the manufacturing process (bonding, melting via laser or heating element). The fused deposition modeling (FDM) process is widely used; it is based on the deposition of a hot and viscous thin plastic filament ┌74. This technology can even be used for the manufacture of closed-pore structures, which frequently occur in nature. This means that porous, material-saving structures, such as sea urchin spines **p. 70**, can be used as examples for lightweight construction in technology. It also means that, aside from biological structures, it is possible to manufacture special components, the loadbearing structure of which is optimized using mathematical algorithms. These possibilities can also be used to produce complex, lightweight, and strong components that combine certain functions and, at the same time, use resources sparingly.

However, plastic components produced via additive manufacturing do not always have the necessary strength for use in highly stressed components. One option for the improvement of strength that is already known from biology is fiber integration. Compared with other additive manufacturing methods, the FDM process can be used to integrate ends of fibers because, while the thermoplastic filament is applied, it is possible to carry a fiber in the print head at the same time. Endless fibers can be aligned to suit the respective imposed load, thereby leading to greater strength in the component. Compared with, for example, steel, the strength of fiber-reinforced plastic in relation to its weight is very great, which means that it is possible to manufacture components of equal strength that are much lighter in weight. This method enables the manufacture of high-performance components of almost any shape for applications in mechanical engineering and in the construction industry.

Production technology III—Functionally graded lightweight concrete structures

Concrete is the most widely used material worldwide, and with an annual consumption of 1.5 metric tons per person, it is the most used substance after water **p. 68**. Thanks to its strength and longevity, it is impossible to imagine our built environment without concrete; it is used in building construction as well as in civil engineering, such as bridge and road building. However, the manufacture of concrete involves two problems that heavily reduce its environmental compatibility. On the one hand, the production of cement—one of the main components of concrete—generates high emissions of the greenhouse gas CO_2. On the other hand, the use of standardized formwork elements in building with concrete means that more concrete is used than would be strictly necessary for structural reasons. These problems are all the more pressing in view of the rapid increase in the world's population and the resulting increase in the use of concrete. One question that arises is how to build more buildings using less material. The formation of biological tissue is a material-intensive and hence energy-intensive process. For this reason, optimization strategies have come about as part of the evolutionary process aimed at forming functioning structures with the least possible amount of material and energy. This is made possible by careful selection and distribution of the components of a tissue or of an organ in accordance with its functional requirements. The resulting functionally graded structures (distribution of density adapted to the function) can be found in all natural tissues and organs exposed to mechanical loads, such as tree trunks, bones, beaks of birds, and exoskeletons of animals on land and in water. The functionally graded structures combine low energy consumption with complex functions, such as mechanical stabilization, shock absorption, temperature control, and—in plant stems—the transport of liquid. Their multifunctionality and modest use of materials mean that these structures are outstanding sources of inspiration for engineers and architects.

The technical equivalents of these biological structures are referred to as functionally graded materials. They were used for the first time in astronautics in 1984, in the form of changeable material compositions using ceramics and metal in order to increase the temperature resistance of structural parts of aircraft. Later, gradations of compound substances appeared in other technical fields of application using combinations such as ceramics with metals, metals with metals, as well as ceramics with polymers. An integrated approach to material selection, processing, and distribution is characteristic of the production of graded materials and requires highly specialized manufacturer technologies. This principle known from astronautics was transferred to the building industry, taking into account the requirements of loadbearing components, material properties of concrete, and framework conditions of manufacturing technologies for large components.

76 *Functionally graded concrete cube that has been manufactured using automated spray technology*

The design of functionally graded concrete components starts with the development of the so-called "gradient layout," which describes the material/porosity distribu-

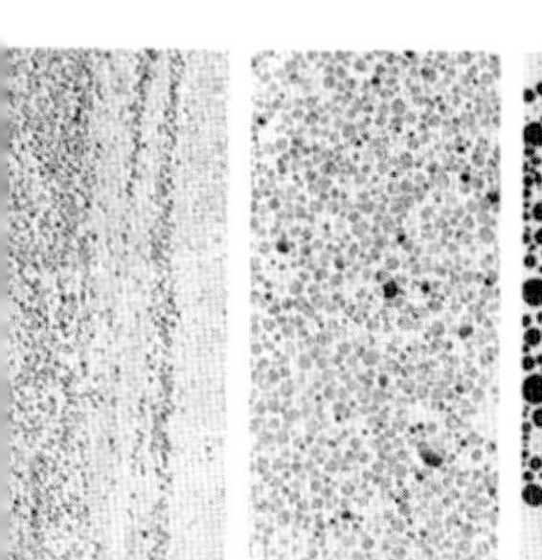
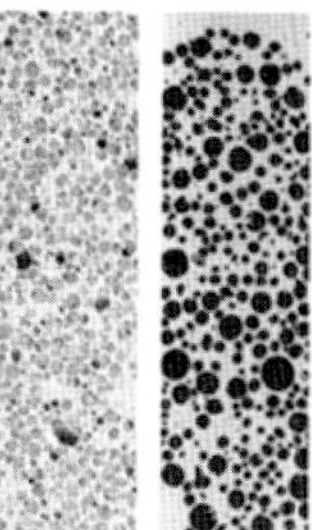
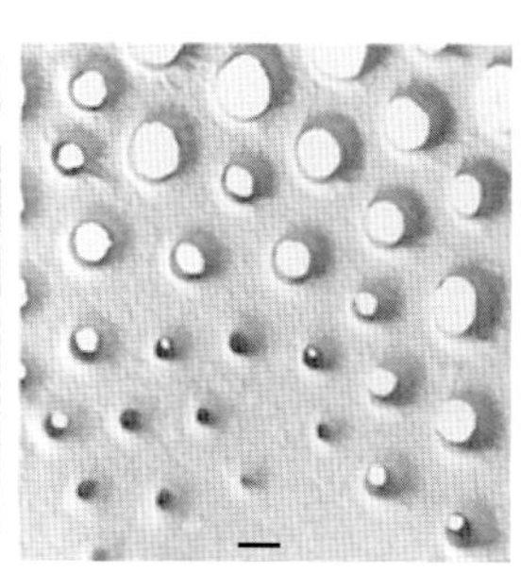

77 *Functionally graded concrete in different orders of size. Scale bar: 1 cm.*

tion in accordance with the external forces acting on the component. The gradient layout is used as a basis for the manufacture of concrete components using two different processes. With the spray process, it is possible to control the density of the concrete. By using a spray system with two nozzles, each of which is filled with a concrete mixture of a different density, a graded density of the concrete is achieved in the component in the desired proportion **p. 70 ⌈58.** The casting process makes it possible to grade the spatial concrete structure by distributing the porosity of the material in a controlled way. In order to make this possible, a three-dimensional formwork structure is built, which, once the concrete has been cast, can be completely dissolved and leaves cavities within the component. Both processes can be used to manufacture spatially graded concrete components in a precise and repeatable way. Compared with conventional, solid concrete components, these components can achieve reductions in mass of up to 60 percent and reductions in emissions of up to 35 percent. Furthermore, the components are very easy to recycle **⌈76,77**.

Multi-material technology: the road to new component technology

In nature, objects can consist of the same material yet have different properties depending on their form and structure. One example of this is the use of solid or porous structures. Using these biological "building strategies," it is possible to generate enormous variations in the properties of materials that consist of the same substance. In technology, such variations are mostly very expensive to achieve owing to the available manufacturing possibilities. Since no material exists that is suitable for all technical applications, the approach up to now has been to select materials and production processes that are as suitable as possible for special purposes and to continue optimizing them. In many cases, components are manufactured not just from one substance but from a combination of materials. This has the advantage that certain elements of the compound structure can be assigned different properties or functions. The conventional combination of materials involves layer, particle, or fiber compounds. Concerning the structure and the production technology, there is almost no limit to the options for this subdivision into individual materials.

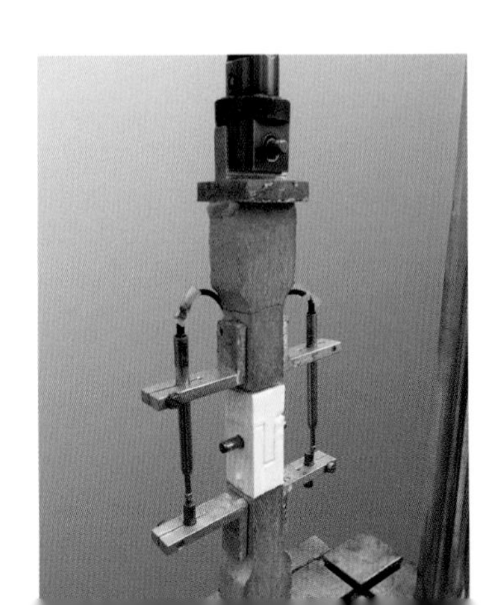

⌈78 *Joining element in a fiber-reinforced plastic/concrete compound component tested for tensile strength*

The manufacturing processes described are constantly being developed further, leading to the combination of the properties of certain materials and the creation of new compound materials.
With respect to their strength, it is often necessary to manufacture components that can withstand both high tensile and compression forces, and hence also bending stresses. Concrete is capable of withstanding strong pressure but very little tensile stress. For this reason, concrete components used in building construction are usually reinforced with elements that can absorb high tensile forces. The conventional material for this application is steel. Fibers made of carbon or basalt have a lower self-weight; in addition, smaller amounts are needed for the building components, which means that they can contribute to more lightweight construction. Furthermore, it is possible to use fibers for the reinforcement of spatially highly complex concrete components **79**. Certain boundary conditions have to be in place for the production of fiber-reinforced concrete components regarding their geometry, surface accuracy, and force transfer. These conditions can be overcome using additive manufacturing technology with thermoplastics. This technology makes it possible to integrate the fibers of the reinforcement and to produce free-form parts that are embedded in the cast concrete like an implant. In this context, plastic implants can also be used to join segments together **78**. The common problem of low manufacturing tolerances in segment connections is avoided due to the flexible deformation of the plastic. This means that component segments can be manufactured with joining elements that are specially designed for the particular load impacting on that element. Generally, these efforts are aimed at transferring interesting biological structures and building principles to technology in order to continue developing manufacturing processes for more efficient functional lightweight building structures.

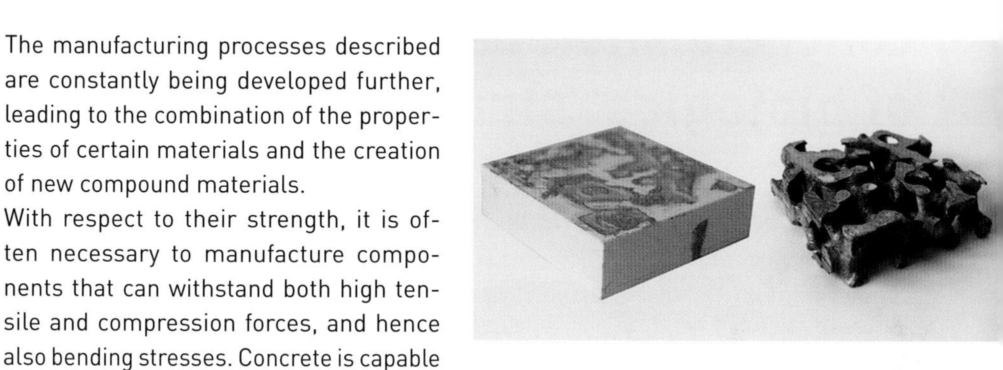

79 *Porous structure of a sea urchin spine (magnified a thousand times), printed in negative form, filled with cast concrete, and heated.*

Rosenstein Pavilion: a lightweight concrete shell based on principles of biological structures

Daria Kovaleva / Oliver Gericke / Frederik Wulle / Pascal Mindermann / Werner Sobek / Alexander Verl / Götz T. Gresser

Natural structural systems that have developed over millions of years illustrate how large loads can be absorbed with very little material. This is achieved by adapting the structural properties to a predominant load profile. If we succeeded in transferring these principles to structures created by people, it would be possible to significantly reduce the consumption of resources in the construction industry. As a contribution to this, the Rosenstein Pavilion ┌80 was developed based on bio-inspired optimization strategies in order to demonstrate the potential of resource-efficient building.

Principles of biological structural systems

Under the motto "structure versus mass," several exhibits in the Lightweight Versatility exhibition space of the *Baubionik—Biologie beflügelt Architektur* exhibition that took place from October 2017 to May 2018 at the Natural History Museum in Stuttgart demonstrated how biological organisms can efficiently fulfill certain functions with the use of as few resources as possible by adapting the characteristics of their tissue to functional requirements. The ability to endure mechanical impact is no exception in this context: with the aim of making optimal use of material, structural tissues can, for example, have a variable density and orientation that correspond to the magnitude and direction of predominant loads. This principle of "functional gradation" can be observed in many living organisms, the cells of which develop into different structures depending on the type of load, material constituents, and the formation processes. Understanding the relationships between structure and

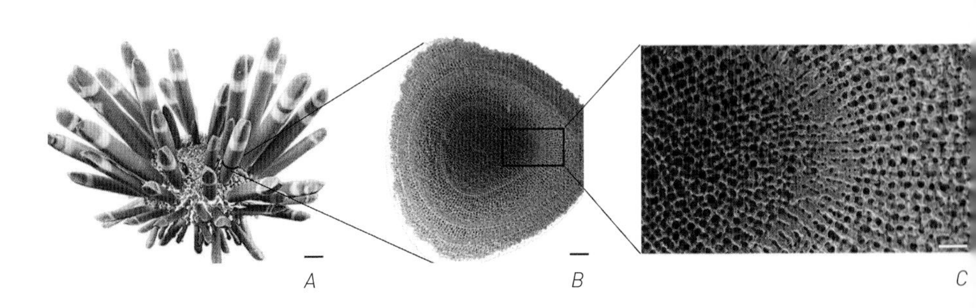

function can help in the development of effective building components and systems. For the development of structures that are mainly subjected to compressive stresses, the principles of highly mineralized biological structures were used, in particular the skeleton tissue of sea urchins and their spines. The inner porous structure—the stereom—of the spines of the *Heterocentrotus mammillatus* sea urchin species shows how the porosity decreases from the center to the outside face of the spine by way of a visibly structured gradation. It is noteworthy that the considerable variation in porosity of 0 percent to 90 percent is achieved solely by the combination of two variable parameters: the diameter of the mineral struts and the size of the pores ⌐**81**. Generally speaking, the denser areas have smaller pores and thicker struts, and vice versa. In order to explore the potential of this construction principle for resource-efficient concrete structures, it was abstracted using scientific methods and then applied in the construction of a weight-optimized concrete shell with functionally graded porosity.

⌐**80** *Photograph of the pavilion in the exhibition space of the Schloss Rosenstein Natural History Museum*

⌐**81** *Photograph of a sea urchin of the H. mammillatus species (A), bar ≙ 1 cm; close-up of the cross-section of a spine (B), bar ≙ 250 µm; close-up of the stereom with varying porosity and direction (C), bar ≙ 100 µm.*

Abstraction of the functional principle

In order to make the principle of functional gradation suitable for technical purposes, it is important to be able to define or determine the dependency between structural characteristics and functional requirements.

In the design of structural systems, it is possible to define the relationship between the density of a structure (porosity) and the amount of the forces acting on the structure. In a first step, the information on the structural behavior is established by simulation using given material properties and load cases. Thereafter, the established stress values are converted into material properties (density) or also geometric characteristics (shape of cross-section) ┌82. As in the case with various living organisms, the structure is essentially influenced by specific material properties, production methods, and all of the functional requirements.

When this principle was applied to the structural system of the concrete shell, the key influencing factors were: the properties of the concrete, the production technology used, and the functional requirements of the exhibition object.

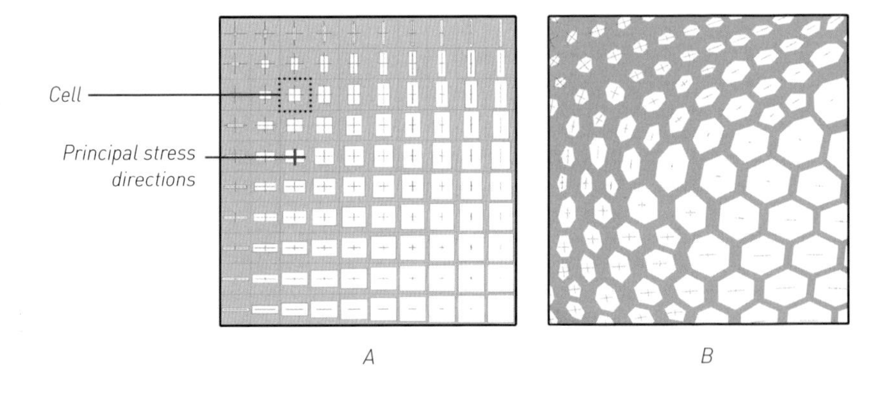

┌**82** *Abstracted model of functionally graded porosity with rectangular (A) and hexagonal (B) cells*

Implementation in the architectural design process

Having been inspired by biological structural tissues, the pavilion was designed as a three-dimensional structure whose properties were adapted to structural requirements and then visualized in the form of functionally graded porosity. The unity of form and function that we often encounter in nature is the result of natural morphogenesis. Therefore, the design of the pavilion was also based on this process as form, structure, and material were to be perceived as an indivisible unit. This procedure was emulated in a computational design process in which the three main steps of a design process—form development, structural analysis, and distribution of material—were integrated in a single digital environment. Requirements, limitations, and boundary conditions were grouped and assigned to each module **⌜83**.

⌜83 *Work process from the design to the production of the pavilion*

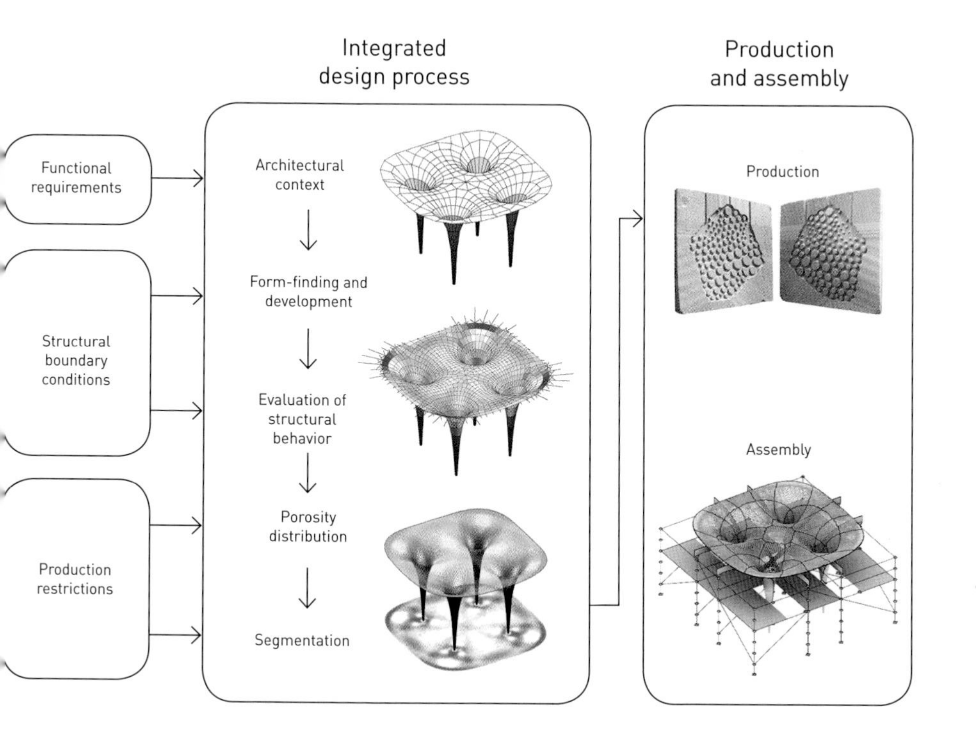

Context of the pavilion

In order to emphasize the architectural relevance of resource-efficient building, the pavilion was designed as a new kind of spatial object in the context of the exhibition space. Firstly, the structure was integrated into the neoclassical surroundings of the museum by positioning the columns in the rhythm of the main architectural elements of the room and by defining the height of the structure to correspond to the tops of the doors and windows ┌**84**. Secondly, the typology of a shell was selected in order to emphasize the contrast between the old post-and-beam system of the neoclassical museum and the lightweight character of future architecture. Furthermore, the area on the ground was kept as open as possible in order to allow the arrangement of other exhibits and permit better circulation of visitors. These design criteria led to the form and structure of the pavilion as a new interpretation of vaulted construction. As a result, the pavilion was designed as a shell that is open towards the ceiling in the shape of funnels and is supported by four columns ┌**84**.

Design process

The intention was to create a combination of structural and esthetic aspects with as strong an expression as possible, which is represented by the convergence of form and structural behavior based on graded material distribution. Following the definition of spatial and functional boundary conditions, an outline design of the shell geometry was developed; this was then analyzed in terms of its loadbearing behavior for the given material parameters and load cases. Owing to the poor loadbearing capacity of the concrete when exposed to tensile stress, a tension cable was placed all around the upper edge of the shell. In this way it was possible to achieve a membrane stress condition in the structure with mainly compression forces. The structural behavior was analyzed and graphically visualized in order to anticipate the required material distribution. Then the calculated stress field was used as input for the modeling of the functionally graded porosity.

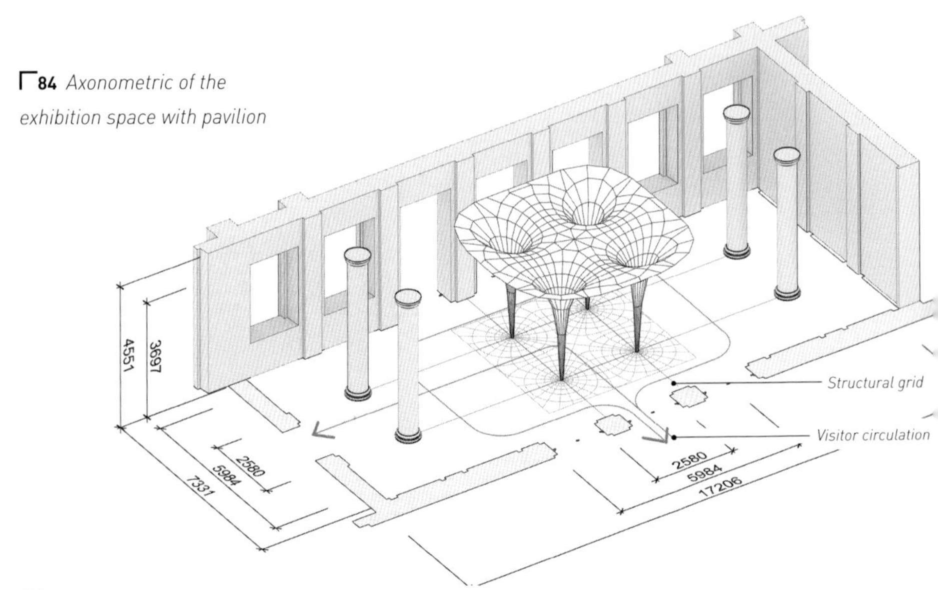

┌**84** *Axonometric of the exhibition space with pavilion*

Material specification for the functionally graded inner structure

Thereafter, the material was specified with graded porosity to reflect the stress conditions in the structure across the entire surface of the shell. Based on the stress values, the surface was subdivided into areas (cells) whose size and orientation correlated with those of the stress field ┌85A. Then the center of each cell was defined as the center of a pore, and the edges as concrete struts ┌85B. Finally, the thickness of the individual struts was determined in order to arrive at the required cross-sectional areas in each case ┌85C.

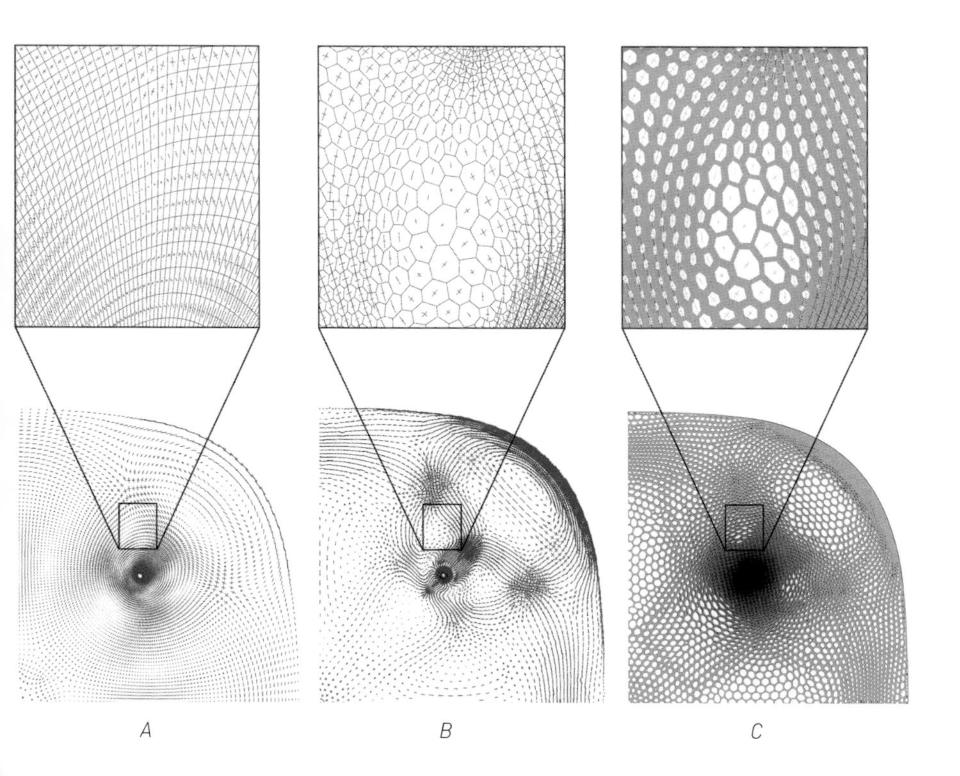

┐85 *Allocation of material to the stress field of the shell. Starting mesh model with stress vectors (A), allocation of cells by size and orientation to principal stress vectors (B) and modeling of the required cross-sections according to the respective principal stresses (C).*

Segmentation

The exhibition was limited to a period of six months. Furthermore, the size of the building components was restricted due to the limitations of production, transport, and construction. For this reason the pavilion was made up of 69 individual segments, of which only 18 were unique owing to the fourfold symmetry of the shell ⌈86. The loads were to be transferred via continuous contact joints between the segments. The joints were located in the dense areas of the segments rather than in the highly porous areas in order to harmonize the porosity distribution with the segmentation layout.

⌈**86** *Layout of segments*

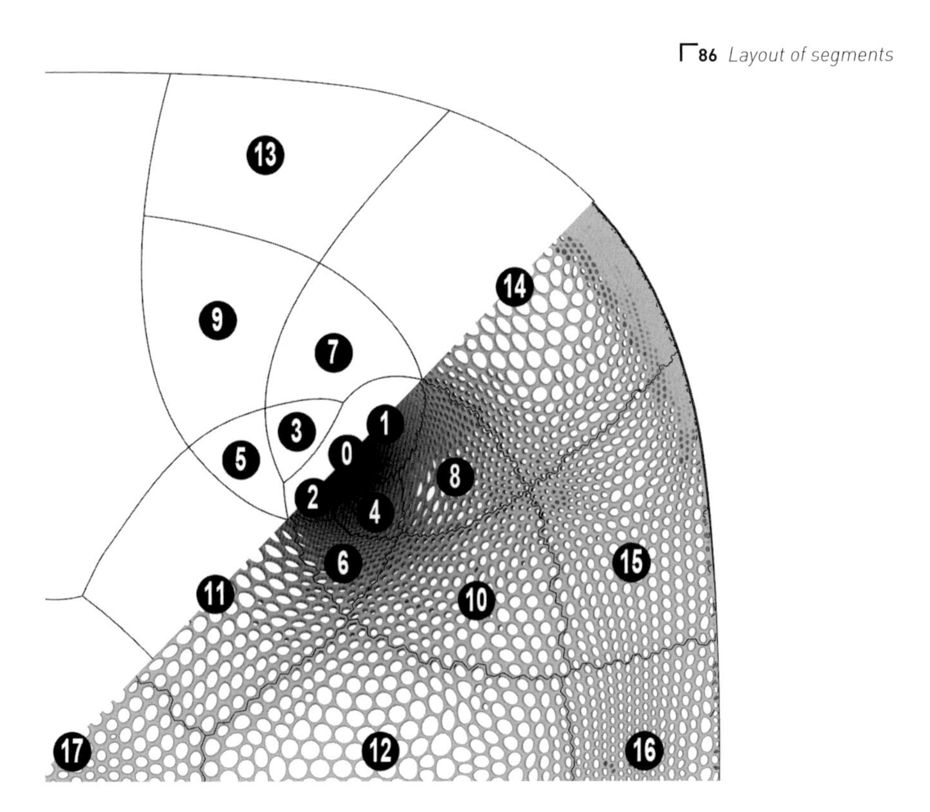

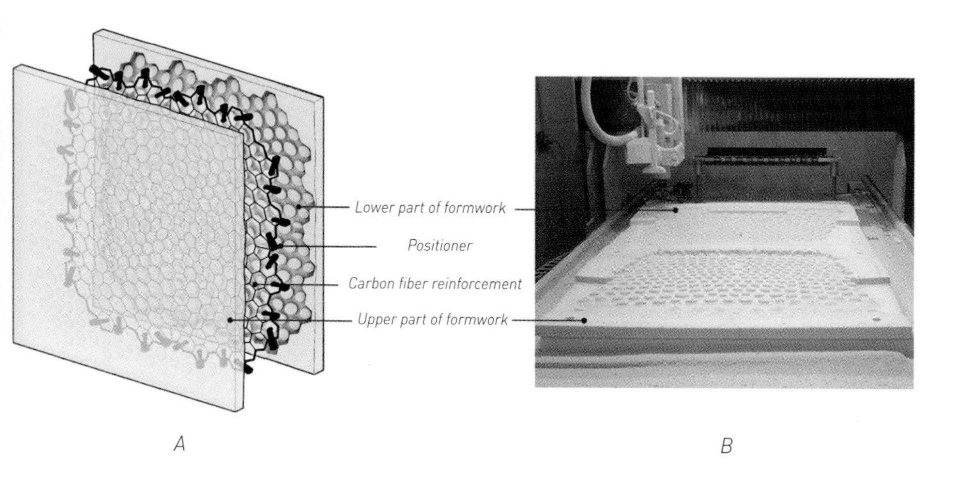

⌐87 *Formwork and reinforcement arrangement for a segment (A) and formwork during processing with a CNC milling machine (B)*

Production

All 69 shell segments were produced using just 18 different formwork units, each of which was reused up to four times. In order to guard against unexpected load cases, all segments were also reinforced with carbon fibers. In addition, a system of connectors was integrated in the edge of each segment in order to ensure that adjacent segments were positioned correctly during assembly and remained fixed in place until the peripheral cable was tensioned.

In order to integrate all of these production requirements, a two-part formwork unit with a double curvature was produced on a CNC milling machine, including a system of channels and cavities for casting, reinforcing, and positioning, for each of the 18 segments **⌐87**. In parallel, precision positioners were produced as fit-in parts using a 3D printing method. In the next step, resin-impregnated carbon fiber rovings were laid along each concrete strut, held in the center with spacers, and attached to the positioners. The fitting of the rovings created integrated textile reinforcement. Once the resin network had been completed, the formwork was coated with release agent, assembled, and filled with concrete. Owing to the concrete's good early compressive strength of 40 MPa after 24 hours, it was possible to remove the segments from the formwork as early as one day after the casting. Thereafter, the formwork could be reused for the production of other segments of the same type.

Assembly

Prior to assembly, the segments were transported in a space-saving manner to the Rosenstein Museum, where the shell was assembled directly on-site. For that purpose, scaffolding was used that consisted of four timber members on steel scaffolding and positioning aids for the columns. First of all, the segments forming the inner vault were placed starting from the columns upwards ⌈**88A**. Then, the adjoining segments were positioned and fixed. As soon as the central segment had been assembled, the cantilevering areas were fitted ⌈**88B**. Finally, the tension cable was inserted along the outside top edge and then prestressed to ensure that the intended structural behavior of the shell—primarily subjected to compression—would be achieved ⌈**88C**. The tension of the cable was also regularly checked during the exhibition.

⌈**88** *Assembly of the structure on the support scaffolding (A), assembly of the structure (B), tension lock and sensors for prestressing the peripheral cable (C), close-up of a segment joint with screw connection (D)*

Functionally integrated: support structure + building envelope

Optimization of bearing capacity + integration of building technology

89 *Vision of a functionally integrated building system using the example of a railway station*

Outlook

The main objective of the project was to demonstrate the relevance of bio-inspired design strategies both for structural systems and for architecture in general. When manufacturing components such as floor decks, beams, or columns, as well as other structures such as shells or bridges, the mechanical properties are adjusted to the structural requirements. In addition, other functions such as thermal insulation, moisture/air circulation, acoustic insulation, and other building physics requirements can be integrated in a building component using functional gradation. For example, by introducing porosity gradients between the dense outer layers and the porous core areas of external walls and roofs, it is possible to achieve components with both structural and insulating properties.

The early inclusion of these principles in the digital design process can help project teams make resource efficiency an integral part of the design work. In parallel, the development of new integrated design and production methods—supported by progress in the material sciences—could ultimately lead to the development of new kinds of structural systems that extend the range of design solutions for a sustainable built environment.

ELEGANCE AND LIGHTNESS: BIO-INSPIRED DOMES

Jan Knippers / Thomas Speck

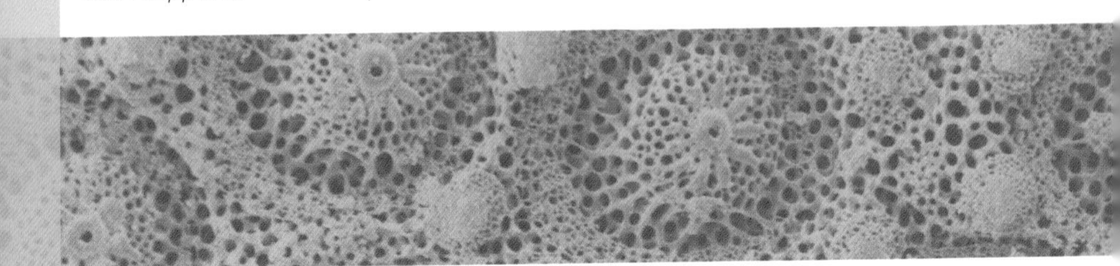

For centuries, master builders have endeavored to create ever lighter constructions. For this purpose, the shapes of domes, vaults, and shells were adapted more and more precisely to the flow of forces. As a result, buildings of unique strength of architectural expression, such as the cathedral of Notre-Dame in Paris (1163), the Sagrada Familia in Barcelona (1882), and the Sydney Opera House (opened in 1973), have been created at various times. A prerequisite for this was a detailed understanding of the structural forces and, especially, a highly developed construction trade that was capable of producing exactly shaped vaults and shell structures able to transfer the applied forces.

However, in the course of the last century, there have been fundamental changes in the factors affecting the building industry. Today, material is cheap, but labor is expensive. Therefore construction methods are today developed with the aim of keeping the labor input required for production as low as possible. This has resulted in a much reduced variety of forms. "Boxes" are created that consist of as many identical components as possible. Whether this involves the consumption of a bit more or less material is of secondary importance.

How can we today manufacture cost-efficient shell structures that are shaped according to the applied loads and are therefore resource efficient, and which open up new opportunities for design in architecture? Nature can supply valuable pointers in this respect. Shells and exoskeletons protect the inner organs of sea urchins, snails, mussels, insects, and many other animals against predators, water pressure, and numerous other potentially dangerous environmental influences. In the course of evolution, an incredible variety of forms and construction principles have developed, which are adapted to a wide range of conditions encountered by animals in their habitats. In this process, the basic principle of evolution has been followed: using resources as efficiently as possible.

How are such natural shell constructions created? In nature, different principles of formation can be observed, which can provide stimuli for technical developments in various directions. Two examples may explain this. The exoskeleton of sea urchins consists of individual plates, and the sea urchin shell grows by forming new plates. At the same time, however every already formed plate grows in size The modular structure of the shells ensures, on the one hand, that the plates can

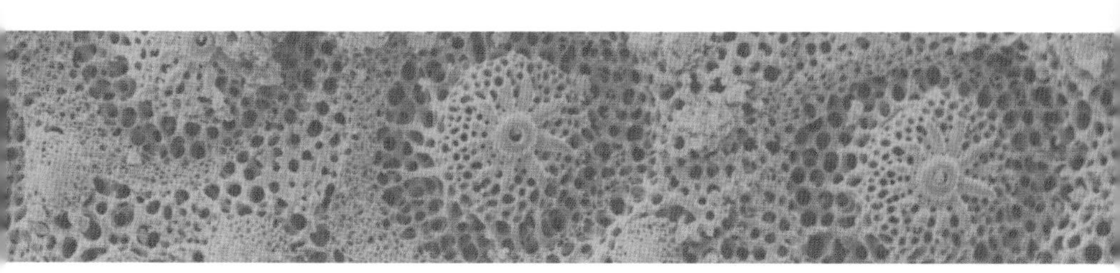

grow independently of each other and, on the other hand, that they are reliably and yet compliantly connected with one another—sometimes via special denticulations. In turn, these denticulations involve a special arrangement of the plates on the shell. What can be transferred to architecture from this example? The sea urchin construction has inspired construction technology to produce complex-shaped shell structures using prefabricated panels of wood, concrete, or other building materials. Compared with shells formed entirely on the building site, the manufacture of such prefabricated individual parts is much less costly. The sea urchin can also provide other valuable pointers for the design of joints and the arrangement and connection of the panels.
Snails, as a second example, use a completely different construction principle. Their shell grows by the snail continually depositing new material at the opening of its shell. To begin, the snail deposits a plastic-like, initially soft layer on the edge of the shell, which it produces and shapes with its body. This layer will then cure and is reinforced from the inside with a mineral material. This additive building process of snail shells can be used as a role model for continuing the development of the 3D printing technology for building envelopes. It would be ideal if, as with the snail, it was possible to first form the shape-giving modeling material and then the structural layer free in space in a continuing process. In this way, it would be possible to omit expensive formwork and supporting structures, which these days, in practice, make shell structures almost unaffordable. Furthermore, the omission of formwork and supporting structures would also be desirable from the point of view of sustainability. Analysis of the growth and structure-forming processes of the shells of sea urchins and snails leads us to two different approaches to making the production of flowing structural forms once again commercially viable. These examples remind us that it is worthwhile to take a close look at rather "simple" living creatures. Sometimes we need to take a second look in order to discover not only beauty but also functionality.

Building principles and structural design of sea urchins: examples of bio-inspired constructions

Tobias B. Grun / Malte von Scheven / Florian Geiger / Tobias Schwinn / Daniel Sonntag / Manfred Bischoff / Jan Knippers / Achim Menges / James H. Nebelsick

In the course of evolution, sea urchins have adapted to a wide range of habitats in the ocean. Particularly conspicuous are the developments in the construction of their skeletons, which feature specific adaptations to their ambient environmental conditions. The sea urchin shells thus have developed many different charakteristics in order to withstand currents, storm events, and predatory attacks, for example. These shells also reveal some very fundamental building principles, which can serve as inspiration for the development of innovative technical constructions. The main focus is on the development of better-performing shell structures, which would be a means of achieving greater resource efficiency and architectural esthetics.

Hard and elegant—the diversity of sea urchin shells

Spiny ocean-dwellers

Sea urchins were not given their name by chance as they resemble their terrestrial namesake, the hedgehogs ┌**90**. Even though sea urchins share spines with the hedgehogs, they are purely marine invertebrates. Sea urchins occur in all oceans and at all depths. In marine ecosystems, they are an important key group because they restrict the rapid spread of algae and excessive colonization of the reef and the ocean floor by other animals, which can be detrimental to the ecosystem, and also because they themselves are an important element in the food chain. Depending on their habitat, the appearance of sea urchins can vary a great deal. Another general distinction can be made between sea urchins with regular and irregular shells. The regular sea urchins ┌**90, 92**, which are mostly spherical, are well known to some of us from times we have spent by the sea, where their spines left painful memories when we accidently stepping on them. The irregular kinds ┌**91, 93** are often of a flatter shape and live primarily hidden, inconspicuously buried in the sand. A special taxon of irregular sea urchins is the Clypeasteroida.[1] This group is characterized by its very strong modular lightweight construction, its effective plate connections, and an impressive diversity of shapes.

[1] *The Clypeasteroida include the sand dollars (in the more specific sense), the sea biscuit, and the pea urchins. Unfortunately, there is no accepted trivial name for the group. For the sake of simplicity, we speak here about sand dollars (in the wider sense) when referring to the Clypeasteroida.*

┌90 *The regular sea urchin,* Diadema antillarum, *does justice to its name in a fascinating way: it features spines measuring up to 30 cm, which it uses in defense against predators. The spines are so effective in deterring aggressors that the space between them is even used by fish as a nursery.*

Sea urchins from a technical point of view

Sea urchins have a strictly hierarchically organized calcareous skeleton (calcium carbonate, calcite, $CaCO_3$), which consists of many, in some cases several hundred individual and often effectively connected plates. Like an exoskeleton, the sea urchin skeleton protects the inner organs. It is, however, covered by tissue and therefore is an endoskeleton. The plates themselves consist of stereom, a highly porous meshwork system of interlaced small rods called trabeculae ┌97.

From a technical point of view, the skeleton system features two impressive characteristics: owing to its high degree of porosity, the weight of the sea urchin shell is reduced; nevertheless, its lightweight construction is strong enough to ensure that the sea urchin skeleton can withstand even strong forces during a storm or other events. Another feature of sea urchins is their modular skeleton consisting of many individual elements, which can produce a fascinating range of shapes. In building technology, prefabricated modular constructions also play an important role because they are usually economical to produce and fast to erect. Sea urchins from the sand dollar group consist of plates that, in most cases, are connected to each other via skeletal protrusions ┌97 and connective tissue. There is another special feature hidden inside them: because of their sometimes markedly flat shape, these species have developed internal support devices that connect the top and bottom sides of the skeleton with each other, thereby forming a structural bridge within the shell. These internal support structures can generally be subdivided

into three types ┌93: (1) *Clypeaster rosaceus*, also known as the sea biscuit, has distinct wall-like freestanding pillars. With its shape, which is relatively rounded rather than flat, this species, whose length is up to 20 centimeters, is probably one of the largest representatives of the Clypeasteroida. The sea biscuit lives mostly on the sediment, where it occasionally hides beneath rocks, masking itself with algae, mussel shells, and suchlike in order to protect itself from predators ┌91. (2) The pea urchin—which, by contrast with the above, is minute, measuring only a few millimeters—has buttresses that, throughout their entire length, are connected to the shell. The skeleton of this tiny creature, which lives exclusively in the substrate, is so resistant that masses of them can be found as fossils that have suffered hardly any damage. (3) Sand dollars, including the very flat genera of *Leodia*, *Mellita*, and *Dendraster*, live either completely or at least partially buried in sand. These often disc-like sea urchins have a meshwork-like buttress system consisting of thin walls that is especially strong at the edges of the skeleton.

Diversity of shape and its (r)evolutionary background

The segmented skeletons of sand dollars feature a great diversity of shape, ranging from highly rounded to strongly flattened, from circular to elliptical in longitudinal section, and from small to large. Skeletons can have very strong shells, with their plates additionally reinforced by internal supports. This diversity of sea urchin skeletons reflects the adaptation of the animals to their specific habitats. In spite of the enormous variation amongst sea urchins, however, some basic shared elements can be recognized in a sea urchin skeleton. For example, sea urchins living today have exactly 20 rows of plates in spite of their big differences in shape. Similarly, the arrangement of the segments, in which three plates meet at one point, can be found in all sea urchins.

91 *The sea biscuit* Clypeaster rosaceus *has masked itself with algae, shell fragments, and sediment in order to disguise itself and protect itself against predators.*

92 *Regular sea urchins are mostly close to spherical and display a distinct pentagonal symmetry. Whilst the variation in the shape of regular sea urchins is already baffling, it is not comparable to that of the irregular sea urchins. Shown from top to bottom are representatives of the genus* Tripneustes *(skeleton with spines),* Tripneustes *(skeleton without spines), and* Arbacia *and* Paracentrotus *(skeletons without spines). Scale bar: 1 cm.*

From a technical point of view, a theoretical structural model can be detected behind the enormous variations in form of sea urchins. In architecture and in building construction, the aspect of diversity of shape due to adaptation as well as the idea of an abstract model are very important, because as a rule buildings are designed to suit the demands of the user, the specific characteristics of the location, and other requirements; these factors alone lead to a great diversity in buildings. In architectural design it is increasingly common to use computer-based methods in order to develop—on the basis of construction principles—digital models that generate geometric variation when certain parameters are changed. When combined with appropriate methods of structural analysis, it is then possible to use the computer to simulate an evolution of load-bearing structures that leads to more efficient structures than could be achieved with traditionally designed systems.

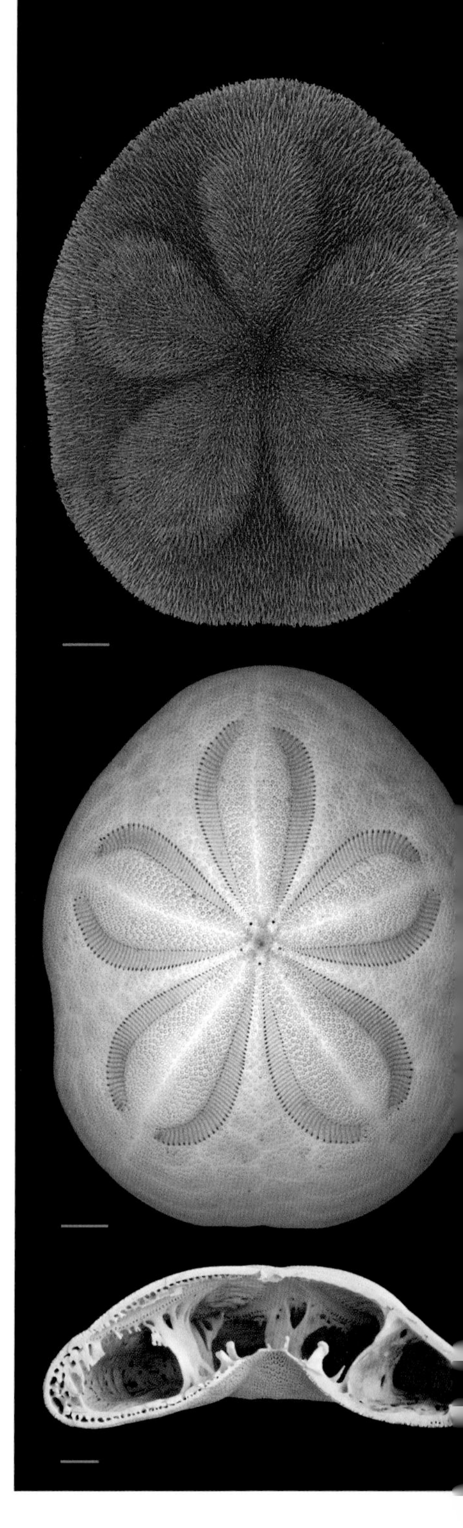

93 *Irregular sea urchins from the sand dollar group (Clypeasteroida) are bilaterally symmetrical (i.e., they have a left-hand and right-hand body half). The shape and curvature of the spines vary widely, and the internal buttress systems contribute significantly to the reinforce-*

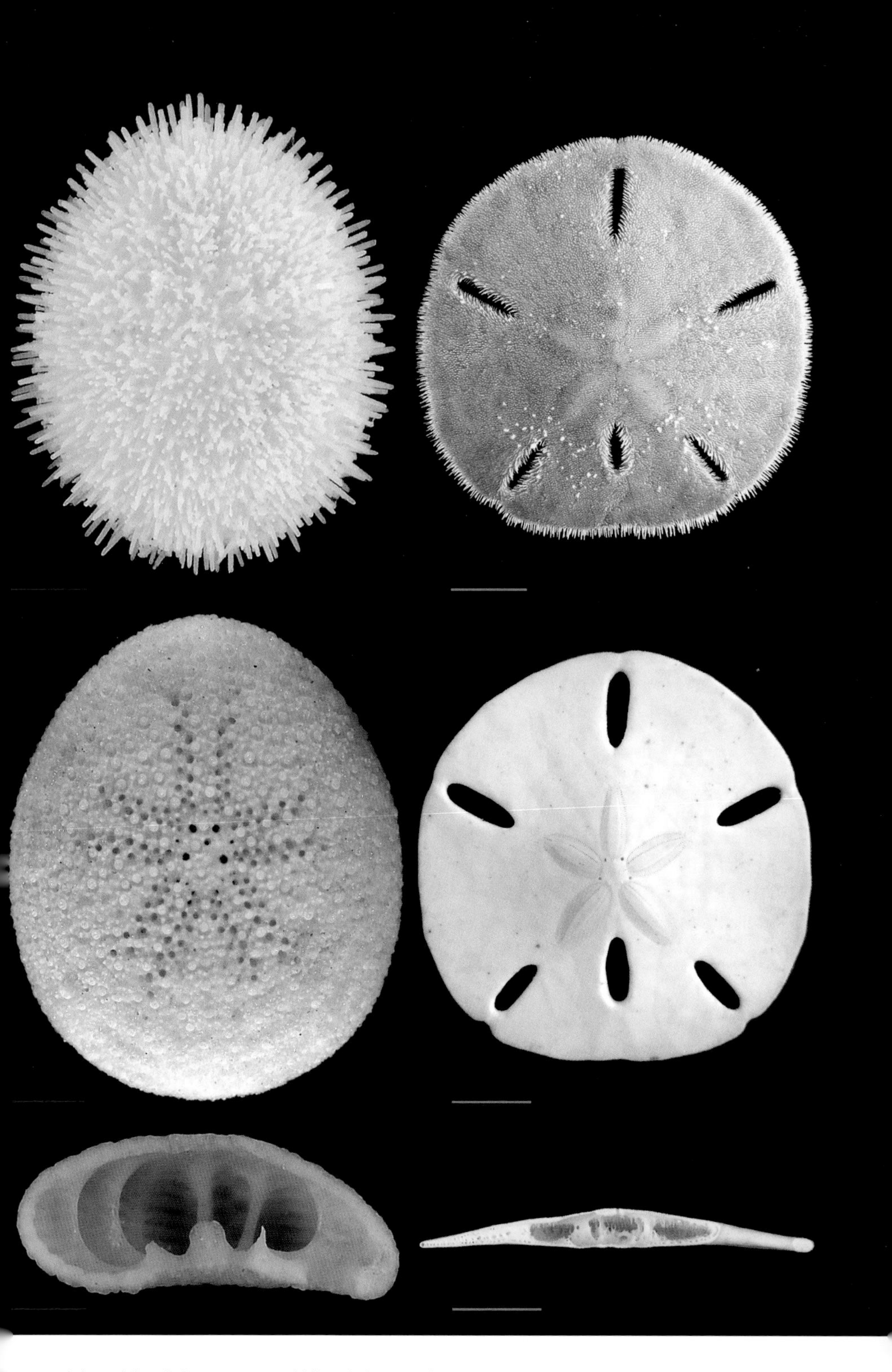

ment of the calcite skeleton. Left: Clypeaster rosaceus; *middle:* Echinocyamus pusillus; *right:* Leodia sexiesperforata; *top: with spines; middle: skeleton without spines; bottom: longitudinal section. Scale bar (gray): 1 cm; scale bar (red): 1 mm.*

Shell structures and their examples in nature

In architecture, the term "shell structure" refers to thin-walled and double-curved structures, which, due to their shape, can be particularly efficient and are therefore often used in buildings with large open spans. Historic examples are domes, such as that of the Pantheon in Rome (completed in AD 128), which made it possible to span large areas using the technical means available at the time. In modern architecture, there are also numerous examples in which free shape shells with curvatures in two directions have a high esthetic value, such as that of the L'Oceanogràfic in Valencia designed by Félix Candela (opened in 2003) ⌜**94**. The double curvature ensures that external loads are transferred through the shell towards the supports exclusively in the form of in-plane forces. This leads to an advantageous structural behavior and optimum utilization of the material, resulting in relatively slender and lightweight constructions. Building such structures is often very costly due to their size, their irregular geometry, and their double curvature. For this reason, current endeavors aim to produce shells from prefabricated elements that only have to be joined up at the construction site. This has already been carried out in the exhibition hall at the State Garden Exhibition (Landesgartenschau) in Schwäbisch Gmünd (2014) in the form of a prototype ⌜**95**.

In many ways, the shells of sand dollars are not dissimilar to the shells used in architecture. It could be said that, at a lower level of the hierarchy, the plates of the sea urchin correspond to the segments of segmented shell structures. The relatively thin sea urchin shells behave structurally like shell constructions in architecture, and can therefore serve as an important source of ideas for the arrangement of modules in segmented shell structures. They can also serve as an example for the development of particularly high-performing module connections. While mod-

⌐94 *L'Oceanogràfic in Valencia (Spain), designed by Félix Candela, is an example of a monolithic (cast in-situ as a single unit) reinforced concrete shell.*

⌐95 *The exhibition hall at the State Garden Exhibition in Schwäbisch Gmünd (Germany) is a prototype for a segmented shell made of beech plywood elements.*

ules in traditional technical constructions often have uniform shapes, the plates of the sea urchin shell feature considerable differences in their geometry and curvature. However, the arrangement of the plates follows a strict basic construction plan, in which three plates always meet at one point **⌐96**. Based on the variation of the plate form and the denticulation, the arrangement of the plates can, on its own, generate an effective shell construction and is therefore an important source of inspiration for biomimetic shell structures.
The connections between the modules are usually weak points in segmented shell constructions because at these transition points the material and geometric continuity is interrupted. In consequence, it is necessary to either optimize the force transfer in the joint or alter the arrangement of the joints in order to be able to build more efficient segmented shells. Sand dollars provide important pointers as to how this optimization can be achieved; this is because they feature a combination of mechanical denticulation **⌐97** and a softer and more elastic tissue embedded within the skeleton, which results in an effective joint.
Internal buttress systems are used to firmly connect the upper and lower parts of the shell of the sea urchin skeleton **⌐93, 98**. Forces can be transferred between the two halves of the shell, ensuring that they are distributed evenly within the shell. Overall, this means that external loads lead to lower internal forces/stresses in the skeleton. From a technical point

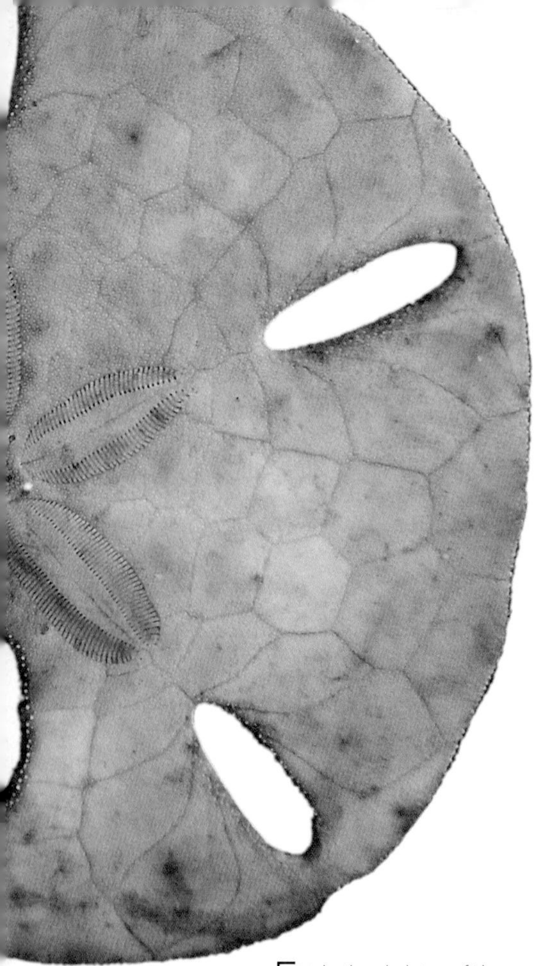

⌈96 *In the skeleton of the sea urchin* Leodia sexiesperforata, *three plates meet at one point (vertex).*

of view, shell structures are thin-walled constructions that span large areas without the use of columns. However, column systems cannot be omitted completely, in particular when the shells only have a low curvature or are completely flat. In this context in particular, the arrangement and geometry of the internal buttresses of the Clypeasteroid sea urchins are of great interest, since they illustrate ways to optimize the structure whilst also reducing the use of construction materials.
It is true that, today, we have wide-spanning shell structures, but their construction often involves comparatively high costs and large amounts of material. Engineers and architects hope that by understanding the structure and load-bearing behavior of the sea urchin skeleton, as well as the transfer of selected construction principles to technology, we can gain better insight for the optimization of shell structures. The objective is to develop shell structures that consist of individual prefabricated building segments. The aim is not only to reduce the consumption of resources and material, but also to pave the way for completely new and efficient lightweight constructions. Clypeasteroida are characterized by many properties that are important for architecture, such as the efficient plate connections and internal buttress mechanisms. For this reason, biomimetic research is currently focusing on these sea urchins, with paleontologists, biologists, engineers, and architects hoping to find new concepts that, on the one hand, are revolutionary in form and function and, on the other hand, extend the understanding of the structure, function, and developmental history of sea urchins.

97 *Scanning electron microscope image of the stereom protrusion at an individual plate that is used to achieve an effective connection of the plates.*

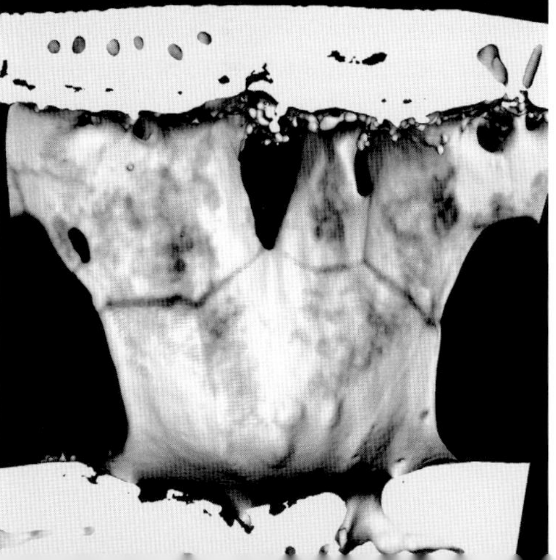

98 *Computed tomography image of an internal supporting pillar of the sea urchin* Clypeaster rosaceus.

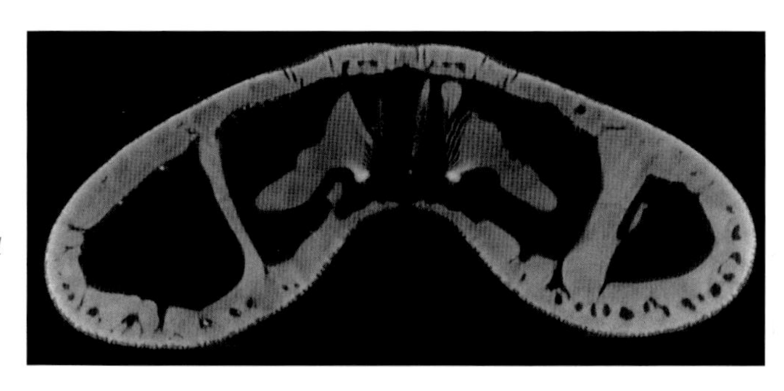

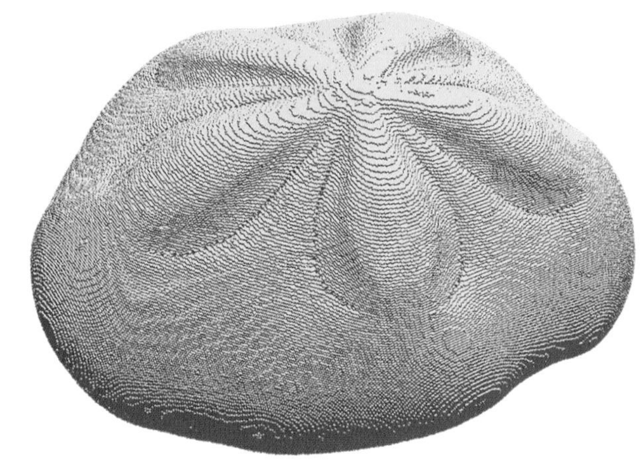

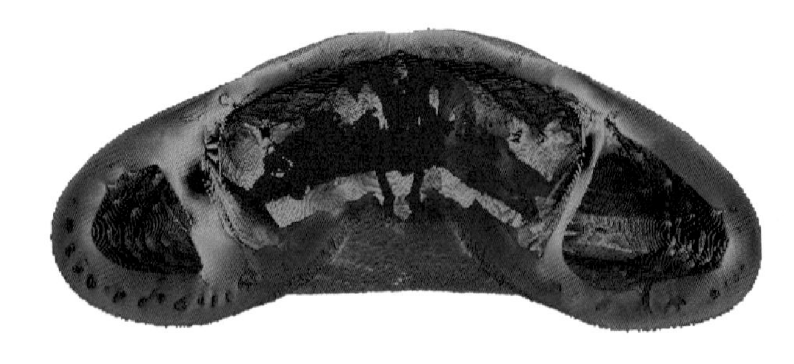

⌐99 *Computed tomography scan (CT scan) and voxel model of the skeleton of the sea urchin* Clypeaster roseaceus. *Top: one slice of the CT scan of the sea urchin skeleton (the brighter the voxel, the denser the material). Middle: external view of voxel model. Bottom: section through the voxel model with color coding of the stresses in the material (red = high stress).*

Sea urchins in 3D

In order to investigate the inner structure and mechanical behavior of sea urchin shells, computed tomography (CT) scans of various sea urchin skeletons were prepared. These scans produce image files that show the material distribution in a very thin section of the sea urchin ⌐99. The brightness of each pixel represents the density of the material; when the area is completely black, this means there is no material, and as the color becomes brighter, the density increases. On the basis of the CT scans, a three-dimensional voxel model (volumetric model consisting of cubes) is created. The word "voxel" originates by analogy from the word "pixel" and is used in a three-dimensional context, with "vo" representing "volume." Voxels are generated only when the brightness and with this also the density is above a specified threshold. In some cases, several pixels of consecutive images are combined to form larger voxels in order to reduce the resolution and hence the later effort involved in the calculations. Subsequently, voxels that are not connected with the actual sea urchin shell are removed and the mechanical loads and bounda-

ry conditions that are necessary for the structural analysis are defined.
The three-dimensional voxel models of the sea urchins make it possible to investigate the mechanical properties of the sea urchin shells in numerical simulations. A mathematical model can be used to describe the mechanical behavior. The equations are similar to those of Hooke's law governing the elastic deformation of solids, which can be used to calculate the deformation of springs. They do not, however, describe the behavior of a single spring when exposed to force, but that of a three-dimensional continuous body. The scientific discipline dealing with this is referred to as continuum mechanics. It provides the basis for computer simulations, which today are carried out in many scientific and industrial fields; examples are the simulation of the crash behavior of vehicles or the prediction of the load-bearing behavior of bridges. These equations of the mathematical model are solved with a numerical model, in this case using the finite element method (FEM). With this method, an approximate solution can be determined by subdividing the domain that is the subject of the calculation into a limited number of elements. The solution shows the distribution of displacements and forces in the sea urchin shell resulting from a certain assumed external load. As the element size is reduced, their number increases and the quality of the approximate solution improves. However, there is an increase in the effort involved in the calculation and, in particular, the time required.
By investigating the sea urchin shell with scientific engineering methods, it is possible to gain a deeper understanding of its functions. Using the mathematical and numerical models described above, it is possible to carry out virtual experiments on the computer that would not be possible using a real preparation. Furthermore, it is possible to visualize and quantify results, such as the distribution of forces or displacements, which could not be observed in real experiments. This means that the simulations not only help in the transfer of ideas from biology to technology, but also contribute to a better understanding of the biological structures—an approach also referred to as "technical biology."

Potential applications of segmented shells in architecture

Tobias Schwinn / Daniel Sonntag / Tobias Grun / James H. Nebelsick / Jan Knippers / Achim Menges

In architectural research, pavilions play a special role because, as temporary structures, they present an opportunity to investigate specific issues without having to fulfill all requirements for permanent buildings. The findings resulting from this investigation can then be utilized in the design and implementation of permanent buildings. In this contribution we describe the context in which the Rosenstein Timber Pavilion was created, and the special issues that were investigated in the project, as well as the knowledge gained from it. In addition, we provide an outlook on other current research topics in the field of segmented timber shells and their application in architecture.

Pavilions as "models for thinking"

One of the essential and characteristic features of research in architecture is the possibility not only to answer research questions on a methodical level but also to gain knowledge based on built projects. In this way a built project can become a catalyst for new findings that go beyond the knowledge of the disciplines involved in the construction process. Pavilions are particularly suitable for this type of research because, in their function as temporary structures, they provide the opportunity to emphasize specific questions without having to meet the whole range of functional and structural requirements of, and demands on, buildings. In this way it is possible to test hypotheses, and the findings can then be utilized in the design of permanent buildings. Thus, pavilions are not only vehicles for material experiments or experimental construction methods, but they are also "models for thinking" on the basis of which new knowledge can be gained and also new questions raised for research.

In this context, the Rosenstein Timber Pavilion, which was designed for the *Baubionik—Biologie beflügelt Architektur* exhibition, can be considered one of a series of research pavilions that, since 2011, have been created at the University of Stuttgart in cooperation with biologists and paleontologists from the University of Tübingen. The preceding projects include the ICD/ITKE Research Pavilion 2011, the exhibition building at the 2014 State Garden Exhibition (Landesgartenschau) in Schwäbisch Gmünd, and the ICD/ITKE Research Pavilion created in 2015–16. These pavilions were used to investigate the transfer of functional principles found in biology to the design, construction, and manufacture of segmented timber shells. It was possible in this process to test hypotheses, validate methods, gain new knowledge, and—along the lines of models for thinking—ask new research questions that were investigated in subsequent projects. In addition to the investigation and transfer to architecture of certain developmental and structural principles of the sand dollar skeleton (p. 104 see contribution on building principles and structural design), the focus was on architectural, structural and production-related questions and objectives. For example, in the case of the Rosenstein Timber Pavilion, this included the objective of optimizing the arrangement of the plate joints from a structural point of view, and of reducing the thickness of the plates and hence the mass of the loadbearing structure compared with previous projects, while maintaining the plates' loadbearing capacity.

Hereinafter we therefore describe the context of the development of the Rosenstein Timber Pavilion, and the new knowledge gained as a result of building the pavilion. Furthermore, we will touch upon those additional questions that are currently being researched in follow-up projects, for example the advancement of the development of the construction systems, larger spans, the issue of the sustainability of segmented timber shells, and the issue of extending existing buildings. Finally, we will discuss the findings gained to date and provide an outlook on the potential rollout of segmented timber shell constructions.

Predecessors of the Rosenstein Timber Pavilion

As mentioned above, the design of the Rosenstein timber pavilion was partially based on findings and questions obtained/raised in the context of preceding research pavilions. The first of these was the ICD/ITKE Research Pavilion 2011 ┌100, for which researchers from the Institute for Computational Design (ICD) and the Institute of Building Structures and Structural Design (ITKE) in cooperation with architectural students from the University of Stuttgart researched historic timber panel connections and reinterpreted these in the context of digitally controlled production methods available. In this context, the researchers investigated the geometry of the plates of the sand dollar skeleton, in which the plates, three at a time, are joined at one point, forming what is known as a Y-arrangement. They also looked into the microscopic connection between the plates of the sand dollar skeleton, which was identified as the structural equivalent of a finger joint. From an engineering perspective, this method of arranging the plates made it possible to create a rigid loadbearing system using flexible connections. From a manufacturing point of view, the focus of this project was on the integration of the production process with the aim of achieving a continuous flow of data from design to the digital control of the machine tool, in this case an industrial robot with milling spindle. To this end, special new processing cycles were developed that enabled the production of the geometrically complex timber connections and the multi-layer polyhedral shell segments.

The exhibition hall at the 2014 State Garden Exhibition in Schwäbisch Gmünd ┌95, 101 that followed was designed and implemented in the context of a research and development project at the interface between research and building practice. The previous project had involved a great

⌜100 *ICD/ITKE Research Pavilion 2011. In this project, historic timber connections were investigated and newly interpreted in the context of the possibilities of digitally controlled production.*

number of building components and complex connection details; therefore, the objectives in this project were to reduce the number of building components in relation to the area covered and to simplify the construction of the shell without, however, diminishing the positive characteristics of the structural system. In addition, the knowledge of the digital design methods and machine control was now to be applied in practice. As a result, a segmented shell was developed that consists of a single loadbearing material plane of 50-millimeter-thick beech veneer plywood. The principle of the Y-shaped joining point of the plates remained unchanged. The connection of the plates primarily enables the transfer of shear forces at the plate edges and, with the help of crosswise screw fixing, to a limited extent bending moments. From a design point of view, the focus was again on the integration of production—this time, however, with the aim of ensuring the producibility of the components during the design phase with the help of agent-based modeling. If one were to draw an analogy to a biological genealogical classification, the exhibition building with its single-layer segmented timber shell and its screw connection is the direct ancestor of the Rosenstein Timber Pavilion.

However, in view of the fact that in the pavilion at the 2014 State Garden Exhibition the lowest possible structural limit of the shell thickness was determined by the additional screw connection, the focus for the 2015–2016 ICD/ITKE Research Pavilion ⌜**102** was initially on alternative timber connections. Having again been designed and implemented at the interface between research and teaching at the University of Stuttgart, the focus for this pavilion was on the plate connections of the sand dollar sea urchin, and especially on the organic components that ensure the additional stability of the sand dollar shell. The basic hypothesis in this project was that timber, as a natural fiber composite material in the form of veneer, should be considered and processed more like a textile, anisotropic material than as a rigid, isotropic material such as steel or concrete, or the crosswise glued veneer plywood used in the pavilion at the State Garden Exhibition. This textile approach paved the way for the application of processing methods used in the field of technical textiles, such as laminating in order to control the bending stiffness of a component, robotic sewing in order to prevent the delamination of elastically bent components, and lacing in order to simply connect building components on the building site. The result

101 *Exhibition hall at the 2014 State Garden Exhibition in Schwäbisch Gmünd. The self-supporting shell consists of beech veneer plywood with a thickness of 50 mm. The characteristic plate connection is able to transfer, primarily, shear forces at the edges of the plates and, to a lesser extent, bending moments.*

was a very lightweight segmented timber shell made of elastically bent timber veneers with a maximum material thickness of 6 millimeters, which did not require any traditional fasteners.

102 *ICD/ITKE Research Pavilion 2015–16. In this project, textile processing methods for timber construction were investigated. The pavilion consists of elastically bent timber veneers with a maximum thickness of 6 mm, which are joined without any kind of traditional fasteners.*

The Rosenstein Timber Pavilion: a segmented shell at the Rosenstein Museum

The Rosenstein Timber Pavilion is a product of this development line, a demonstrator for segmented timber shells that was developed by the TRR141 Collaborative Research Centre (Biological Design and Integrative Structures) as part of the research project entitled "The sand dollar skeleton as biological example of segmented shells in building construction." The pavilion is the result of cooperation between the ICD, the ITKE, the Institute for Structural Mechanics (IBB) at the University of Stuttgart, and the Invertebrates, Paleontology, and Paleoclimatology Working Group at the University of Tübingen. One of the key research questions investigated in this project was to what extent the plate arrangement of the sand dollar skeleton is the result of structural optimization. Starting from the construction-oriented optimization of the pavilion at the State Garden Exhibition in terms of its plate geometry, the development of the Rosenstein Timber Pavilion focused on the optimization of the plate arrangement and the joint layout from a structural point of view. To achieve that, the material distribution within the sand dollar skeleton was analyzed and modeled, and the loadbearing behavior of the sand dollar shell was simulated in order to be able to deduce mechanical principles (**p. 114** see also sea urchin in 3D). In parallel, the agent-based method of shell segmentation was extended in order to incorporate feedback from structural analysis. As with the pavilion at the State Garden Exhibition, the producibility of the building components was one of the parameters considered in the modeling of the plates from the start of

103 *Rosenstein Timber Pavilion. The global shape of the pavilion is the result of the boundary conditions of the space in the Rosenstein Museum, as well as the exhibition concept and the circulation layout through the exhibition. From the perspectiv of the visitors, the openings in the segmented shell provide a frame for special exhibits in the exhibition space.*

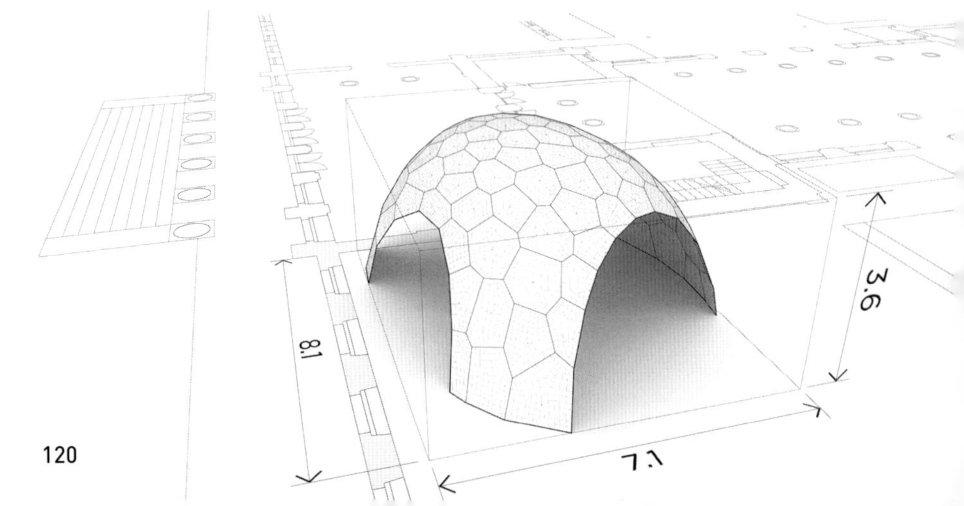

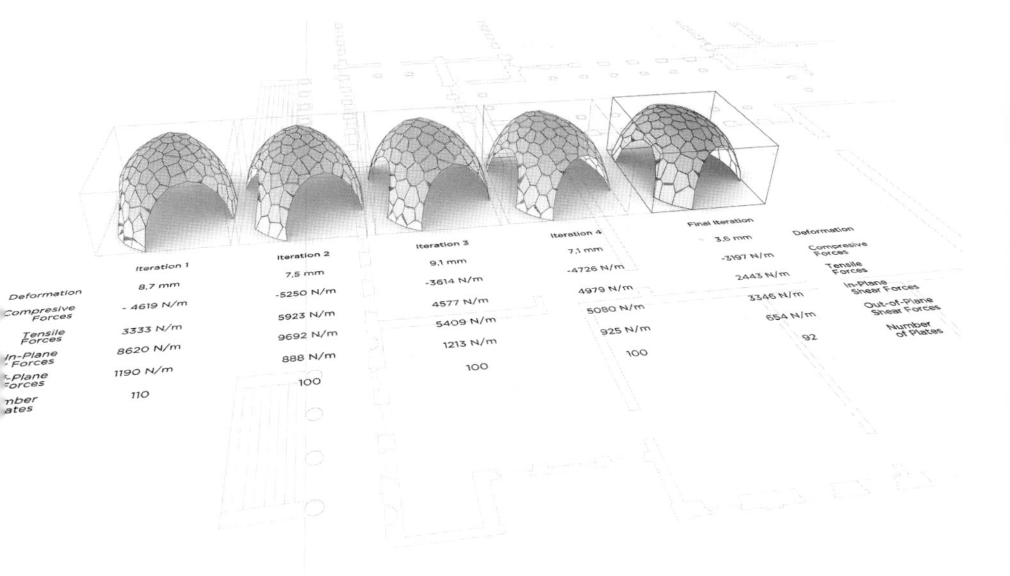

104 *Optimization of the plate arrangement. The plate arrangement of the Rosenstein Timber Pavilion is the result of structural optimization, with the aim of reducing the connection forces and increasing the rigidity of the overall structural system.*

the design process. The structural optimization of the overall shape and of the plate and joint arrangement reduces the forces acting in the plate connections and, in addition, leads to greater rigidity of the overall structural system **103, 104**.
The result of the optimization is the specific plate arrangement of the Rosenstein Pavilion that consists of 92 polygonal beech veneer plywood plates with a thickness of 20 millimeters. With a weight of only 25.4 kilograms per square meter of covered area, the shell spans about 7 meters, which was made possible by the close integration of parametric design, structural optimization, and robotic production. The shape of the pavilion is based on the specific boundary conditions of the Rosenstein Museum space, the exhibition concept, and the circulation layout that guides visitors through the exhibition. From the perspective of the visitor, the openings of the segmented shell provide a frame for special exhibits in the extended exhibition space. The pavilion itself is also part of the exhibition, and unfolds its effect through its material, its individual plate geometry, and the lightweight structural system. Visitors can walk around it and thereby appreciate its characteristic connection details **105–107**.

105 *Interior view of the Rosenstein Timber Pavilion. The pavilion itself is an exhibit, but also frames other exhibits along the exhibition path, as in this case the segmented shell made of graded concrete, which can be seen in the background between elements of the timber pavilion.*

106 *Exterior view of the Rosenstein Timber Pavilion. The pavilion is a special lightweight building with an extremely low weight per area, which has been achieved with a shell that is extremely thin compared with the span.*

107 *Connection detail of the Rosenstein Timber Pavilion. The plates are mitered at the narrow side. The rounded finger joints and crosswise arranged fully-threaded screws make it possible to transfer shear forces at the plate edges and, to a lesser extent, also bending moments.*

The completion of the pavilion demonstrated that the Clypeasteroida (the scientific name of the sea urchin family to which sand dollars belong) are suitable as biological examples for segmented shells in building construction. Not only was the arrangement of the plates geometrically optimized, for example for reasons of production technology, but also the loadbearing capacity of the segmented shell was improved by optimizing the plate arrangement and the joint geometry. If we apply the method of reverse biomimetics (i.e., the application of traditional engineering methods in biology), the structural analysis of the sea urchin skeleton shows that the plate arrangement and overall shape in sea urchins is also determined by structural parameters.

Discussion and Outlook

The findings regarding the plate arrangement and joint geometry are particularly important from a biological point of view because they raise the question to what degree these aspects are the result of evolutionary conditions and what influence mechanical factors have on them. From an architectural and structural engineering point of view, it was particularly important to find out that there is a close interrelationship between global geometry, component geometry, and joint geometry, which much restricts the scope for finding solutions for structurally viable segmented shells. It must be said, however, that the principles of these interrelationships and their mechanisms have not yet been fully understood. Furthermore, there are other research issues that are being investigated in parallel and follow-up projects.

┌108 *Visualization of the timber pavilion for the 2019 Federal Garden Exhibition in Heilbronn. The pavilion will be completed in the spring of 2019, consist of 400 individual components, and have a span of more than 29 m.*

For example, a segmented timber shell is being planned for the 2019 Federal Garden Exhibition (Bundesgartenschau) in Heilbronn, which is the subject of research and building practice; the focus here is primarily on the development of the construction of the segments and their connections, as well as on the development of the manufacturing process. This pavilion, which is to be completed by the spring of 2019, will consist of about 400 individual robotically manufactured timber segments and have a span of more than 29 meters ┌**108, 109**.
In parallel to the development of the Rosenstein Timber Pavilion, the ecological and economic effects of segmented timber shells were investigated in another research project. In this context it has been possible to demonstrate, amongst other things, that the two construction systems for segmented timber shells described above, which were developed for the 2014 State Garden Exhibition and the 2019 Federal Garden Exhibition respectively, have a significantly lower global warming potential than comparable shells made out of concrete and are not more costly to produce.

In the context of increasing urbanization and the associated subsequent increase in the density of cities, we are currently also investigating the possibility of adding additional space on top of existing buildings using lightweight segmented timber shells. In this context, it is particularly important that the shells can be adapted to the existing loadbearing structures in terms of geometry and support conditions ┌**110**.
The relevance of segmented shells in construction is increasingly borne out by buildings that are going up outside the confines of academia. Examples are the Dagsturhytte (hiking cabin) near Hammerfest in Norway and the Elephant House in the Zoological Garden in Zurich. Nevertheless, the technical hurdles impeding implementation are still considerable, in

particular with respect to modeling, simulation, and production. For this reason, additional research will focus on lowering the technical hurdles that currently make the application of segmented shells in architecture difficult.

The Rosenstein Timber Pavilion is a milestone in the research and development of segmented timber shells in terms of the performance of its structural system and the conservation of materials. As one of the four demonstrators in the *Bionik: Biologie beflügelt Architektur* exhibition, the pavilion also shows the potential for transferring structural principles from biology to architecture. As well, the research and design history of the Rosenstein Timber Pavilion shows how findings from teaching and research can be transferred to building practice in a stepwise process. Taking the pavilion as a "vehicle" and model of thinking, it is possible to formulate research questions in the context of the university, to suggest hypotheses, and to test these across several disciplines; this is generally not possible in the same way in general building practice because of the many disciplines involved and the lack of integration. It is therefore important to further promote the transfer of knowledge to building practice. This requires, in addition to educating and training the next generation of architects and engineers, future research and transfer projects. The aim is to be able to utilize the ecological and economic potential of this new construction method on a broader scale.

109 *Construction details of the timber segments of the timber pavilion for the 2019 Federal Garden Exhibition.*

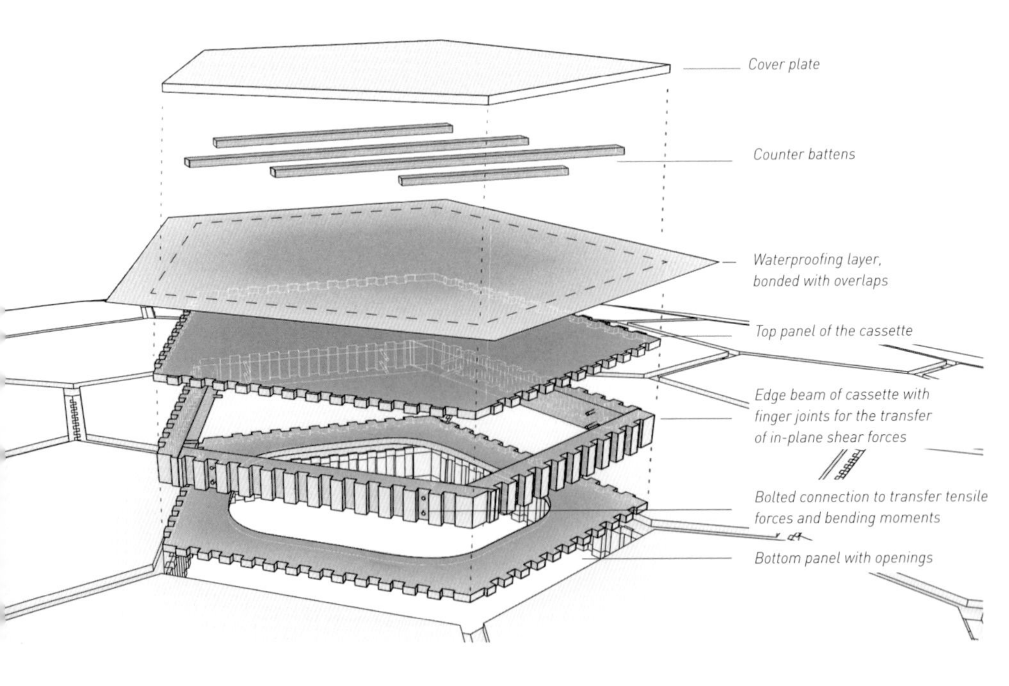

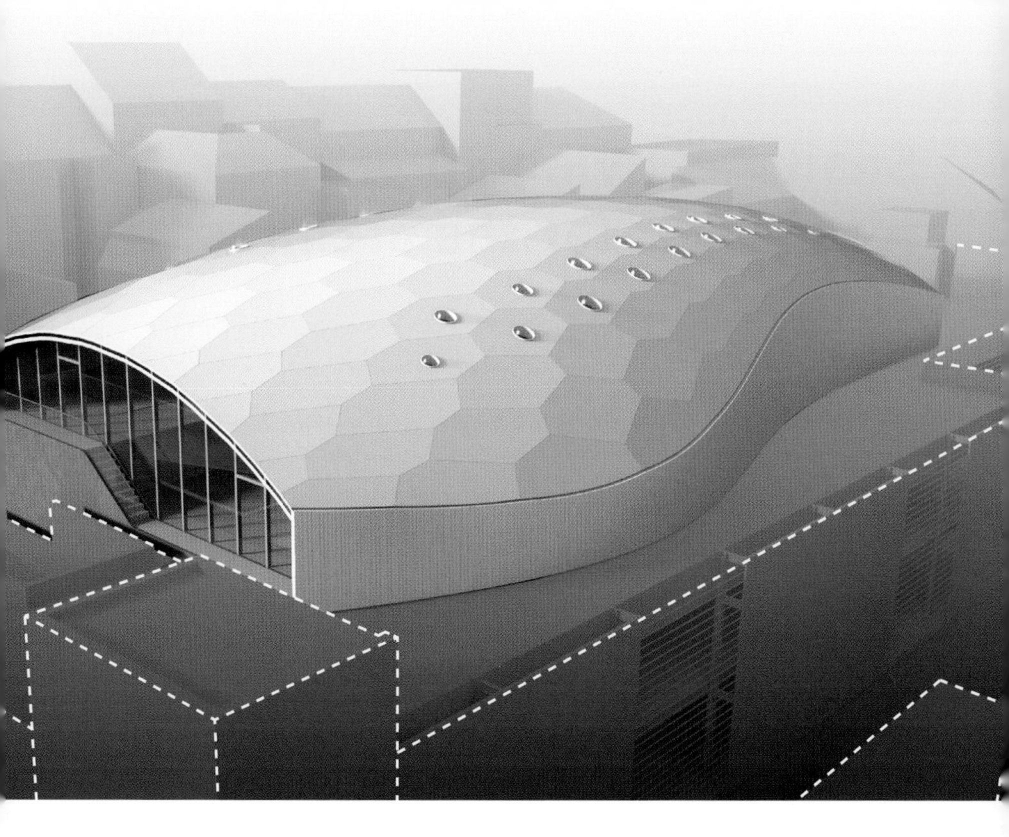

110 *Proposal for increasing the density in an urban context by adding space on top of existing buildings using lightweight segmented timber shells*

Snails as living 3D printers: free forms for the architecture of tomorrow

Christoph Allgaier / Benjamin Felbrich / Frederik Wulle / Emna Khechine / James H. Nebelsick / Achim Menges / Günter Reiter / Renate Reiter / Armin Lechler / Alexander Verl / Karl-Heinz Wurst

Snail shells are some of the most fascinating structures in the animal world. The diversity of shape and structure of the shells is astonishing. The soft body of the animals is capable of generating a high-strength material compound using a production process that has developed over millions of years of evolution and is outstandingly suited to a continuous process of shell building. In spite of the wide range of shapes in the different species and the immense diversity, all snails use the same formation process, which is based on an additive procedure. When considered throughout the growth phase of a snail, the process can be compared to a continuous 3D printing process. However, unlike the additive print process, where the material is added in stacks, snails add material from a gland zone at the edge of the shell. The study of this process holds the promise of exciting innovations for production technologies.

Variety of snail shells

Snail shells can vary widely in shape; many have bizarre shapes while others are esthetically very pleasing ⌈111,112. However, irrespective of how fascinating we find these "works of art," they are the product of a living animal involved in a continuous struggle for survival. Together with squids and mussels, snails belong to the phylum of mollusks (Mollusca). The soft body of the snail is a constant target for predators, and the simplest form of protection is an armored exoskeleton that surrounds the animal. This is all the more important in view of the fact that snails can only move relatively slowly, using a single muscular foot on their underside. For this reason, the scientific name of snails is Gastropoda

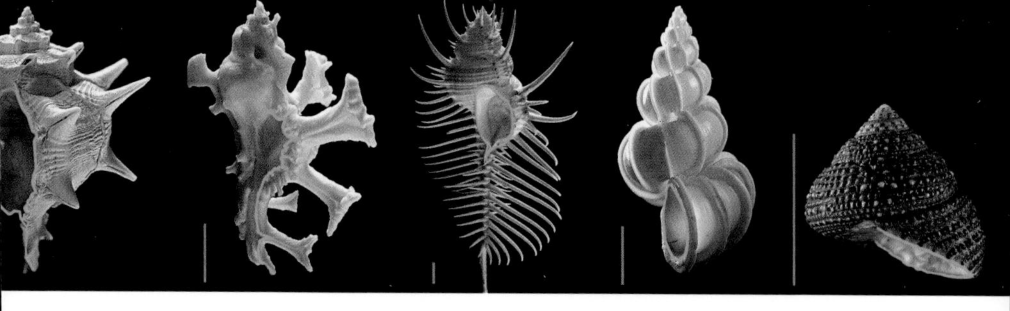

⌈111 *Snail shells with protrusions such as spines, ridges, and ribs or with roughly ornamented surfaces. Green line: shell margin and position of the mantle edge during growth. Scale bar: 1 cm.*

("belly-footed animals"). The snail shell is produced by the soft body in special gland cells. The body skin surrounding the inner organs, the "mantle," separates the shell from the body.

Even though most snail species live in the sea, snails have colonized almost every habitat on earth during the 500 to 600 million years of their evolution. Their shells are correspondingly diverse. Marine snails usually have thicker-walled shells compared to those of land snails. Some snail species have shells less than 1 millimeter thick, while others boast shells measuring over 80 centimeters in length. Furthermore, the shells are often sculptured (i.e., formed into spines, ridges, or keels), and/or the shell surface is covered with protuberances, ribs, or a fine micro-sculpture ⌈115.

⌈112 *Different snail shells show variations of the principle of a tube coiled around an axis. Green line: shell margin and position of the mantle edge during growth. Right-hand shell: longitudinal section; arrow: the point where the soft body is attached to the shell. Scale bar: 1 cm.*

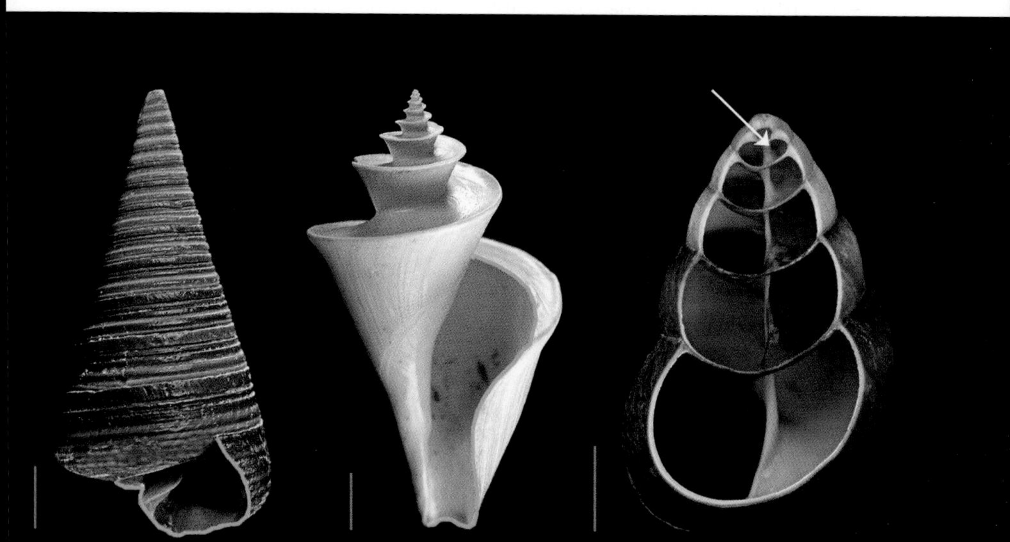

⌐113 *The shell consists of two different layers, the periostracum (P) and the ostracum (O). Living snails often have a shell with an intact periostracum. However, as can be seen here, it can sometimes become detached near the apex. Scale bar: 0.5 mm.*

Hard shell, ingenious core

The snail cannot leave its shell completely, because at one point—on the inside of the tip of the shell—it is fused with the shell. When the soft body grows, the snail adds substance to the external margin of the shell, which results in the growth of the structure. In more detail, the shell construction involves two processes. In the first step, an external organic form-giving layer is created, and this is reinforced from the inside with an inorganic material in the second step. The organ that constructs the shell, the so-called mantle, first produces a thin, protein-rich membrane called the periostracum and then adds one or several hard layers of calcium carbonate ⌐113. Ultimately, the shape of the shell is determined by the activity of the living tissue of the animal. The entire soft body of the animal can move freely backward and forward within the shell. In order to be able to begin building the shell, the mantle edge and the shell margin must come into contact. Sometimes the activity pauses, for example when the animal withdraws into the shell. This means that the snail shell does not grow uninterrupted, but in repeated phases.

Shell growth throughout the entire width

The secretion of the mantle epithelium takes place in a band-shaped zone of productive tissue, the so-called mantle edge. In that region, the newly formed periostracum is attached to the margin of the shell in the periostracal groove and extruded over the entire length of the periostracal groove, which occurs in a continuous process ⌐114. When it is still fresh, the soft periostracum membrane is brought into a certain form through typical movements of the mantle edge. The layer then hardens and, at the top end of the mantle edge, is reinforced from the inside with calcium carbonate, thereby completing the shell, a material compound consisting of an organic outer layer and an inorganic inner layer.

Freely formed

During the hardening process of the newly extruded periostracum layer, it is supported and formed by the mantle edge Many snail species are known for protu-

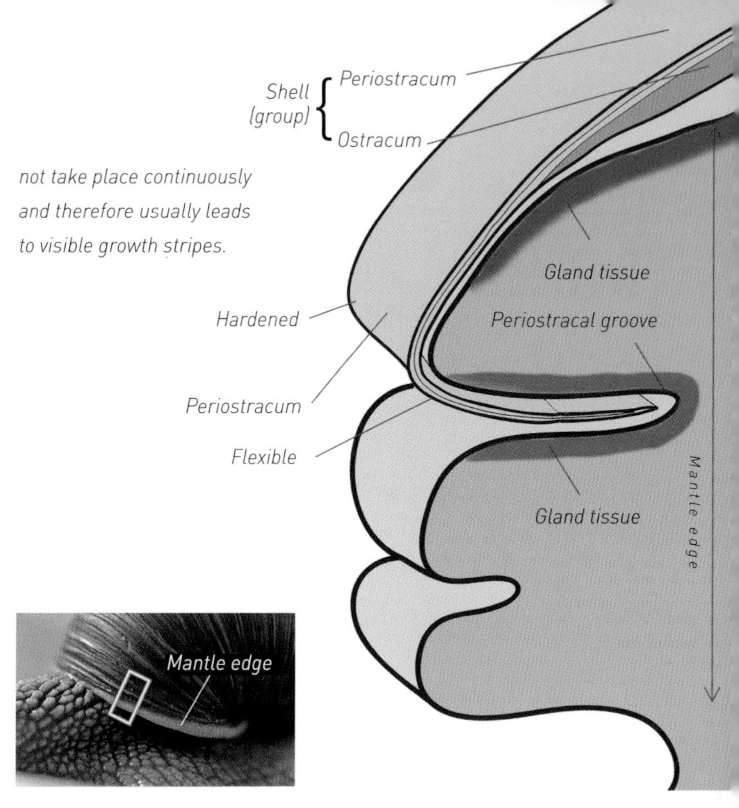

114 *The 3D print head of the snail: The snail shell is formed by the soft body at the mantle edge with its many glands. Two different formation zones are located in this area. At first a flexible membrane, the periostracum, is attached to the existing shell margin, which is extruded from the periostracal groove. Once this has hardened, reinforcing calcium carbonate layers are applied from the inside along a range of glands located farther up along the mantle edge. The growth process does not take place continuously and therefore usually leads to visible growth stripes.*

berances and ornamental, three-dimensional structures on the shell surface. All these variations are generated by the respective forming movements of the mantle edge during the growth at the margin of the shell. This means that the design of the shape of the shell takes place here. When looked at in more detail, it can be seen that the elements are repeated (i.e., they are periodic structures). The accretional growth and form generation are based on various construction programs that are innate to the snail. Once a certain constructional activity has been completed, the mantle edge is reset for a new form element. In the case of land snails, these processes, which take place in periodic form in these snails too, create the micro-sculptures that we frequently find **115**. The importance of these surface structures in the micro-range is still largely unknown.

115 *Shell surfaces of pulmonates (land snails with a lung) with micro-textures. Left: Roman snail (*Helix pomatia*); middle:* Helicigona lapicida*; right:* Monachoides incarnatus.

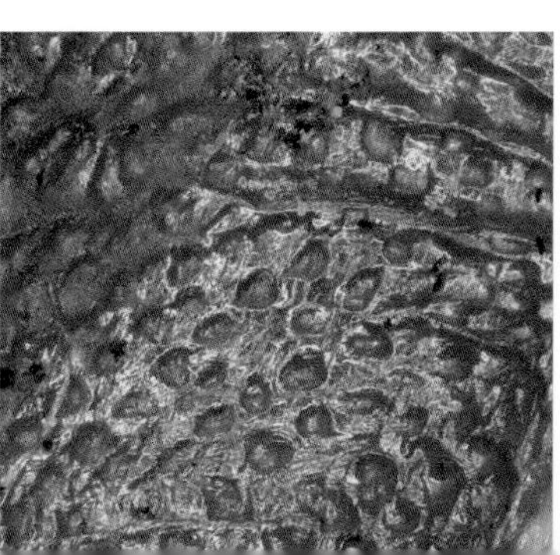

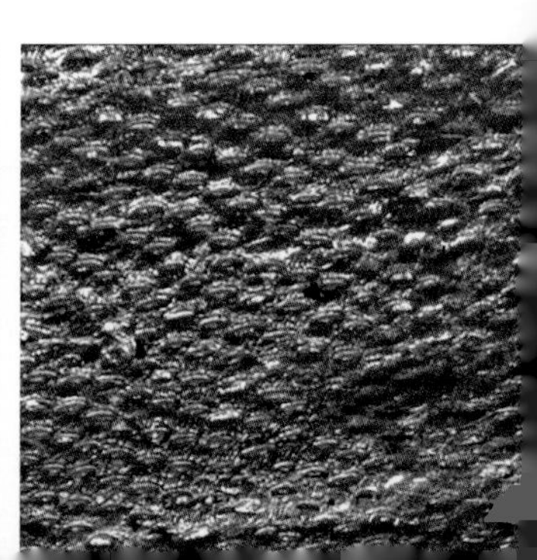

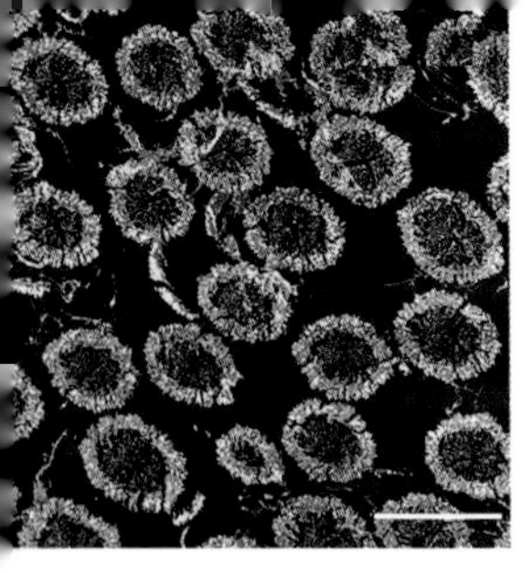

┌116 *Image of crystalline areas in a monolayer of poly-L-lactide acid (PLLA), taken with a scanning force microscope. The cutout of the image is 20 µm x 20 µm; the scale bar of 0–20 nm is relevant for the height.*

┌117 *Image of partially crystalline areas in a monolayer of poly-benzyl-L-glutamate, taken with a scanning force microscope. The cutout of the image is 2 µm x 2 µm; the scale bar of 0–10 nm is relevant for the height.*

From biology to architecture

Structured biopolymer monolayers for building up the formable periostracum membrane

There are many diverse challenges that have to be faced by the properties of the periostracum membrane. Initially, the membrane is very thin and soft, and can therefore be formed easily. However, once it has been formed, it must be stabilized until it has chemically cured and hardened, and is supported by growing calcium carbonate layers. The mantle edge plays an important role in giving the shell its form and supporting it; furthermore, the biological materials used for building the shell must have properties that allow this forming process to happen.
One important property is the ability of the periostracum to emerge from the plane into three-dimensional space at certain places. At these places, the membrane must be less stiff than in the areas that are less heavily curved. One option for creating differences in the bending stiffness is to modify the structure of the membrane. In this context, this means that the membrane is made up of units with different degrees of stiffness. For example, the base lamella of the membrane can be soft and flexible, and hard, stiffening structural elements are embedded therein, arranged in a very specific pattern. When we arrange stiff elements in a line, for example, the bending stiffness along this line will be greater than in other areas of the membrane. Polymer physicists use this principle in the production of ultra-thin layers made of so-called biopolymers. These molecules are simplified models of the protein molecules of the periostracum. Using a self-assembly method at the water surface, it is possible to initiate crystallization of these molecules in some areas, where they become hard and stiff. In other areas, however, the biopolymers are in a softer and more flexible state. The spatial arrangement of these structure elements is significantly influenced by the properties of the molecules and the preparation conditions of these ultra-thin layers. This can be illustrated with the examples of the monolayers of a polylactide and polypeptide ┌**116,117**. The presented images show that it is possible to generate different arrangement patterns of the hard, stiff areas. This approach can be used for a targeted modification of the membrane's bending stiffness.

From the snail shell to the building envelope

The continuous growth process of a snail shell can be compared to additive manufacturing processes, the principles of which are also based on the addition of material. However, when taking a closer look at the growth of snail shells, we can detect that the growth principles are different from the conventional methods in manufacturing technology. Taking into account the biological example and technical possibilities for implementation, the function principles are described below using a model ┌118. This model is used for transferring the innovative bio-inspired approaches to the manufacture of components for use in architecture.

The biomimetic model focuses on the functional separation into a form-defining and a loadbearing layer (in the snail, periostracum and ostracum). First, the form-defining layer generates the form and it is then reinforced with the structural loadbearing layer, which adapts to this given form. In order to produce an envelope, both layers are generated flat in the direction of growth. The growth can be in any direction, which means that the envelope can be curved. A shape with a double curvature is generated by an additional deformation of the form-defining layer in cross-section. In the extrusion process, this post-extrusional forming takes place when the material is soft and formable. During this part of the process it is also possible to create other textures, such as patterns on this layer. This subsequent modeling of the printed shell can be adapted to suit special functions (e.g., self-cleaning). The necessary strength of the form-defining layer for the stability of this of the continuing manufacturing process is achieved with targeted hardening of the material. In the technical implementation, the connection between the two layers has to take place differently from the biological example, because scaling effects do not permit simple bonding of the loadbearing layer to the substrate.

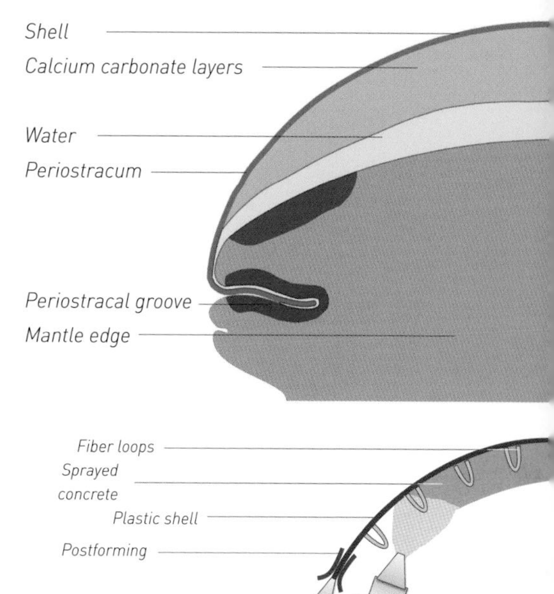

┌118 *Biomimetic transfer: biological snail shell growth (top); model of technical manufacture of building envelopes (bottom).*

The extrusion of a plastic shell is limited to a certain width. In the case of the snail, the membrane sides are connected to the adjoining snail shell. This connection strategy of the membrane sides that occurs in nature is modified in the technical application (i.e., several lengths are arranged next to each other in order to achieve a wider envelope).

The innovative approaches of this biomimetic model—the function principles of the snail—are now transferred to the manufacturing technology for manufacturing building envelopes. To do this, fibers and sprayed concrete are used in additive manufacturing in addition to the customary plastic materials.

┌119 *Test specimen consisting of several 8-cm-wide HDPE strips welded together, including fiber loops for the connection with the concrete*

3D print technologies make it possible to design forms freely and to use several materials functionally in one component. In the fused layer modeling process (FLM), thermoplastic filament is heated beyond its melting point and deposited in layers as threads above each other. The conventional FLM process is based on extrusion from a relatively small circular nozzle. To produce a membrane in this way, the print head would have to move along several lengths of each layer, step by step, which is not very efficient for the creation of such a structure. For this reason, we pursue the biologically inspired approach of continuous shell extrusion in the direction of the structure. Technically, this is implemented using a plastic extruder that processes granulate. The material is heated and melted therein and then extruded. The extruded material ends in a wide-slotted nozzle that forms a thin, wide component. Through the movements of the extruder in space, this membrane can be created in almost any shape. Then the warm and flexible structure is actively cooled using airflow in order to harden it and hence make it resistant to form changes.

The plastic shell is printed in individual lengths that are then welded together. This produces the form-defining layer, which is then reinforced with concrete that is sprayed on. In order to achieve a better connection between the plastic membrane and the concrete, fiber loops are woven into the shell. In this way it is possible to manufacture an almost free-form solid envelope that, in addition, has special characteristics, such as water permeability or the ability to self-clean **┌119**.

Intelligent form design

In recent years, the 3D printing process and, in particular, the FLM have become significantly more popular with architects and designers. The reason for this is their versatility in application when the path involves the relatively quick and simple manufacture of complex forms, together with their uncomplicated technical structure. As a result, this method of additive manufacturing has become a popular tool in architectural model building.

FLM-related techniques are also used for actual-sized buildings. Here, much larger

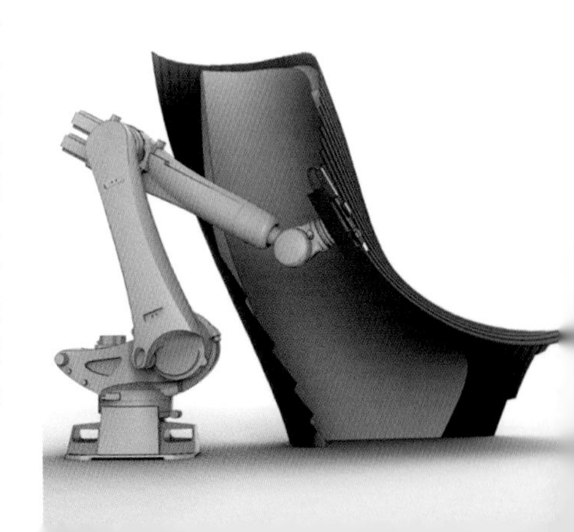

3D printers are required than are available in the trade, and use other materials such as concrete or clay. In their basic function, however, they hardly differ from their smaller relations: a nozzle is moved in three directions (x, y, z) and deposits materials on top of each other in horizontal layers. Architects who work with this method have to produce a building design in the form of a virtual 3D model. Intelligent software then translates this virtual geometry into machine commands that are executed by the respective "printer."
However, this way of functioning involves considerable restrictions. By depositing material on previous layers, it is not possible to create overhangs without expensive support structures, which heavily restricts the achievable form diversity. As well, the application of fine textures on printed components is possible only to a limited extent, and the structures are frequently still quite coarse due to the output of large quantities of materials. This is where snails may be able to help—as a source of ideas for large-format 3D printing techniques. The manufacturing method in the form of a continuous shell extrusion presented here was inspired by this biological example ⌜**120**. However, the design process obviously changes due to the larger space that has to be filled and the degree of texturing. As a result, a virtual model can no longer be split up into horizontal layers as before. In view of the fact that the fabrication machine is considerably more complex, the forms to be created can be designed with greater freedom, but this also involves a more complicated machine control system. Furthermore, it is possible that the printed thermoplastic layer undergoes deformation before the concrete is applied and assumes a slightly changed form.
In order to be able to predict these aspects, we simulate the entire fabrication process at an early stage in the architectural design.
This means not only that the form of the printed component fulfills the requirements for spatial quality and strength, but that efficient manufacture can also be guaranteed. It must be said, though, that conventional approaches to computer-assisted design reach their limits at this point. Modern solutions based on robotics may be able to assist in this situation; in these solutions, an imagined control unit—a so-called robotic "agent"—is used to assist in the development of favorable construction strategies with the help of various optimization methods. Based on such an "agent" or "behavior-based" control mechanism, the computer supports architects in assessing the advantages and disadvantages of potential solutions in extremely complex simulation environments and in making relevant decisions. For example, in this process it is possible to include the foreseeable deformation of the shell and the limited working space of the printing robot in the design of the shell.

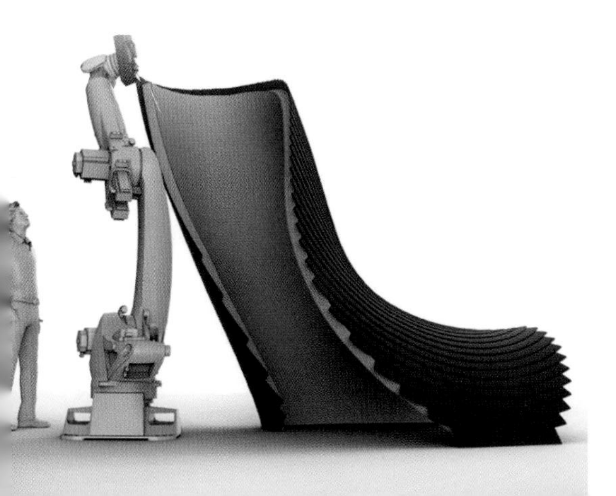

⌜**120** *A component with a complex form is created using the stepwise application of additional polymer strips (dark). This is reinforced with sprayed concrete (light) in a step-by-step process.*

Evolutive approaches to explorative design methods in architecture

Yaron Malkowsky / Anna K. Ostendorf / Nico van Gessel / Long Nguyen / Daniel Lang / Achim Menges / Anita Roth-Nebelsick / Ralf Reski

Current studies on the evolution of selected moss species reveal exciting new insights into the genetic mechanisms that lead to the creation of new species. One of these moss species, the spreading earthmoss, has been used in science as a model organism for many years, and its genetic information has been completely decrypted. This makes it and other members of its family ideal research objects for the transfer of these genetic mechanisms into algorithms—defined computational processes—and for their use in the developmental process of product design and architecture.

There is no doubt that no theory on the origin of species has molded our understanding of the worldwide diversity of species (biodiversity) in the same way as Charles Darwin's theory of evolution. Although Darwin was not the first to tackle this question in his studies, his work—for the first time—presented a comprehensive and well-founded approach that explains the underlying mechanisms of evolution. Based on the observations he made during his research trips, and his work on the biological materials collected and the fossils found on these trips, Darwin established the basic pillars of his theory, which he published in 1859. Fossils reflect the continuing changes occurring in nature. They make it possible for us to draw conclusions about shared ancestors within lineages. Evolution is a process in which species evolve from their ancestors in small steps. Darwin described the force driving evolution as natural selection. Changes can only take a foothold when they prove viable in the predominant environmental conditions. However, for new species to become established, they need to go through a process of reproductive, behavioral-biology, seasonal, geographic, or genetic isolation within a group of individuals of a species, what is termed a population. Over the course of the 20th century, Darwin's theory of evolution was expanded by the field of genetics. The theory was further underpinned by the advent of population genetics, by the discovery of DNA[1] as the carrier of genetic information, and lastly, by the development of scientific methods in molecular biology and bioinformatics.

[1] *See glossary* **p. 141**

Evolution as the driving force of diversity and variation

A basic tenet of evolutionary theory holds that the increase in morphological diversity—the diversity of shape and form in the blueprints of living beings—is made possible through genetic changes and selection. Nowadays, biologists can trace these changes to the genetic code of the species, its genome, or even down to the single genes of an individual. In this case, the small changes described are random mutations of the DNA components. Such mutations can often be detected and characterized. In spite of this, it is mostly impossible to link these directly with a certain functional change or morphological characteristic. Instead, it has been shown again and again that biological processes are based on highly complex genetic networks of different genes and their gene products. They depend on constant feedback between genes and their products, and from the respective environment. Put simply, genes are translated from a DNA sequence into a sequence of transition molecules of RNA components and then finally into a protein ┌121. Modern methods in molecular biology have made it possible to find out how highly regulated each of these steps is. This regulation applies to the accessibility of a gene on the DNA, to the activation of its decoding, to the structure of the RNA molecules and their subsequent modifications, through to the longevity of a protein after its formation. There is also the fact that not only proteins but also RNA molecules themselves can perform a wide range of biological functions. In eukaryotic organisms—creatures with a cell nucleus—the protein-coding genes are usually made up of exons and introns. Exons are areas that contain information for the structure of proteins. The introns lie in between these and do not have a coding function, that is, they do not contain information. The process of removing the introns is called "splicing." It is an indispensable step in the process of producing a functional protein. However, sometimes parts of exons are also removed in the process, which leads to a new gene product, and hence—possibly—to a new function of a protein. This process is referred to as

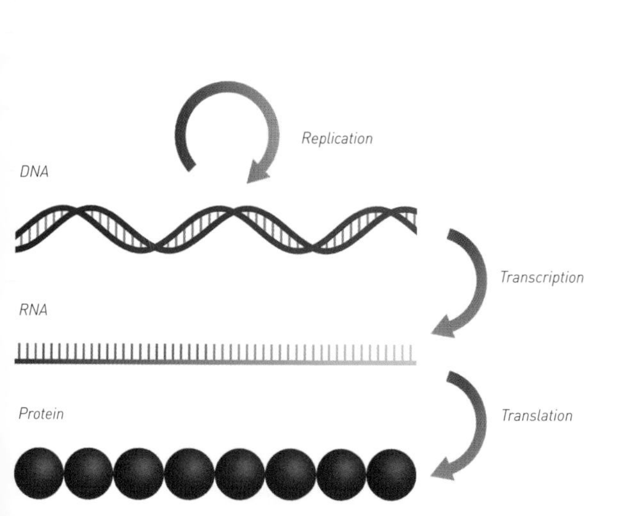

┌121 *The path from the DNA to the protein is a closely dovetailed and highly regulated biological process. Top: duplication of the DNA as part of cell division (replication). Middle: decoding functional sections on the DNA (gene) and translating into RNA molecules (transcription). Bottom: translating the RNA molecules into a protein (translation).*

"alternative splicing." In this way it is possible that additional gene products with a changed function are created without there being further genes in the genome. In addition to the protein-coding genes, a large part of the genetic information is composed of so-called noncoding DNA. We know today that a large part of this noncoding DNA contains transposons. These regions of DNA can spread themselves or copies of themselves in the genome through "jumps." When they carry out these jumps, they are able to also transfer adjoining DNA sections. This can lead to a dramatic change in the overall genome, and may explain how new genes are generated. Therefore, in addition to the exterior adaptation of shape and function, organisms are also subject to processes on the genetic level that favor the creation of diversity. Even though such genetic mechanisms are obviously critical in terms of evolutionary development, their role in the emergence of new species remains largely unclear.

Mosses and genetics

For the investigation of evolutionary processes at the genetic level, it is important to choose a suitable group of organisms that has already been well researched. An example is the Funariaceae, a family of mosses that does not contain too many species and includes the small spreading earthmoss ┌123. Funariaceae occur worldwide on open or disturbed surfaces. In these places they grow either in single tufts or in the form of loose turf. The part of the moss plant that carries the leaves is called the gametophyte. Gametophytes have small, rosette-like stems surrounded by small leaves. On the side facing the substrate they form stringy, root-like structures (rhizoids) for the purpose of anchoring. Following fertilization, a sporophyte grows on the gametophyte. It consists of a spore capsule on a stem, which often extends above the moss cushion. Inside the spore capsule, spores are formed that are hardly visible to the naked eye. In Bryophytes, the opening mechanism of such a spore capsule is often extremely sophisticated. Within the Funariaceae, there are considerable differences between the species. The range of forms includes spore capsules with complex

⌈122 *Intricately constructed spore capsule of the tropical Funariaceae species* Funaria calvescens *with a sophisticated toothed rim along the capsule opening, which allows the spores to discharge depending on the relative humidity.*

toothed rims at the opening of the capsule that can open or close depending on the relative humidity ⌈122 through to completely closed, spherical spore capsules whence spores can emerge only when the wall of the capsule tears open ⌈124.
The spreading earthmoss of the Funariaceae family is an annual plant, which is visually rather inconspicuous. It can often be found at the banks of drying-up lakes and in floodplains ⌈125. The spores of this pioneering species can survive long periods in the ground and, given the right conditions, can grow up quickly when it colonizes open areas in small tufts. The life cycle of the spreading earthmoss is very short, lasting approximately eight weeks, and is ideally completed before the water level rises again. The spore capsule looks like a simple sphere. It does not have any complex structures that would facilitate the release of the spores. In spite of its

⌈123 *Typical Funariaceae representatives. From left to right: the bonfire moss (*Funaria hygrometrica*), the Norfolk bladder moss (*Physcomitrium eurystomum*), and the spreading earthmoss (*Physcomitrella patens*).*

⌜124 *Independent of wind and weather—the spore capsule of the spreading earthmoss simply bursts open as soon as the spores are mature.*

⌜125 *Drained lakes or dried-out riverbanks are the typical habitat of the spreading earthmoss. At such locations the plants have little time to fulfill their life cycle and produce spores that can survive the next flooding.*

inconspicuous appearance, for years the spreading earthmoss has been used internationally as a model organism for biological studies. The fact that it can be easily cultivated in the laboratory, as well as its short life cycle, means that it is an ideal research object, making it possible to study how plants adapt to new habitats, for example. Thanks to specific methods and the successful mapping of the genome of the spreading earthmoss in 2008, molecular biologists are able to generate specific changes in the genetic code and thereby activate or repress specific genes.

What we can learn from the genetics of moss

Not knowing that DNA carries the genetic information, Darwin posited that geographic isolation and a resulting barrier to reproduction is a driving force in the evolution of species. However, as shown in molecular biology, spontaneous changes in the genome can also lead to reproductive isolation. Using the Funariaceae as models, it is now possible to find out how changes in the genomes are related to morphological and functional innovation and diversity.
Such changes may involve the duplication or shifting of parts of the genome, or whole genome duplication. In the case of the Funariaceae investigated here, these occurred time and again in the course of evolution. For successful sexual reproduction of eukaryotes and the number of parental chromosomes—the DNA packaging units—must equal. Therefore, a duplication of the chromosomes owing to genome duplication represents a barrier to reproduction. It is assumed that the evolution of morphologically simpler species such as the spreading earthmoss and its close relatives is characterized by duplication events and the subsequent loss of individual chromosomes. But there are other factors, such as the transposons described above. Perhaps the conspicuously variable form of the spore capsule can also be traced back to such changes ⌜126.

126 *A direct comparison of the size of (A) bonfire moss, (B) Norfolk bladder moss, and (C) spreading earthmoss illustrates how different the spore capsules of the Funariaceae can look.*

A B C

Evolutionary design

In biology, every manifestation within a population is primarily based on a genome (i.e., the genetic information of an individual). These genomes have mutated in the course of evolution. In sexual reproduction they are combined with each other so that a new set of variants is created in the following generation.
Using so-called evolutionary algorithms, it is now also possible to apply these mechanisms in the field of evolutionary design of products, architecture, and art. Everything starts with a simple population, the digital genomes of which—in the form of numerical series—present random design variations. Gradually, new design variants are created through step-by-step mutation and the re-combination of the digital genomes. As in the natural selection process, every design variant is evaluated against defined design criteria and only the good ones are retained for the next evolutionary step. Over time, this leads to continually improving variants until finally a set of best suitable design variants is achieved. Normally, the sole purpose of these processes is the improvement of certain factors. However, an important characteristic of evolutionary processes is their strength of innovation, which again and again produces surprising new results. It follows that evolutionary approaches in design may lead not only to optimization but also to the exploration of new solutions.

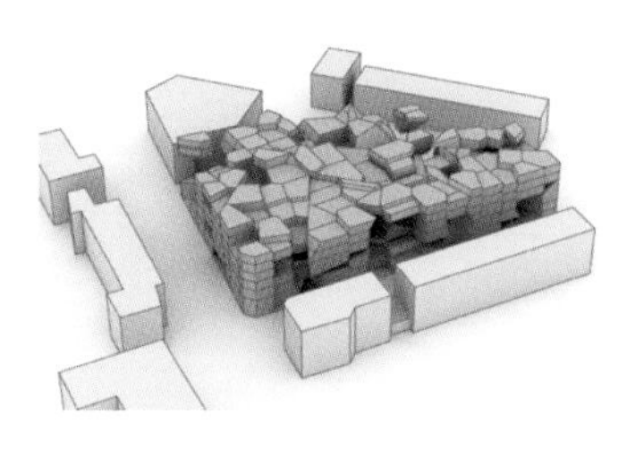 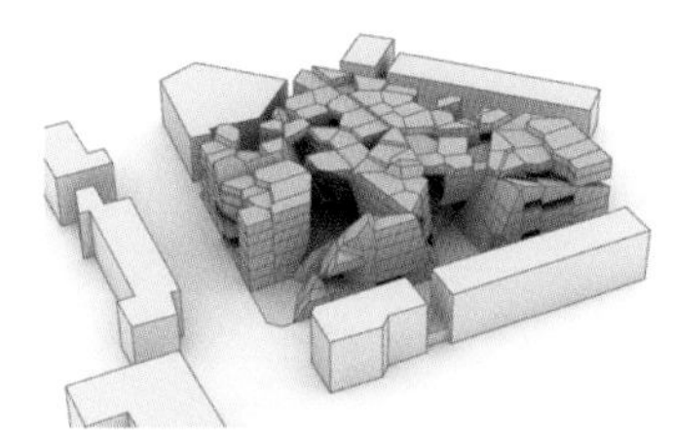 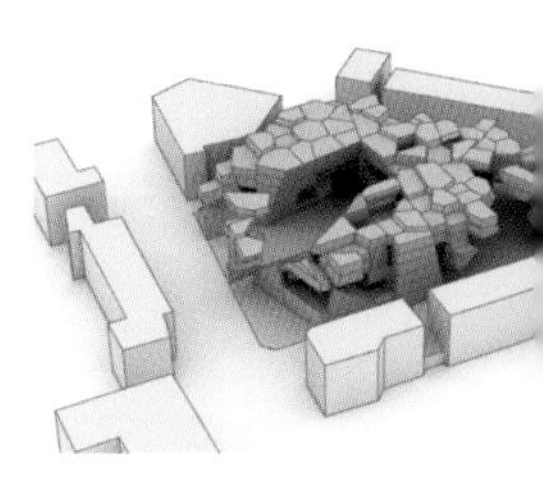

Transfer of evolutionary mechanisms to evolutionary design

The objective is to use selected genetic mechanisms of biological evolution to develop algorithms that allow the design to evolve analogously to the processes in nature. This makes it possible to utilize the innovative power of evolution and to proceed along new avenues in product design and architecture. However, two aspects must be taken into account in this endeavor: firstly, the variability of the size of genomes, and secondly, the importance of the noncoding DNA.

The digital genomes used in evolutionary design usually have a fixed size. This represents a simplified working model and reduces the computing time required. However, the variable size of genomes of the different species of Funariaceae illustrates that it is important to be able to modify the size of the digital genomes generated on the computer over the course of the evolution. Another factor is the simplified relationship between the genome and the resulting design compared to nature. In order to achieve free evolution of design these simplifications must be eliminated. Furthermore, the presence of noncoding DNA indicates that not every variable in the digital genome has to have a mandatory direct influence on the design. The seemingly superfluous variables are not necessarily decisive for the design of the following generation. However, if they are assessed as potentially useful as part of the selection mechanism, they are retained as part of the genome.

The part of the algorithm that converts the digital genome into a design is also referred to as digital embryogenesis. In biology, embryogenesis describes the development of the embryo following the fusion of the genomes of the egg and sperm cells. This analogy with biology indicates how the new type of design develops from the digital genetic makeup. The embryogenesis must be sufficiently complex that it does not limit the diversity of the possible design results and, at the same time, that it is able to benefit from the growing size of the genome. Tests carried out to date indicate that the complexity of this digital embryogenesis has heavily influenced the outcome of high-quality design variants. The structures that contribute to the evolution of the individual moss plant are similarly complex. Even though it is relatively easy to understand the individual steps involved, it is difficult to grasp how they all work together. Assuming that the developed evolutionary algorithm is helpful in solving the one specific design problem, it doesn't necessarily follow that this will apply to all design problems. The applicability of the evolutionary algorithm therefore depends heavily on the type of design problem and the algorithm has to be readjusted every time ┌ **127**.

The above prerequisites must be met before the genetic mechanisms of biological evolution, such as genome duplication, can be simulated digitally. Furthermore, processes such as alternative splicing or transposon jumps make it possible for new products to be created from one and the same gene. These different variants will then again be the starting point for

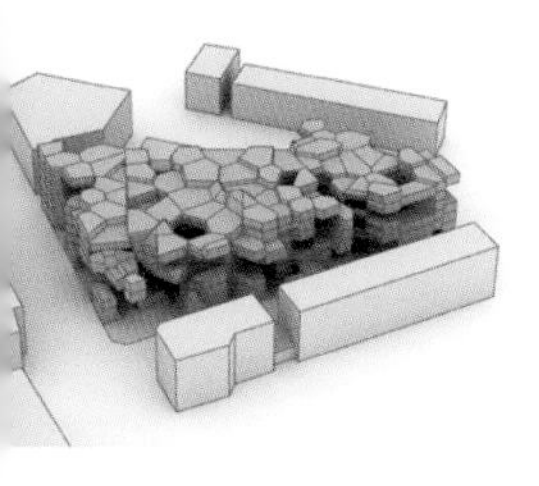
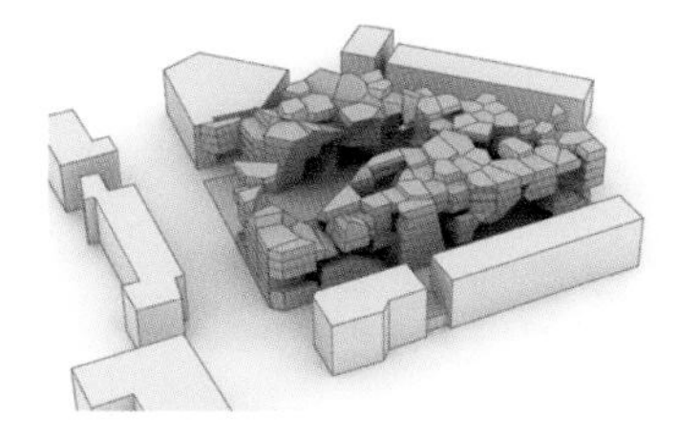
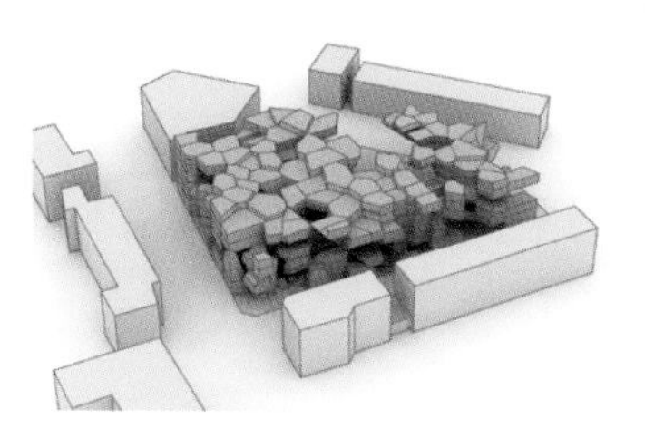

new design variants. We can conclude that understanding the processes underlying biological evolution and their implementation in evolutionary algorithms constitutes a key to fully utilizing design diversity and design innovation in product design and architecture.

127 *Development of urban apartment blocks (dark gray) using evolutionary algorithms. In this case, a specified genome size was used together with a complex embryogenesis.*

Glossary

Algorithm	*Stepwise process or set of rules to be followed in calculations*
Chromosome	*Packaging unit of the DNA*
DNA	*Deoxyribonucleic acid, molecule, carrier of genetic information*
Embryogenesis	*Development of the embryo after the fusion of the genome of the egg cell with that of the sperm cell*
Encoding	*Containing information for making a gene product*
Eukaryotes	*Organisms in which the cells have a cell nucleus*
Exon	*Coding section of a gene that is decoded to produce a protein*
Gene product	*For example, a protein produced after a gene has been transcribed and translated*
Genome	*Total of the genetic makeup of a creature*
Intron	*Noncoding section of a gene that has to be removed before the transcript is translated*
Molecule	*Contains at least two equally linked atoms*
Morphological	*Relating to exterior shape or form*
Mutation	*Spontaneous modification of the genetic makeup*
Protein	*Protein molecule*
RNA	*Ribonucleic acid, a transition molecule that is created when decoding the DNA and is used (e.g., as a pattern for proteins)*
Splicing	*Removing the intron sections of a gene*
Splicing, alternative	*Removing the intron sections including certain parts of the adjoining exon areas or incomplete intron removal*
Transposon	*DNA area that can spread itself or copies of itself in the genome through jumps*

BRANCHED LOAD SUPPORT SYSTEMS

Jan Knippers / Thomas Speck

Branched systems are of fundamental importance in all domains of nature. In the context of building construction, systems that transfer forces are of particular interest—for example, the crown of a tree, the reinforcing veins in the wings of insects, the widely spread web of a spider, or the inner structure of a bone. The latter consists of many small bone trabeculae that form a branched system of compression and tension struts, which stabilizes the bone at the exact points where loads impact on it.

It is said that Gustave Eiffel took this as an example for the design of his famous tower in Paris. Whether this is actually the case is not undisputed, but Eiffel was certainly an ingenious engineer, and his 312-meter-high tower was the world's highest building for many years. It consists of 7,300 metric tons of iron, which, melted down, would result in a cube with an edge length of less than 10 meters. Eiffel belongs to the generation of engineers who, in the second half of the 19th century, promoted construction with iron. Towards the end of the 19th century, railway station buildings and bridges were built with clear spans that would have been completely unthinkable a few years earlier. They are constructed in the form of branched iron frameworks in which the orientation and dimension of each individual member has been designed exactly to suit the respective load, just as is the case in a bone. Branched frameworks such as that of the Eiffel Tower are drawn and calculated, manufactured to the exact detail, and finally assembled. In the nodes of the frames, the forces come together and are diverted. At these highly loaded points, the construction is joined together by bolting or welding, or in some other way. The nodes are the points in the construction that need the most careful consideration. By contrast, plants, bones, and other natural branching systems are generated in a continuing growth process. In this process they not only grow in size but, at the same time, continuously adapt their shape and inner structure to the forces acting upon them, and in that way change and improve their loadbearing capacity. There are no joints or other discontinuities. Like the bone trabeculae, all twigs and branches of a tree are homogeneously grown together. Plants are of particular interest because they develop quite different forms of ramification. Some feature a main axis from which significantly smaller side shoots branch off. In others, the main axis itself divides into two or three main axes of (almost) identical size, which in turn undergo further ramification. Within these two

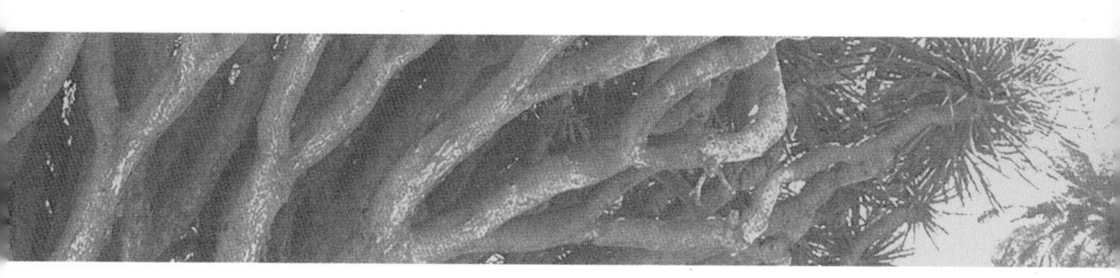

main groups in the world of plants we can find innumerable different types of ramification, which are capable—sometimes with very different structures—of reliably supporting the load of their own weight, as well as the wind and snow loads impacting on them.

Using modern imaging processes such as microcomputer tomography (μ-CT) or magnetic resonance tomography (MRT), it is possible to investigate not only the exterior shape but also the inner composition of such biological ramified structures and to compare them with each other. The resulting digital images can be transferred—via a few intermediate steps—into an engineering simulation model that can provide information on the inner stress and deformation conditions, and hence on the mechanical function and capability of the ramified plant structure.

From plant branchings to technical support structures

Katharina Bunk / Florian A. Jonas / Larissa Born / Linnea Hesse / Claudia Möhl / Götz T. Gresser/ Jan Knippers / Thomas Speck / Tom Masselter

Bridges and roofs are often supported by branched steel columns. Their production is usually expensive and consumes a great deal of energy. In nature, plants manage to form similarly strong and frequently even more complex branch systems through natural growth processes. They can effortlessly withstand mechanical loads, such as their own weight, wind pressure, snow load, or the heavy weight of fruit. In order to find out about the success strategies of ramified trees and shrubs and to learn from them for architecture, we need more than a detailed look at the form of ramification and inside the plants. We also need computer models and new materials and methods for the production of branched support structures in building construction to succeed in transferring the biological concepts to technology.

Plant branchings as example and inspiration

Trees and shrubs look very different from one another. Even within one species there are sometimes big differences in size, appearance, and the form of growth. The same applies to the connections between trunk and branches, and the branch ramifications themselves. Depending on the form and size of the plant, as well as various external factors, a wide range of branching patterns are formed. An important role is played by external and internal forces acting on the plant, such as the plant's own weight, sometimes involving mighty branches or heavy loads of fruit, and strong effects of the weather such as wind or precipitation. In addition, plants constantly compete for sunlight. The successful plants are the ones that can outdo their competitors in height and width, by growing taller and/or by more effective ramification. As the result of all these factors, a huge diversity of branching patterns exists ⌈128. How can we find suitable models from this profusion for the optimization of architectural support structures for buildings or bridges?

⌈**128** *The Oriental paperbush (Edgeworthia chrysantha) shows hierarchical branchings in height and width.*

┌129 *Detail of the ramification of the Oriental paperbush (*Edgeworthia chrysantha*), with three branches of almost identical diameter (left), and branched columns at Stuttgart Airport—each with three or four equivalent struts (right)*

In this context one must always remember that a direct transfer is not possible. Even though they look similar, the ramifications of plants and architectural structures differ in many aspects ┌129. Plants can react to specific local loads through increased growth and by depositing material in certain regions. By contrast, support structures in construction are static. Likewise, the functions of the support structures differ in nature and technology. In plants, these structures are responsible not only for mechanical stabilization but also for the transport of water to the side branches, leaves, and fruit, and for the transport of photosynthesis products (sugars) from the leaves to the storage organs. In technical applications, support structures primarily serve structural stability but, increasingly, are also used for other functions, such as integrating, for example, drainage, ventilation, heating, or lighting. Plant ramifications are not connected at their apices. When exposed to load, they are forced to bend downwards (e.g., under snow loads or fruit hanging from the tree) or are deformed laterally (e.g., through wind load). This leads to bending stresses in the branches. In architecture, branched columns mainly carry roofs or flat elements that connect the ends of the columns firmly with each other. In this case, the imposed forces act for the most part in the direction of the columns. Consequently, when looked at in more detail, the term "tree column" does not fit very well for the designation of these branched architectural columns. A direct transfer or a copy of nature is not something that promises to be successful for the reasons stated. If we want to draw lessons from natural branchings for technology, simplification and abstraction of the basic functional principles is always necessary.

Why branched columns?

One success strategy of plants is to create as large a (leaf) surface as possible for harvesting energy from sunlight with as little building material as possible. The ends of the trunks and branches are not restrained. At these points the plant continues to grow. By contrast, the ends of the branched supporting elements in buildings are firmly attached to other parts of the building. Often they are directly attached to the roof of the building. The advantage of branched columns versus unbranched

┌130 *The columnar cactus (Cereus sp.) has constrictions between the stem and the often large and heavy side branches.*

columns is obvious: the structure to be supported—for example a roof—can be more slender and more lightweight, because the distances between the endpoints of the branched supports are smaller. Furthermore, a roof construction with branched columns at the same height as a roof construction using unbranched elements—with the same quality of support—provides significantly more open space on the floor. In view of the fact that the form of the branched columns affects the load transfer and the thickness of the columns, the design is aimed at finding the most favorable form.

A wide choice

Most trees we are familiar with from our local forests and parks have substantial lateral branches. These "typical tree ramifications" are characterized by their size, their mechanically strong wood, and their growth rings, which in our latitudes are quite pronounced.
However, when searching for biological role models, our attention is also frequently drawn to branchings of a somewhat different kind. These sometimes don't reveal their special features until looked at more closely, but there's more to it. For example, columnar cacti are frequently (much) thinner at, of all places, their points of ramification—seemingly the points where strength matters most—than at their stem and side branches, which is a result of the way the side branches are grown ┌130. Together, biologists and engineers were able to demonstrate that the form of this narrowing at the point of

⌜131 *Canary Islands dragon tree (*Dracaena draco*) with numerous hierarchical ramifications*

⌜132 *Longitudinal section through the branching of a* Dracaena marginata *tree. Scale bar: 1 mm.*

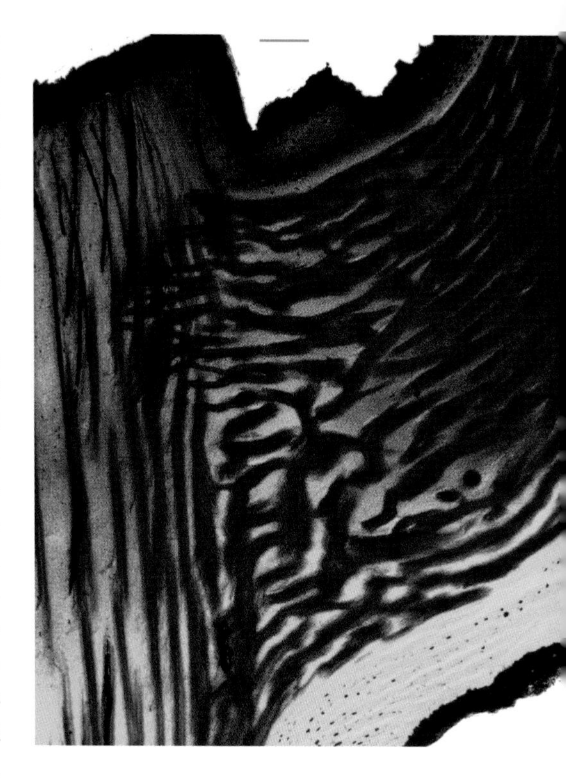

branching constitutes a special adaptation of the columnar cacti, which store large and heavy quantities of water in the cortex of their stems which enable them to survive phases of drought. This form of the branching region facilitates the distribution of mechanical loads in the main stem and the side branch, making it possible to support greater loads.

The dragon tree too (genus *Dracaena*), which ranges from small houseplants to imposing trees **⌜131**, employs a special trick for forming strong ramifications. Lignified fibers embedded in soft ground tissue are adapted in arrangement and orientation to the loads acting on them **⌜132**. In this way, the branching region is reminiscent of fiber-reinforced composite materials like those used in lightweight construction for the manufacture of sports articles or parts of automobiles, as well as, increasingly, in building construction.

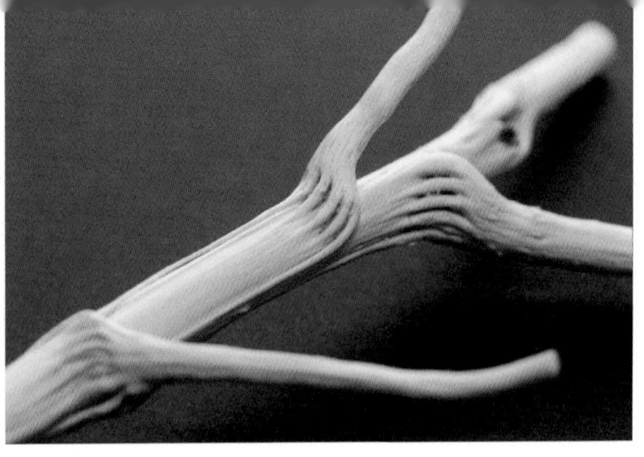

133 *The dwarf umbrella tree (*Schefflera arboricola*, left) has in its ramifications finger-shaped elements that connect the branch with the main stem, which are not visible unless the cortex is removed from the lignified part (right).*

134 *The X-ray imaged obtained via computed tomography show the emergence, path, and joining of the individual "fingers" in a branching of the dwarf umbrella tree.*

The secret of the Araliaceae

Another very special stem–to–branch connection can be found in the dwarf umbrella tree (*Schefflera arboricola*), which is a popular houseplant **133**. At first glance, seen from the outside, its ramification appears to be quite ordinary, but a look inside brings one or two surprises.

When we cut off a branch of the dwarf umbrella tree and remove the green tissue (botanically: cortex or bark), a ramification is revealed that consists of finger-like wood strands. These run individually from the main stem into the branching and only merge into a solid side branch there **133**. This type of ramification can also be found in other species of Araliaceae, but up until now it could not be detected in any other plant family. But here too, the same applies: no finger-like ramification is 100 percent identical to any other, which means that each ramification looks a little bit different, differences being found in the number of individual strands, the embracing of the main stem by the fingers, and the gaps between them. Is this type of ramification a strategy of the Araliaceae to save material, or is its main purpose to avoid critical loads?

In order to answer these questions, the inner structure of the ramification was analyzed in more detail. By making very thin cross-sections (thinner than a sheet of paper) through the ramification, it is possible to investigate the individual fingers in detail and to follow their path throughout the entire branching region.

In order to understand how such ramifications are developed, test plants are decapitated (i.e., cut off at their tips). The plant reacts to this injury by forming a ramification below the cutting point, which we can witness with the help of time-lapse photography. In addition, some of the plants are scanned using high-resolution computed tomography, a process that is similar to X-ray photography in the hospital. This provides insights into the inner structure of the ramification and also facilitates a detailed three-dimensional reconstruction of the exterior shape—both important steps from the biological role model towards a technical implementation and, at the same time, the key interface between biologists and engineers **134**.

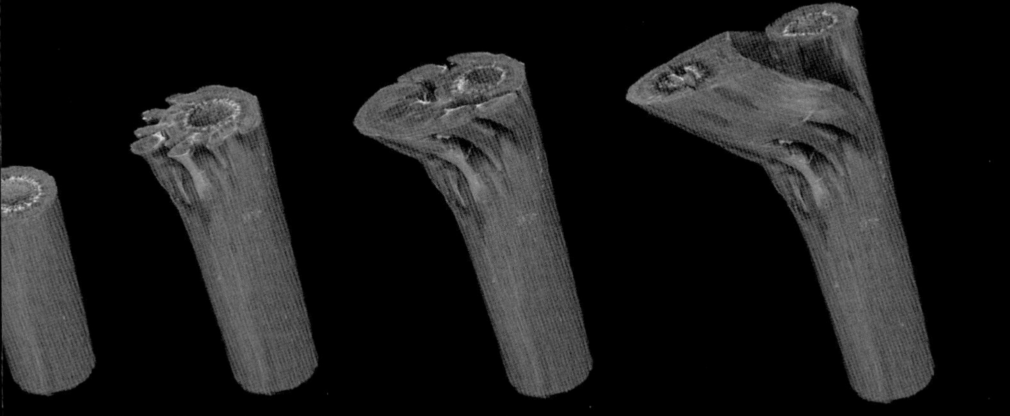

From the plant to the computer model

Advanced technical methods such as computed tomography make it possible to generate digital three-dimensional images from real objects. Based on these images, it is possible to build models and carry out mechanical simulations on the computer (e.g., in order to investigate the influence of various forces on a ramification) ⌈135. This helps to answer important questions, for example, for what type of load is a certain ramification particularly suitable? How is the form of the plant adapted to naturally occurring loads?

Similarity between the branchings of plants and those in architecture is sought not only in the external shape but, above all, in the loadbearing function. In order to be able to investigate the behavior of plant ramifications when exposed to the plant's own weight, wind, or snow, virtual geometric and mechanical models are generated from the data of the imaging processes. In addition to the outer shape

⌈135 *Geometric model of* Schefflera arboricola*; exterior envelope with cavities in red (left), mesh for finite element analysis (center), result of a virtual load test: the extent of the deformation is visible via the color changes (right).*

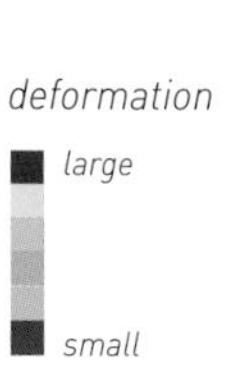

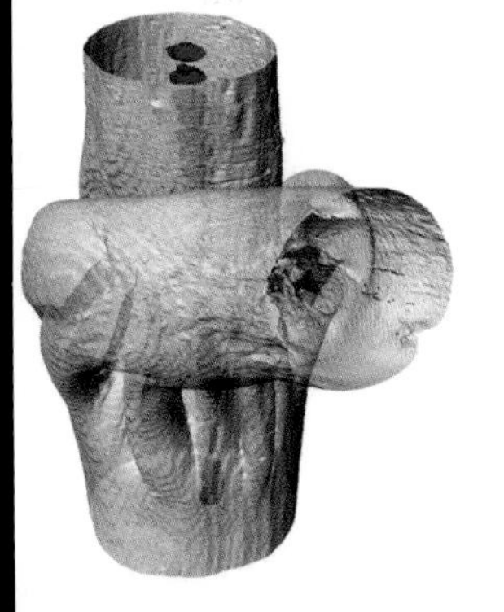

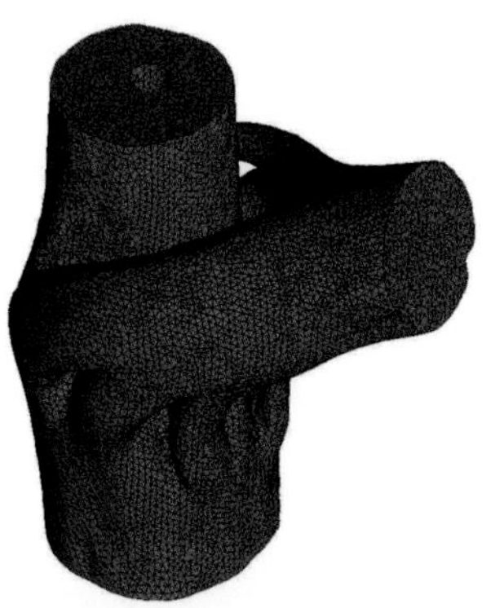

136 *Branched grid-shell construction made of steel tubes at King's Cross Station in London*

of the ramifications, these also contain information on the internal structure. It has been shown that the material is not a uniform one. Instead, the internal structure is complex, with very different physical and mechanical properties. For example, there are areas with a different density, as well as cavities and different fiber arrangements. The fibers frequently run along the plant axis, which is advantageous for resisting bending moments—such as those mainly occurring in plants.

In both biology and technology, ramifications can be subdivided by their angle and number of branches, and by their arrangement and number of ramification levels (hierarchies). We know ramifications with branches of a different thickness, in which there exist one main branch and several thinner side branches, but also ones in which all branches are equally thick. The latter can often be found in technical support structures. The simplest example is the typical branch fork, which represents a ramification with two (approximately) equally thick branches in one level. But both in nature and in architecture, we find ramifications with a symmetrical structure of three or four comparable branches, such as those of the Oriental paperbush (*Edgeworthia chrysantha*) and of the roof supports of the Stuttgart airport building **129, 141**. When the ends of two "branches" are reconnected with each other (which only occurs in technical solutions), a third type of structure is created: a gridshell. Such gridshells are highly efficient load-bearing structures that can be used for the construction of large open spans—such as that of King's Cross Station in London **136**.

⌈**137** *Radial braiding machine with braiding yarns (inside on white and red bobbins), filler yarns/ stationary threads (outside on blue bobbins), and robot (center in orange)*

⌈**138** *The dance around the maypole. Braiding is placed around a maypole with two types of cords, which are guided by dancers who move around the pole in opposite directions.*

The "maypole dance" for producing lightweight loadbearing structures

Load analyses and computer models derived from the model of plant ramification are used to gain an understanding of the forces acting in a support structure. In addition, a suitable building material must be selected. Plants obtain their loadbearing capacity mostly from stiff lignified fibers that run along the stem and side branches and are embedded in a more elastic ground tissue. The individual fibers form fiber bundles and are firmly bonded with the ground tissue, which enables them to jointly absorb forces in the structure (e.g., the tree trunk). In other words, they form a natural fiber-reinforced composite. It is not only nature that relies on such a high-performance material based on this principle. Fiber-reinforced plastics are used by engineers for many technical components that have to be both lightweight and sturdy. In these materials, plastics are combined with strong artificial or natural fibers in order to achieve mechanical reinforcement. The fibers have the task of absorbing the forces acting upon them. Of course, this means they always have to be arranged in the component such that the forces run along their axis. Otherwise, it would not be possible to fully benefit from their potential strength.

How is it possible to produce ramified technical structures in which the fibers are consistently arranged such that the forces can always be optimally absorbed? One solution is the textile braiding process ⌈**137, 139**. The principle of textile machine braiding is similar to the dance around the maypole. In this dance there are two groups of dancers who hold cords in their hands and dance around the maypole in opposite directions. They circle around each other, and the cords are braided around the pole ⌈**138**.

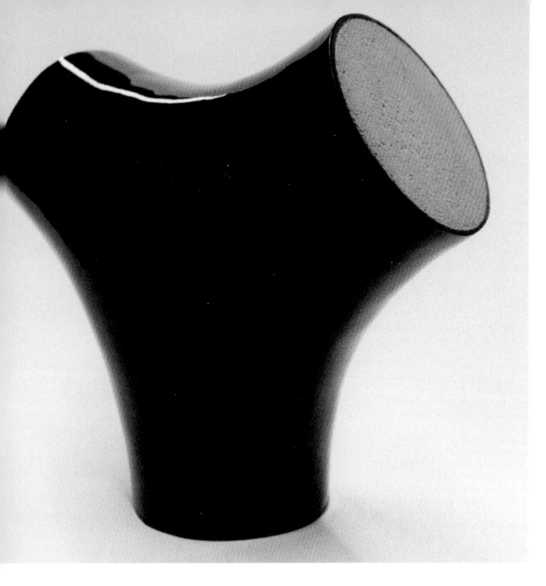

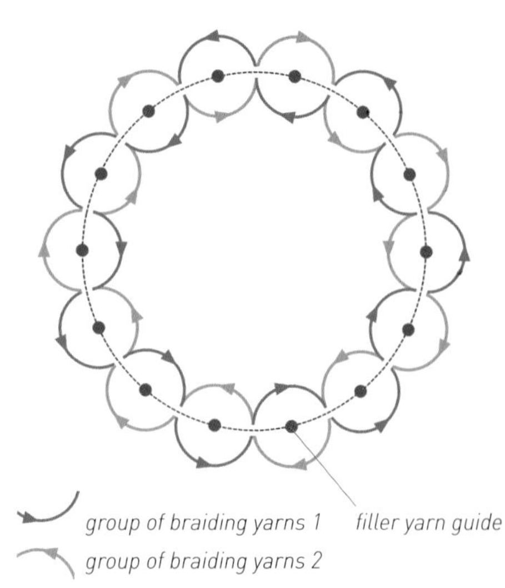

┌139 *Braiding principle of triaxial braiding (right), concrete-filled branched node made of fiber-reinforced concrete composite plastic (left) (arm diameter 125 mm)*

In the braiding machine there are bobbins instead of the dancers from which the threads are pulled **┌137**. They too are divided into two groups and move in opposite directions, and their paths cross over continuously. Instead of the pole at the center, a robot pushes a so-called braiding mandrel through the center of the braiding process. This determines the ultimate external geometry of the component. It is possible to carry out the braiding on round, angular, straight, or curved mandrels, depending on the component geometry required. By adjusting the movement speed of the bobbin carriers or of the mandrel that is pushed through the machine, it is also possible to adjust the angle at which the braiding yarns cross over. This gives the yarns their direction, following which they are soaked in plastic and thereby bonded. In addition to the braiding yarns, it is also possible to insert so-called filler yarns. Their bobbins do not move and the yarn is only pulled off and deposited on the mandrel by its advance. This also makes it possible to reinforce the component in the direction of its axis. This type of braiding is referred to as triaxial braiding (fibers oriented in three directions) **┌139**, which comes closest to the layout of fibers in a plant. In plants, however, the fibers are never braided, though they can have a similar structure as the result of fusing together. The braided structure deposited on the mandrel is then soaked in plastic and cured. After that, the mandrel can be removed, resulting in a strong hollow structure. Owing to the orientation of the yarns, such a hollow structure is optimally suited to absorbing stresses resulting from pulling, bending, or twisting. Only compressive forces cannot be transferred adequately. For this reason, the ramified hollow structures used in architecture are subsequently filled with concrete, which is ideally suited to absorbing compressive forces.

The interdisciplinary cooperation of biologists, engineers, and architects is focused on the detailed investigation of the biological role models, the necessary understanding of their secrets of success, and simplification and implementation in technical materials and constructions. This is the only way to achieve the transition from plant branchings to technical supporting structures.

New branched loadbearing structures in architecture

Florian A. Jonas / Larissa Born / Claudia Möhl / Linnea Hesse / Katharina Bunk / Tom Masselter / Thomas Speck / Götz T. Gresser / Jan Knippers

Branched loadbearing structures have a long tradition in architecture. After centuries of application, the principle of this construction method is still valid today and results in good structural systems. It is obvious why this is so: owing to the form-active design, slender branched columns are effective supports for roofs and floor decks.

Form-active loadbearing structures permit wide spans

As early as the Middle Ages, master builders knew how to use arches and vaults in their designs to create large open spans that appeared very elegant. To this day, many of these structural systems baffle us with their "audacity" ⌜**140A**. Here too, a construction method inspired by nature played a role, but only at an esthetic or formal level rather than a functional one. Whereas in the Middle Ages stone was still the main building material, in recent decades it is primarily steel that has been used for branched pillars and columns, for example in bridges or buildings ⌜**140B**. However, the manufacture of branched nodes, which frequently consist of cast steel, is expensive. An alternative could be a hybrid construction with an outer hull of fiber-reinforced plastic and a concrete core.

A well-known example of branched columns is the structural system of Stuttgart Airport. Whereas the space close to the ceiling and above the heads of the air passengers is available for the branched loadbearing structure, the circulation level is large and generous and encumbered only by the widely spaced lower parts of the columns ⌜**141**.

A

B

⌜**140** *(A) King's College Chapel, Cambridge (1515): masonry; (B) branched pillars of Pragsattel Bridge, Stuttgart (1993): steel construction*

┌ **141** *Branched columns support the roof of Terminal 3 at Stuttgart Airport.*

┌ **142** *(A) Branched columns with reduced cross-section height of the horizontal element; (B) the horizontal element spanning non-branched columns with the same spacing as in (A) needs to be thicker because the spans and the bending moments are larger.*

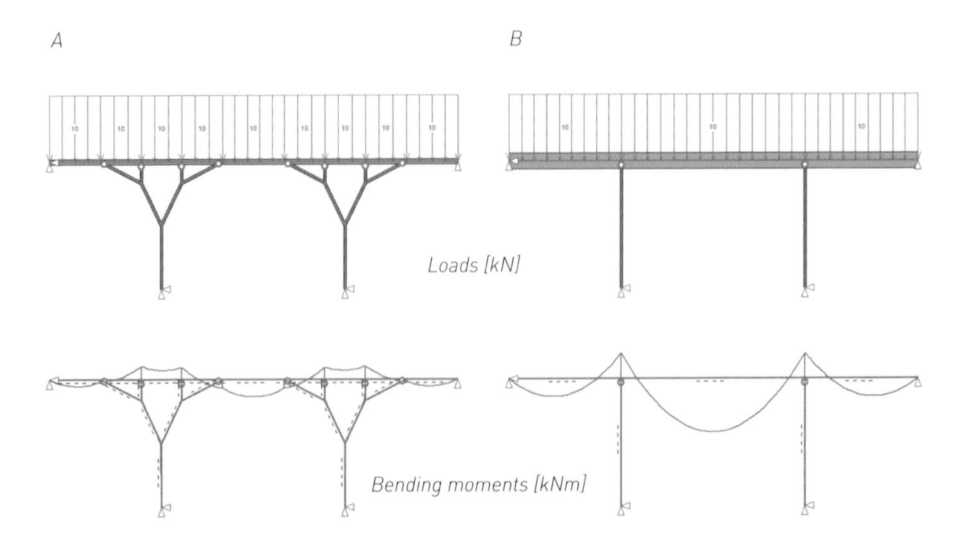

Branched columns not only make efficient use of space, they also have other advantages: the branched columns provide many support points for the horizontal loadbearing element, such as the roof or the deck of the bridge. This effectively reduces the distance between two columns to be spanned by the horizontal element. Smaller spans lead to a reduced construction height. In turn, this means that less material is needed for the horizontal element, reducing the overall weight of the construction.

⌈143 *Comparison: (A) internal forces of a branched column with tension member; (B) example of internal forces in a tree.*

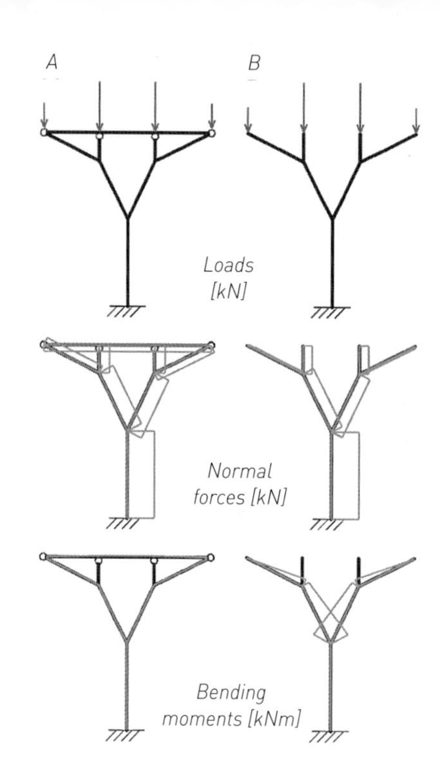

The loadbearing characteristics of a branched column are quite different from those of a natural tree, which is why the frequently used designation "tree column" is misleading. The ends of branched columns—the column heads—are connected via horizontal loadbearing elements, as in the slab of a building or the road deck of a bridge. The loads are primarily transferred as normal compression forces. By contrast, the branches of trees have free ends and respond to loads—such as their own weight and external loads such as those of wind and snow—by bending. For this reason, natural ramifications in plants are primarily exposed to bending loads. The difference can be clearly seen in the diagram of internal forces **⌈143**.

Branched columns, as shown in **⌈141**, are of a slender construction. This means that the ratio of the diameter to the length of the bars is small. The loadbearing capacity of slender structures exposed to compression depends on the strength of the material used as well as on the resistance to buckling (i.e., to stability failure). Stability failure occurs when the loadbearing structure deforms under a load—like a ruler that deflects when exposed to axial compression.

Finding the form of branched columns

In the design of branched columns, their geometry plays an important role because it determines the distribution of the internal forces. A geometry needs to be found in which the bending moments are as small as possible, therefore requiring only small cross-sections in the members. To achieve this, a number of different experimental and analytical methods are available.

An experimental approach was taken by Gaudí, for example: he used hanging models for designing the main loadbearing structure of the Sagrada Familia (Barcelona). To do this and to define the form of the ribs and vaults, he hung defined weights from a cable network and used the deformed model as the basis for the design of the building.

In the second half of the last century, Frei Otto's working group continued the development of experimental methods for determining the geometry of branched structures. By hanging weights from threads, it was possible to identify branch configurations that are suitable as effective loadbearing structures. Branched structures can also be formed experimentally by fibers saturated in resin that, at one end, are attached to the grid of a plate and, at the other end, converge in one point. Owing to surface tension, a balance is achieved between the resulting attractive force and the retained threads **⌈144A, B**.

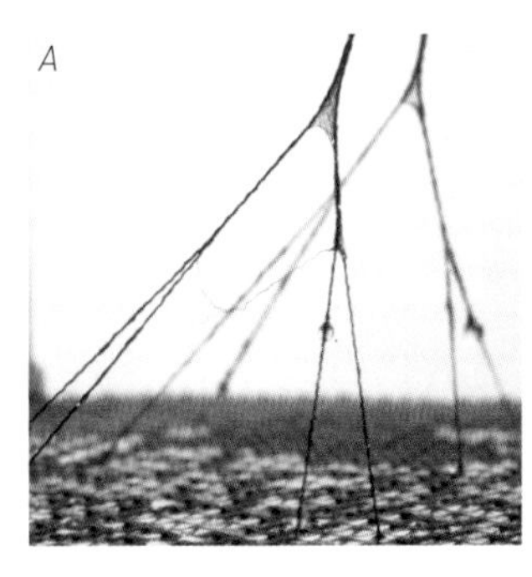

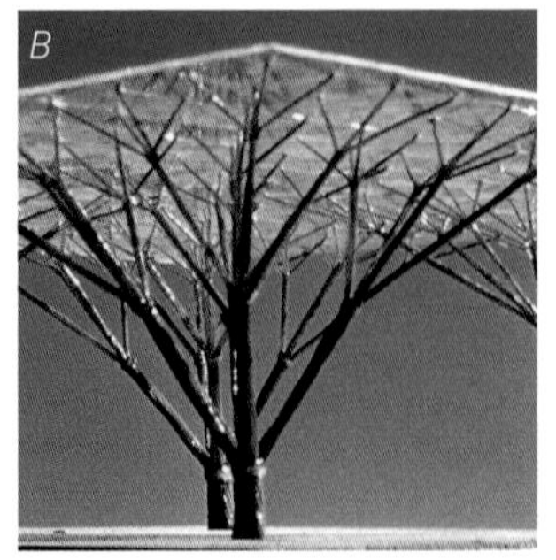

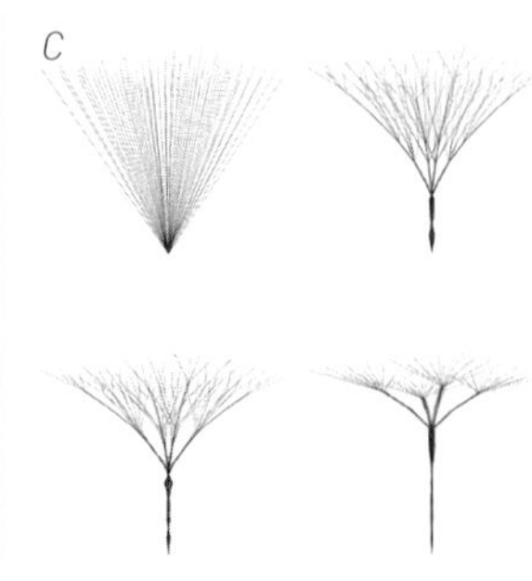

144 *Experimental determination of form: (A) thread model (ILEK); (B) project study "Tree structures" (ILEK); (C) digital determination of form: computer simulation*

Nowadays, the advent of new technologies has significantly changed the methods for determining the form. Instead of working experimentally, form-finding processes can be simulated using a range of computer programs **144C**. For example, the structure optimizing methods help to find a branching geometry that transfers a certain load with the minimum amount of material.

How branched columns are built today

Today, branched columns in buildings or branched pillars in bridge building are frequently manufactured from steel or reinforced concrete. The disadvantage of the reinforced concrete construction lies in the comparatively expensive formwork and reinforcement work.

When steel tubes are used, several tubes have to be cut precisely and then welded together. As a rule, the surfaces of the cuts are complex and therefore the welding work is expensive. Alternatively, a connection node made of cast steel is used at the intersection of the bars **145**. This ensures a continuous transfer of forces at the transition between the individual bars. In this constellation, each tube is welded to the connection node instead of joining several tubes at one point. In view of the fact that the manufacturing of cast steel nodes requires complex molds for high-temperature casting, they only make sense when the node geometry is repeated several times in the building.

145 *Manufacture of a cast steel node: (A) cooling of the cast; (B) mechanical finishing work on the component*

How branched columns can be built in future

Many plants have a heavily branched loadbearing structure, which is particularly evident in the crown of large trees. The mechanical properties of the loadbearing structures of plants are determined by the complex interaction of very different structural hierarchy levels, which include the external shape (m–cm), the tissue structure and arrangement (cm–mm), the cells (mm–µm), the organelles (µm–nm), and the macro-molecules (≤ nm), and are optimized by adaptation, using growth processes throughout the life of the plant. At several of these levels of the hierarchy, the plant relies on construction principles based on lightweight fiber-reinforced composites (e.g., fiber-based tissues and filamentous cells and/or macromolecules in the form of fibers such as cellulose). It has been proven repeatedly that the fibrous elements of plants are oriented in a load-adapted manner (i.e., in accordance with the loads acting on them) (see "From branchings to technical support structures"). This principle was adopted for the fiber arrangement of a newly developed hybrid node **⌈139, 146, 147**, transferred to a branched model **⌈148**, manufactured using a braiding machine **⌈149**, and implemented in a branched support structure **⌈150**. One of the challenges of this method is the manufacturing of a branched textile hull in which the threads are continually guided—adapted to the load—through the branching point **⌈146**.

The braiding process is one of the oldest known textile processes, and is extremely well suited to the manufacture of three-dimensional textiles with fibers continuing. The machine employed for the hybrid node **⌈149** uses 216 threads at the same time, which allows it to also manufacture larger cross-sections such as those required for a loadbearing structure.

In one step of the process, two of the tree arms are braided with a continuous flow of fibers **⌈146A**. The braiding is repeated for all pairings of arms **⌈146B, C** in order to obtain a coherent textile hull **⌈146D**.

⌈146 *Steps for braiding the branching with coherent fiber arrangement: (A) braiding from the first to the second arm; (B) braiding from the second to the third arm; (C) braiding of the last pair of arms (3 to 1); (D) detail of a braided branching with carbon (black) and glass fibers (white)*

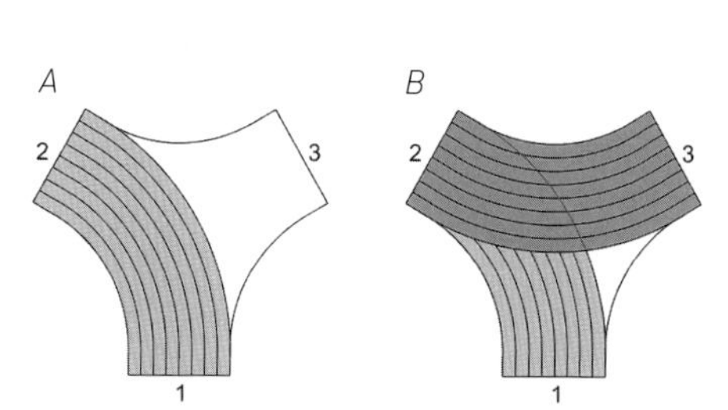

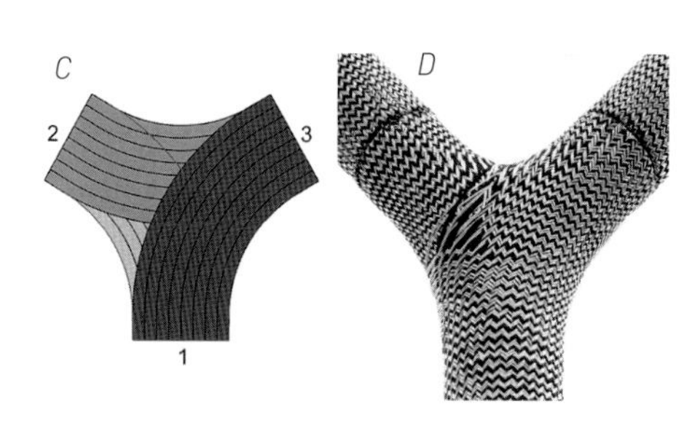

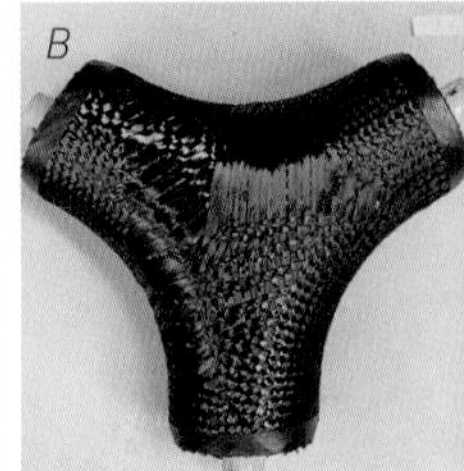

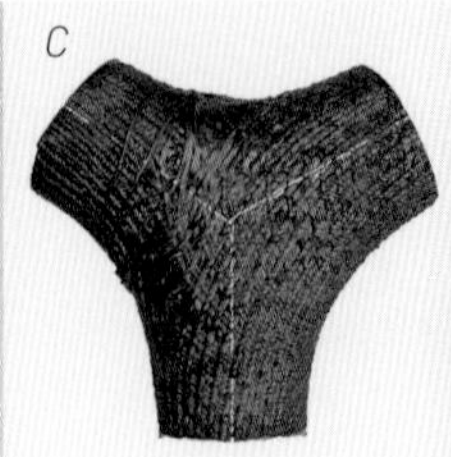

147 *Production of a hybrid node made of fiber-reinforced plastic (FRP) and concrete: (A) braiding cores are milled from foam; (B) dry textile hull after braiding; (C) fiber-reinforced plastic component after impregnation; (D) the hull is filled with concrete.*

The loadbearing hybrid node consists of a fiber-reinforced plastic hull and a core of concrete. The manufacturing process involves four steps **147**. (1) Firstly, a core with the selected geometry is milled using a lightweight foam blank **147A**. (2) Secondly, the core is enclosed by braiding, resulting in a branched textile hull, which at this stage is still flexible. (3) Thirdly, the textile hull is made rigid by impregnating it with resin **147B**. The braiding core is removed **147C**. (4) Finally, the rigid hull is filled with concrete, serving as formwork and reinforcement at the same time **147D**. Once the concrete has cured, a high-strength structural node has been made.

To demonstrate the braiding process that had been developed, a branched structure with a height of 6 meters was produced **150**. The freestanding column with a textile hull consisted of seven nodes and 15 rods with a diameter of up to 127 millimeters. The branched nodes are single-plane nodes, meaning that the axes of each of the three arms lie in one plane.

New design scope for branched loadbearing structures

The demonstrator for the exhibition **150** was developed using a digital model **148**. In this model, the length of the rods, the diameters, and the opening and turning angles of the arms of the branches are variable parameters. The model is built such that the detailed geometry of each node is issued on the basis of the configuration of the overall structure and can be used directly for producing the component (e.g., milling the cores). In addition, the manufacturing limits imposed by the braiding technology have been taken into account, and the range of parameters has been restricted accordingly.

For the application of fiber-reinforced plastic (FRP)/concrete nodes in buildings, it is important that they are geometrically variable and have sufficient loadbearing capacity. In load tests, such three-armed node structures made of FRP and concrete with an arm diameter of 125 millimeters were able to resist compressive forces of up to 1,700 kN. This means that these branchings are suitable for use as slender columns in two- or three-story buildings or for lightweight roofs. Following the development of the new manufacturing process and the successful passing of the initial load tests, the next step is to devise ways in which these innovative branched nodes can be integrated in conventional multistory buildings and industrial shed structures **151**.

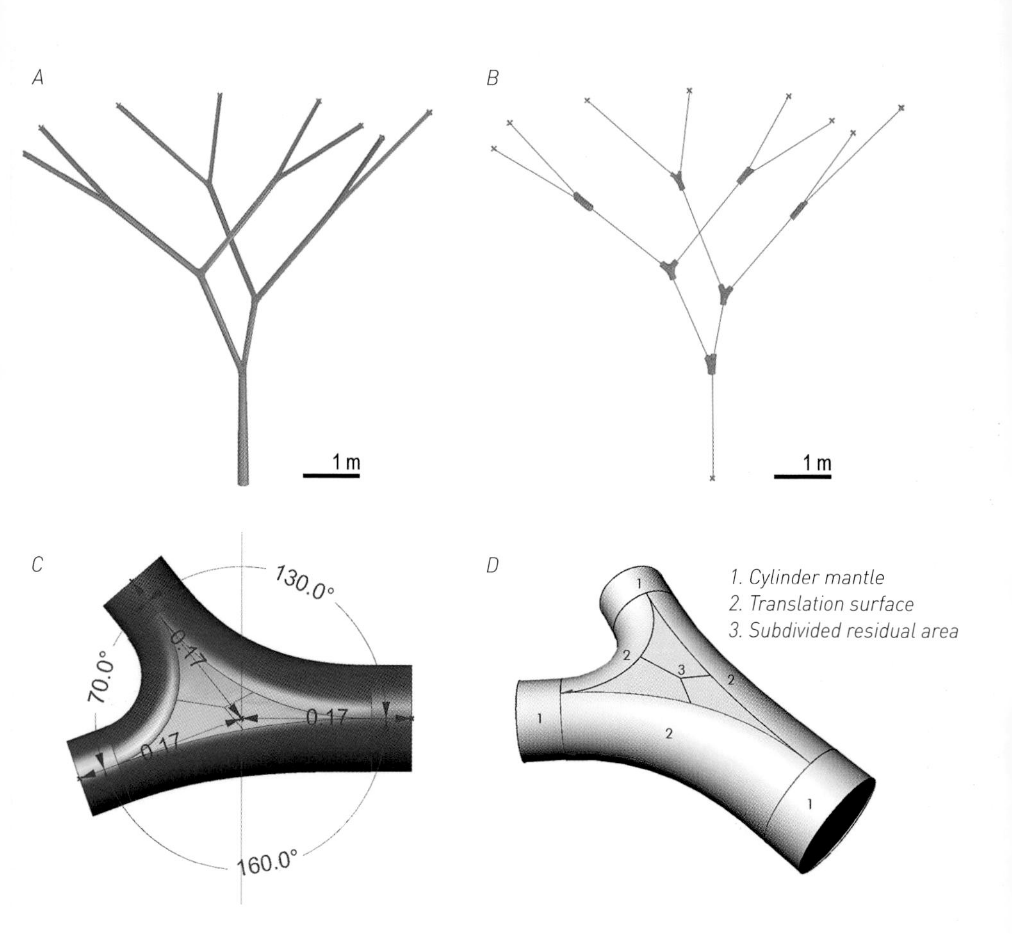

148 *Digital parametric model: (A) final geometry; (B) nodes and axes emphasized; (C) detail of a node generated in relation to the overall structure in an automated process; (D) geometric surfaces for generating a plane branching*

FRP/concrete nodes are a possible alternative to traditionally manufactured nodes for branched loadbearing structures. Owing to their attractive design options and efficient loadbearing capacity, they are suitable not only for new buildings but also for the extension of existing structures.

149 *Radial braiding machine with a branched braiding core. The braiding process is operated by a robot arm.*

150 *Branched demonstrator in Schloss Rosenstein at the* Baubionik—Biologie beflügelt Architektur *exhibition in the Museum of Natural History, Stuttgart (2017/18): branched column with braided textile hull consisting of carbon and glass fibers.*

151 *Loadbearing node made of fiber-reinforced plastic (FRP) and concrete; in the background the demonstrator with braided textile hull and the plant that served as model,* Schefflera arboricola

The plastid skeleton: a source of ideas in the nano range

Bugra Özdemir / Pouyan Asgharzadeh / Annette Birkhold / Oliver Röhrle / Ralf Reski

All life on earth relies on the conversion of solar energy into chemical energy through the process of photosynthesis, in which the greenhouse gas carbon dioxide (CO_2) is absorbed and oxygen (O_2) is released. The green parts of plants are capable of performing this reaction. This is where we find chlorophyll, the green pigment that captures sunlight. Chlorophyll and all components of the conversion process do not exist freely in the plant cells, but are located in certain "reaction spaces," the chloroplasts. These are part of what are called organelles, small reaction spaces within the cell that are separated from other cell components by a double membrane of lipids and proteins.

Plastids with skeleton

Chloroplasts are normally lens-shaped ⌐152. But they can also change their shape, that is, they can grow and divide. For a long time it was not known what causes these changes, what structure gives the organelles their shape, and what is responsible for changes in that shape. We biologists were able to demonstrate that the chloroplasts of a moss, the spreading earthmoss (*Physcomitrella patens*), contain five different so-called FtsZ proteins. When we mark these FtsZ proteins using genetic methods by attaching the bright-green fluorescing GFP protein, microscopic images reveal protein filaments and networks ⌐153. It is noticeable that each FtsZ protein is characterized by a pattern that is different from the other four. These patterns are reminiscent of the cell skeleton that occurs in the cytoplasm of every higher cell (eukaryotic cell), giving it its shape and helping it to change its form. For this reason we proposed the analogous term "plastid skeleton" for these FtsZ filaments in the chloroplasts. Microbiologists have been able to demonstrate that similar cell skeletons occur in bacteria, determining their shape and triggering division. Here too, an FtsZ protein is involved. When this is mutated in bacteria, they take on the shape of a thread at certain temperatures. This is also where the abbreviation FtsZ comes from: filamentous temperature-sensitive mutant Z. This finding is particularly exciting from the point of view of evolution, because the chloroplasts of plants evolved from bacteria about one and a half billion years ago. We can therefore surmise that the FtsZ molecules of bacteria are similar to those of chloroplasts not only in their composition and sequence but also in their function.

In this research project, biologists from Freiburg University and engineers from Stuttgart University have got together in order to uncover the secrets of the plastid skeleton in mosses. This is very challenging, because the structures investigated

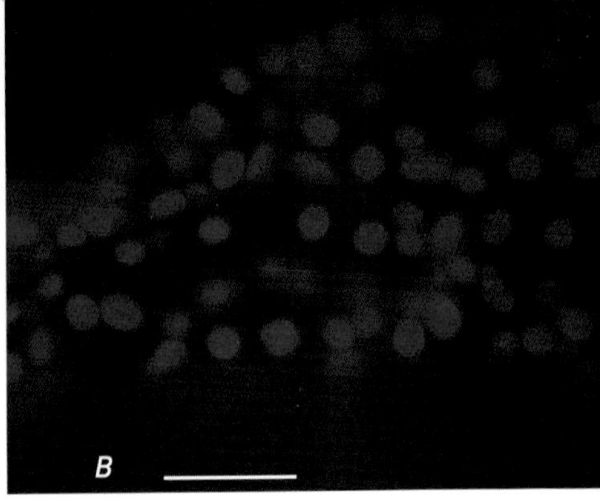

152 *Cutout from a small leaf of the spreading earthmoss (*Physcomitrella patens*). Light microscopy using a Zeiss Axioplan2 microscope shows the green-colored chloroplasts. (B) The same cutout using fluorescence microscopy shows the red inherent fluorescence of the chlorophyll. Scale bar: 20 µm.*

are minute: the moss plants themselves measure only a few millimeters, their chloroplasts have a diameter of just a few micrometers, and the FtsZ protein filaments have a thickness of a few nanometers. To make these visible, high-resolution microscopes are needed. We use confocal laser scanning microscopes for this purpose, special light microscopes that scan the structures with laser beams of certain wavelengths and then put together the individual light points to create images **153**. Because these images are produced from living cells in which the molecules are constantly moving, no two images are the same. For this reason it is necessary to make a great number of different images in order to obtain a good overview of all possible structures of the plastid skeleton. Since all of these images are electronic, the tests create a huge amount of data, which can be automatically processed in computers. For this, special methods are developed with which it is possible to describe the recorded structures of the individual protein networks with mathematical equations, thereby making them comparable.

From image to model

In microscopy, 2D layer images are created from 3D structures, a process known in medical imaging. Depending on the resolution, the amount of data, and the microscope, the distance between the individual images can vary. In order to actually produce 3D images of individual objects, a 3D geometry has to be created from the 2D images. The smaller the distance between the image slices, the more accurate the models. When the distance becomes too great, there is too much uncertainty about the space in between, and assumptions have to be made. This can lead to errors.

Once the models have been completed, they must then be converted into computer models. For this, a grid network has to be created. We can imagine how such a grid network functions if we compare it with Lego blocks: if we only have very big Lego blocks—analogous to a coarse grid network—we can only build a coarse structure, which can only approximately replicate a complicated object. If we choose smaller Lego blocks—or a finer

⌐153 *(A) A single chloroplast under the Leica TCS 8T-WS confocal microscope. An FtsZ2-1 network shown in green. (B) The same image; here the chlorophyll is also shown in bright red. Scale bar: 2 μm.*

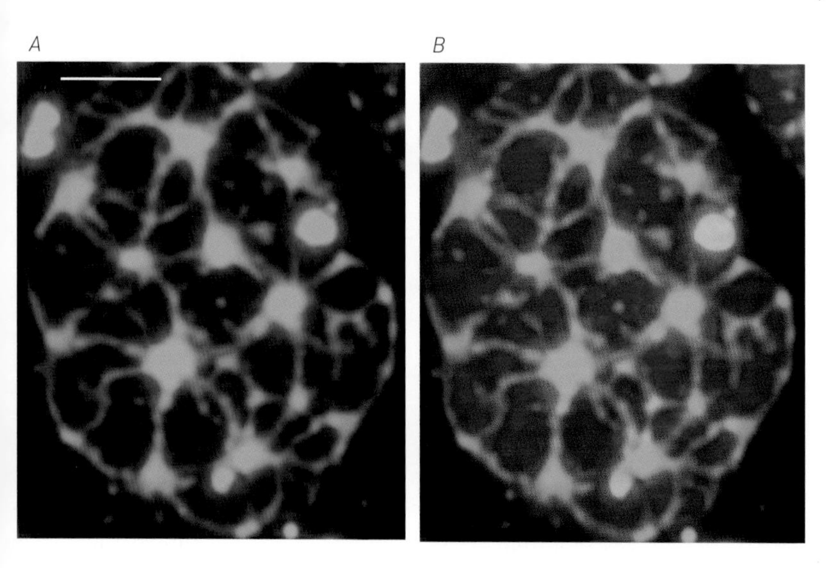

grid network—we can replicate the structure much better.

However, such a detailed replication also involves a large amount of data. After all, the geometry and position of each individual Lego block has to be determined. If we now want not only to reconstruct the geometric variables of the model but also to obtain information about how its function relates to its structure—for example, if we want to carry out a simulation of its mechanical strength—then we need to solve a set of mathematical equations for each Lego component. A very detailed model obviously increases the precision of the information/simulation, but at the cost of the general computing time. For very high resolutions, we need to use one of the supercomputers that have been purchased for several million euros by certain computer centers, such as the High Performance Computing Center Stuttgart (HLRS). This means that, taking practical considerations into account, a good balance has to be struck between computing time, resources, and precision.

In this way it is possible to achieve a mathematically exact description of the different FtsZ networks of the plastid skeleton and to differentiate them. Initial results show that the five FtsZ networks differ from each other; one hypothesis is that, together, they form what is known as a tensegrity structure **⌐154**. Such a structure consisting of bars and tensioned cables was initially invented by two architects and refers to a stable construction that uses only a minimal amount of material.

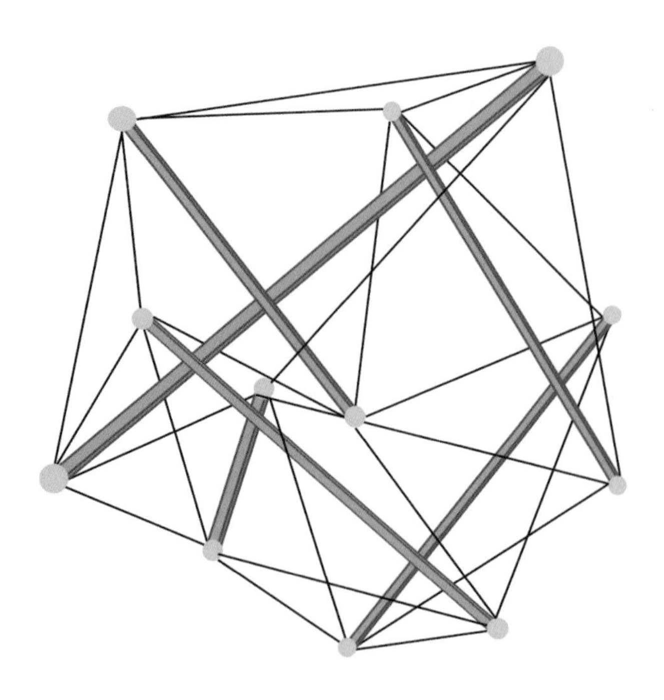

154 *Model of a tensegrity structure, a strut system in which the struts are connected with each other by tensile elements (such as cables). The tensile stress in the elastic parts (black) stabilizes the system and makes it dynamic.*

In our ongoing work we want to check the hypothesis that the plastid skeleton is a tensegrity structure, and investigate how the plastid skeleton changes when exposed to loads, during growth, and in the division of chloroplasts. To this end, we have already carried out initial tests using a scanning force microscope, which we can use to mechanically scan the chloroplast surface and measure even minute forces at the nanometer scale. The objective of our project is to shed light on the dynamics and mechanics of the plastid skeleton, to describe it mathematically, and to use this information to derive general principles that could be used at much larger dimensions (i.e., in engineering and architecture).

In order to achieve this objective, we will take the path of "reverse biomimetics." This means that the detailed analysis of the plastid skeleton will be used to establish hypotheses and models; furthermore, it is intended to produce functioning prototypes (demonstrators). This transfer from a very small scale to a much larger one—from nanometer to centimeter—will lead to new findings and hypotheses, which in turn will be examined using specific genetic changes of the moss. The knowledge gained in this process will then lead to improved models and demonstrators. In this way, not only can architects learn from nature, but biologists can learn from engineers and architects. That is the particular scientific attraction of this project.

Abstracting instead of copying: in search of the formula for success

Nicole Radde / Debdas Paul / Manfred Bischoff

For thousands of years, we have drawn on examples from nature for our technical inventions. We frequently observe animals and plants directly to see how they have solved a certain problem, and then we transfer this solution to technology. But would it not be fascinating to develop new technical solutions with natural methods rather than just transferring existing solutions from nature to technology? Beyond specific solutions to individual problems, there is the issue of general strategies natural systems use to function reliably and to achieve a fascinating combination of efficiency, adaptability, and robustness. We are not talking here about the known strategies of evolution, but about the success formula underlying the blueprints evolution creates. One idea for getting to grips with this natural plan is based on the observation of formal analogies—abstract relationships between what seemingly is not related. We are talking about the search for nature's mathematical formula for success.

Abstraction as a driving force of science

The anecdote about Newton and the apple is very well known. We find ourselves in 1666; Sir Isaac Newton, an English natural scientist and civil servant, is 24 years old. According to legend, he was just contemplating the question of what it might be that keeps the moon orbiting around the earth when, on a beautiful autumn day under an apple tree in his garden at his home village of Woolsthorpe in the north of England, he fell asleep. It wasn't long before he was rudely awakened from his dreams by a falling apple ⌐155.

If we believe his own statements, this event is supposed to have given Newton the idea that the apple falling vertically to the ground is governed by the same physical laws as those governing the moon orbiting the earth. This inspiration led to the discovery of the laws of gravitation, which in turn laid the foundation stone of classical mechanics. Newton had succeeded in establishing a comprehensive physical theory that underpinned Kepler's previously empirical laws of planetary motion (i.e., based on observation and measurement).

With a view to bionics, what is so significant about this story? Let's embark on a play of thought, and ask ourselves what the moon and the apple have in common, the movement of which we are, after all, concerned with here. Apart from the fact that we could refer to them both as round

⌜**155** *Sir Isaac Newton (1642–1726)*

objects (in an idealized way), we probably couldn't think of anything else. In particular, we cannot detect any commonality between the trajectory of an apple that falls straight to the ground and the elliptic orbit of the moon around the earth. So how do these two objects and their movements fit together?

Let's have a closer look at the three axioms (principles) formulated by Newton. The first axiom, the principle of inertia, says that a mass does not change its motion without the influence of a force (i.e., it remains at rest or continues to move at a constant velocity). The second axiom, the so-called law of force, states that the force is equal to the mass of the object multiplied by its acceleration ($F = m \cdot a$); it thus establishes a relationship between the force F of an object with the mass m and the resulting acceleration a. The third axiom states that every force exerts an opposing force (i.e., two bodies always influence each other mutually through the force of gravitation). You may now ask again what these principles have to do with an apple and the moon. To answer this question, we will try to draw conclusions from these principles for both objects. Neither the falling apple nor the moon move uniformly. From the first axiom we can conclude that force is acting on both of them (i.e., the force of attraction emanating from the earth), which decreases proportionally to the square of the distance to the center of the earth ⌜**156**. In both cases this force causes acceleration in accordance with the second axiom. The apple falls to the ground with increasing speed; the moon continuously changes the direction of its movement at any given point in time. The third axiom states that both the apple and the moon exert an opposing force on the earth and that we therefore have to consider the systems apple–earth and/or moon–earth together. It is, of course, pretty obvious that we can disregard the force exerted by the apple on the earth compared with the gravitational force exerted by the earth on the apple. The gravitational force of the moon is about one-sixth that of the earth; in other words, it is significantly smaller.

After contemplation of the above, the commonalities between the apple and the moon become clear: they are governed by the same physical principles and natural laws ⌜**157**. Both trajectories are just practical examples that can be described with the same mathematical formulae, albeit with different parameters and initial conditions. If we threw an apple horizontally with enough speed, it would in fact—like the moon—orbit the earth. Similarly, if the moon were to start its movement from a position of rest, it would—like the apple—fall to earth. Newton's axioms provide us with an abstracting description using physical laws and mathematical formulae that allow us to establish a connection between both objects and phenomena.

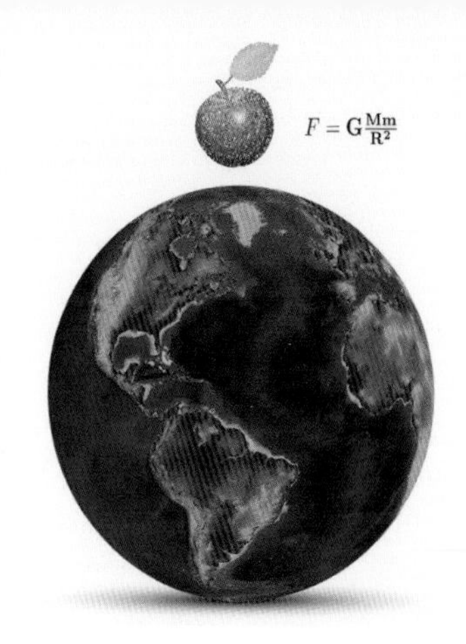

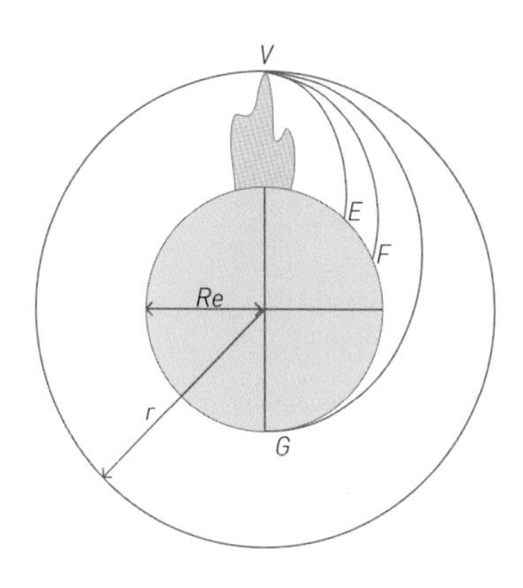

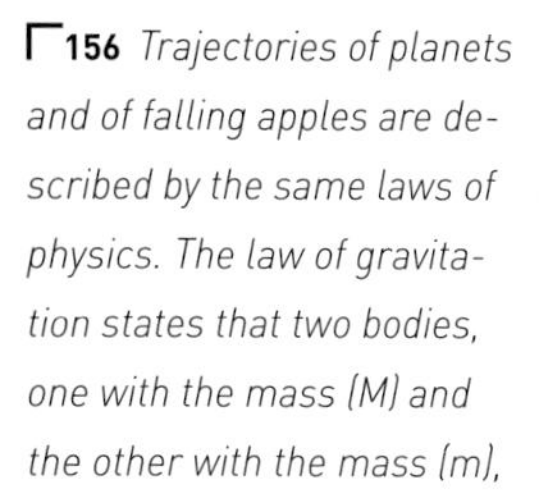

156 *Trajectories of planets and of falling apples are described by the same laws of physics. The law of gravitation states that two bodies, one with the mass (M) and the other with the mass (m), exert a force (F) on each other that is proportional to the product of their two masses and inversely proportional to the square of their distance (R). Here, (G) refers to the gravitation constant.*

157 *Trajectories E, F, and G with different initial horizontal speeds*

Abstraction and analogy

With his conclusion relating the apple to the moon, Isaac Newton had a stroke of genius. He developed a theory that provides a general, overriding explanation for seemingly completely different phenomena. Rather than collecting empirical values from a thousand tests with a thousand apples, which are dropped from a thousand different heights, to enable him to predict, by way of approximation, the outcome of test number 1,001, he has created a uniform mathematical formalism that correctly describes the movement not only of falling apples but also of thrown stones and shot arrows, not to mention the movement of celestial bodies. Not only did he describe these processes, he also understood them.

This is all the more remarkable because the force exerted by the falling apple on the earth—not only does the apple move towards the earth, but the earth also moves towards the apple—is so small that it practically cannot be measured due to the gigantic difference in mass. However, in the motion of the earth–moon system, this mutuality cannot be disregarded. The fact of having discovered this and quantified it is the actual step of abstraction that makes Newton's achievement so outstanding. Simpler laws of falling bodies that ignore this mutual effect had already been established by Galileo Galilei half a century earlier.

Science is full of such abstracting models. And it is true that a suitable abstraction is necessary in order to be able to detect general principles and find important generalizations (i.e., to be able to come to general conclusions based on the observation of completely different objects). An important tool in the development or discovery of new laws, principles, and models is analogy. In analogy, directly observable or purely formal similarities between different phenomena are used to draw conclusions from what is already known and can be explained about what is not known and cannot yet be explained. A classic example is the 19th-century idea of a model of light as a wave, which today has been replaced by the theory of relativity and quantum field theory. It gave substance to the analogy between the mechanical waves in acoustics and the electromagnetic waves in optics, and not only provided an explanation of phenomena that could be observed experimentally but also made it possible to predict phenomena that could not yet be observed experimentally.

Substantive and formal analogies

The analogy between acoustic and optical waves described above is referred to as a substantive (also material or physical) analogy, because there is a direct similarity at the level of the phenomena observed. However, we often come across abstract, formal analogies.

Nowadays, models in the natural sciences are usually described via mathematical formulae. We speak about a formal analogy when two different natural science phenomena can be expressed with the same equations. For example, certain models in financial mathematics describe the development of the price of a purchase option for a portfolio consisting of several shares using the exact same mathematical equation that is used in natural science to calculate chemical reactions in a fluid in flow. Another popular example is the analogy between the equations of electrodynamics and mechanical vibrations. For each physical variable in the one world we find the mathematical equivalent in the other: the electrical capacity corresponds to mass, resistance corresponds to damping characteristics, inductivity to spring constant, the difference in electrical potential to displacement, strength of current to force, and so on. The same system of equations also describes the phenomena of hydrodynamics and thermodynamics, in each case with different interpretations of the mathematical parameters involved. The formal analogy that the authors of this chapter want to utilize in a shared research project establishes a relationship between the processing of signals in molecular networks and the vibration behavior of load-bearing structures, for the modeling of which the same mathematical equations can be used.

In his 1892 essay "On the Methods of Theoretical Physics," the physicist and philosopher Ludwig Boltzmann expressed this idea exceedingly clearly: "The most surprising and most far-reaching analogies were discovered between seemingly completely disparate natural processes. It seemed that nature had built the most diverse things to the same blueprint or, as the analysts wryly say, the same differential equations apply to very diverse phenomena. For example, thermal conductivity and the diffusion and distribution of electricity in conductors follow the same laws. The same equations can be applied for the solution of a problem in hydrodynamics and in potential theory. The theory of fluid vortices and of gas friction shows the most surprising analogy with that of electromagnetism, etc."

An example from biology

Another well-known and fascinating example at the interface of biology, mathematics, and physics is the Hodgkin–Huxley model for the description of nerve signals in the stimulation of nerve cells.

Signals are propagated in the form of nerve impulses via long nerve cell projections, the axons. A mathematical model

that describes this process was named after the two physiologists Alan Hodgkin and Andrew Fielding Huxley. They received the Nobel Prize for Medicine in 1963 for their groundbreaking work on the occurrence of action potentials in the giant axon of the Atlantic squid.
What is remarkable here is that this model contains the principles/laws of an electric circuit, as they are known in electrical engineering, even though with respect to the exterior appearance there are practically no commonalities between a nerve cell and an electric circuit with resistors and condensers.
Like Newton's laws of force, the Hodgkin–Huxley model made it possible, for the first time, to describe with the same model many experimentally observed phenomena that are nevertheless very different in each individual case.

Bionics with differential equations

The distinction between formal and substantive analogies takes us back to bionics. When it is possible to describe the behavior of a natural system and of a technical system using the same mathematical equations, it follows that certain characteristics, such as efficiency, capability, functionality, and robustness, must be transferable. To remain with the example of electrodynamics: from known devices for attenuating electromagnetic vibrations, it is possible to directly derive suitable measures for the attenuation of mechanical vibrations with the help of this formal analogy. Likewise, it should be possible to transfer efficient strategies from one world to the other through formal analogies between natural and technical systems. The fact that the analogy used is based on purely formal similarities represents the special challenge. The external appearance of the biological example and of the technical implementation can, however, be completely different.
The far-reaching work of Newton as well as that of Hodgkin and Huxley utilizes the principle of abstraction for the discovery of higher-level laws, principles, and models. Using abstract mathematical formulae and models, it is possible to discover commonalities between an apple and a planet, between the price of shares and chemical reactions, or between nerve impulses in living organisms and electric circuits, that are not visible in the external appearance. Perhaps this approach can provide new stimuli to the fascinating field of bionics research.

Functionalist, organic, and biomimetic architecture

Gerd de Bruyn / Oliver Betz / Manfred Drack / Mirco Limpinsel / James H. Nebelsick

This contribution represents an attempt at defining and determining the position of architecture that, since the beginning of the Modern Movement, broke with its conventions and wanted to prove that it was up to date and was open to contemporary developments in science and technology. In view of the fact that architecture is also an art that gives us more than just comfort and security, it suits the contradictory nature of human beings, who feel most comfortable between tradition and progress.

The functionalization of architecture

Ever since their entry into the modern era, architects have had to withstand the enormous pressure to deny their creative authority. Their artistic authority was questioned to such an extent that they themselves no longer wanted to uphold it. At the same time, the belief in "strong authors" waned. People no longer associate large, complicated buildings—the completion of which involves many experts—with a single person. Almost everybody knows that, when it comes to complex tasks, even the most ingenious architect is replaced by large teams whose bosses ensure that the "signature" of the designing practice remains recognizable. The style expressed in that signature is a vestige of the anachronistic character of architecture as art. Relativizing the artistic claim and the author of the design in architecture led to a widening of its remit and an increase in its functional value. At the same time, there was increased interest in its technical and scientific input. This enormous shift in values was ushered in by the debates on functionalism that took place in the wake of the French Revolution and the Industrial Revolution. The demand was for buildings that prioritize functionality (*utilitas*) and are no longer in step with construction (*firmitas*) and esthetics (*venustas*)—three values that were traditionally considered to be of equal rank. The dominance of purpose heralded the end of the idea that—in architecture—art, science, and technology form a unit. From then on, architects had to decide whether they wanted to continue practicing art or lean towards science **⌜158**.

⌜158 *Architecture as a combination of science, art, and technology: Francesco Borromini, spiral staircase in the south wing of Palazzo Barberini, Rome (1627–38)*

The birth of the original genius

In the 19th century, architecture and engineering started to take opposing positions. The engineers employed a more modern style than the architects, who called themselves modern, and the avant-gardes were mostly interested in re-establishing the lost unity of architecture. The two dominating personalities in Europe and the USA—Le Corbusier (1887–1965) and Frank Lloyd Wright (1867–1959)—continued to consider their métier to be art, and themselves to be outstanding proponents of the art of building ⌜159.

The mystification of their authorship seemed an appropriate means of resisting the denial of creative authority. The heroization of the architect made a Goliath out of a David. This was based on two ideas: (1) the wishful thought that esthetics and function could coincide (in accordance with the motto "what is functional is automatically beautiful"), and (2) the hope that the fate of architecture could be made dependent on a few geniuses.

In order to be able to explain what happened outside the limelight of their impressive achievements, we will discuss two movements that, to this day, represent an underestimated line of development in modern architecture. We are talking here about functionalist and organic architecture. However, the idea here is not to establish a historic pedigree for "biomimetic architecture," which is currently appearing on the horizon, but to understand how these movements differ and what they make of architecture. The latter point is important, because we always have to think of the consequences that are triggered when architecture is associated with terms such as expressionistic, rationalistic, functionalist, or biomimetic.

159 *Architecture as synthèse des arts: Le Corbusier, Villa Savoye, Poissy near Paris (1928–31)*

The schism in architecture

Not every move towards greater specificity automatically brings a benefit, especially because greater specificity of architecture always meant a reduction rather than an emphasis of its inherent characteristics. The reason for this is that its most important and most longstanding claim is to be a discipline that synthesizes other disciplines within it. Just as the horizon of the meaning of old terms narrows over time—as an example, let's take the term *τέχνη*, which in ancient Greek meant art, craft, and science and was not, until the Modern period, reduced to what we understand by technology—architecture loses richness when we define it more specifically. Somebody like Le Corbusier noticed immediately that the modern differentiation and autonomization of the arts goes against the definition of the art of building as a *synthèse des arts*. When the disciplines that worked together in architecture took their leave, architecture remained empty. The architects responded either by turning vice to virtue and making functionality the overruling objective or by doing the opposite, that is, attempting to replace the departed arts (painting, sculpture, music, and so on) with their own resources.

The avant-gardists opted for both. In architecture, the focus on certain purposes was rarely concrete enough to be able to derive from it the appearance and esthetics of a building. Although the points Le Corbusier made in his famous *Five Points of a Modern Architecture* (1923), probably the most prominent definition of modern architecture (free plan, free facade, ribbon windows, pilotis, and the flat roof that can be used as a garden), were meant to increase the functional value of architecture, they were also intended as esthetic principles and, as such, were much more effective. Cube-shaped buildings, horizontal windows, and flat roofs symbolized a functionality that tended far more towards art than towards function. Even though they are devoid of decoration, the buildings of Gropius, Mies van der Rohe, Rietveld, Melnikow, and others demonstrate more esthetic confidence than the extensively decorated Art Nouveau villas. Like abstract sculptures, they rose up from the site and proudly presented their sophisticated proportions, subtle coloring, and sometimes also noble building materials.

Nature as example

Given that the increased functional value of these fascinating architectural works of art was not trusted by contemporaries, a dispute about the true function of architecture flared up in the 1920s. Was traditional architecture perhaps, after all, more useful than the functionalist? Conservative architects maintained this view and were not even wrong in that. Even within the Modern movement, controversies arose. The most important one was provoked by the proponents of organic architecture. They were serious about finding out how buildings function better, and to what extent this changes their appearance and layout. In their search for examples that offer a perfect synthesis of form and function they chanced on nature or, more precisely, on the fascinating phenomenon of living organisms.

Of course, this was not really new. The belief that art is modeled on living nature because of its beauty and vitality had already gained ground in the 18th century. The arts were to absorb as much of that as possible in order to avoid the risk of being stifled by rules and conventions.

In the 19th century, with the emergence of modern biology, another aspect appeared that some universal geniuses like Leonardo da Vinci (1452–1519) had already contemplated 400 years earlier. Leonardo noted that not only does nature express itself in beautiful forms, but living organisms are (nearly) perfectly organized. After he exposed the arteries of human corpses with a scalpel, he proposed that the water and supply routes of Italian cities be newly organized, taking the blood vessels as an example. The whole thing was intended as a contribution to modern urban hygiene and to combating the plague. It thus follows that Leonardo is the originator of organic urban design.

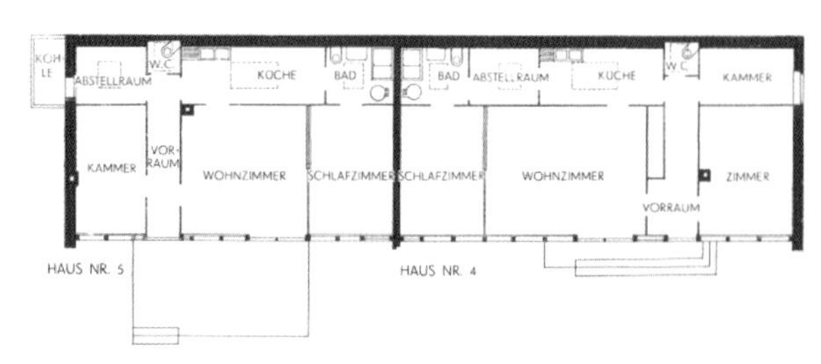

160 *Organic residential plan layout: Hugo Häring, houses for the Werkbund estate, Vienna-Lainz (1930–1932)*

Organic building

Given that form and function appear to be inseparable in nature, the proponents of organic design wanted to adapt this principle to an architecture that was no longer just to appear—but was actually to be—functional. The declared starting point was a layout plan that reflected actual needs, organizing spaces in the way people move therein. Owing to the demand for "light, air, and sun," it was no longer allowed to design facades that contradicted the layout plan for esthetic reasons, for example in order to achieve symmetry. The external appearance was to mirror the internal arrangement (Hugo Häring) and was to develop from this as "organically" as the entire house should from the surrounding landscape (Frank Lloyd Wright) **160, 161**. Shapes of buildings that result from a "better"-functioning plan layout do not necessarily deviate from right angles and straight lines. Organic architecture that wants to be functionally superior to functionalistic buildings does not necessarily look different from the latter. The fact that a house is organic in its design does not necessarily show on the outside—at least not at first sight. The appearance of the building can change significantly when the straightforward right angles and straight lines of the layout are replaced by curves. Taking into account, however, that there are hardly any better reasons for curved walls than for straight ones, we have to admit that the flowing forms of organic buildings purely symbolize purposes rather than fulfilling them; this is also true of the rectangular designs that are generally referred to as Bauhaus architecture. One might even suggest that the "organic" architects had triggered an even more independent formal vocabulary precisely because they wanted to produce buildings that were functionally superior to those of their competitors. When you think of Frank Gehry and Santiago Calatrava, the accusation of pursuing Formalism with esthetically overdone organic designs applies in the same way as it does to the Art Nouveau style or Deconstructivism **162**. However, that is not really a bad thing. Formalism means that architecture maintains a com-

mitment to art, even when it is described as "functionalist" or "organic" in order to declare it as the opposite. Do we have to conclude, then, that esthetically successful biomimetic architecture will not take its cues from nature and technology any more than organic architecture does?

161 *Unity of house and landscape: Frank Lloyd Wright, Fallingwater (1937)*

Outlook on biomimetic architecture

We would like to go even further and state that the term "biomimetic architecture" cannot be justified until the scientific input derived from biology has become secondary and its esthetic transformation into architecture has become the primary feature. We believe that productive misunderstandings and "far-fetched" reinterpretations of scientific findings and methods are constitutive for their transfer into architecture and art. But we are talking about the future! For now, we can only detect efforts to utilize biomimetic products in technical details (Flectofin, p. 11) or to mold expressive shapes (research pavilions) resulting from the technical transfer of fascinating natural structures ⌐163. In view of the fact that these pavilions can be entered and remind us of Ludwig Wittgenstein's famous dictum "Architecture is a gesture," it would not be out of place to call them biomimetic pioneering buildings or refer to an anticipation of biomimetic architecture.

At this stage, two things are desirable: firstly, that imaginative visualizations are created as part of biomimetic research that become popular amongst architects and lead to more inspiring designs; and secondly, that those few architects who participate in biomimetic research remove themselves a little bit from its enchantment and consider that, in architecture, many things we can learn from nature will have to remain metaphoric. Architecture is science and art. The authorship of biomimetics-inspired buildings cannot permanently be delegated to objectifiable processes. We will not be able to talk about biomimetic architecture with the same confidence as we talk about organic or functionalist architecture unless the subjective authorship of the design is once again vested in the designing architect.

There is one further point: architecture informed by biomimetics will not be genuinely legitimate unless buildings become more ecological and the progress unleashed by science and technology becomes obvious—also in the eyes of the layperson. It goes without saying that architecture understood in this way must achieve high esthetic standards. We do not emphasize this in order to claim that art is a mandatory part of architecture. Instead, this has to do with the fact that architecture never only gains when it goes through a process of examination by science and technology; it also makes sacrifices. As a result, we humans also win and lose. In the best case, we will have the benefit of healthy and well-functioning spaces that strengthen us physically and psychologically. In the worst case, we lose some of our identity. People are contradictory in nature; they project themselves into the future but also cling to the past. Architecture takes this into account if it finds an expression for our rational as well as our irrational needs.

162 *Organic formalism: Frank O. Gehry, Guggenheim Museum, Bilbao (1993–97)*

163 *Biomimetic architecture: ICD/ITKE Research Pavilion, Stuttgart University (2014–15)*

The biomimetic promise

Olga Speck / Johannes Gantner / Klaus Sedlbauer / Rafael Horn

Technical progress in recent centuries has brought enormous prosperity to a part of humankind. Our modern lifestyle is largely based on material wealth. In order to satisfy the corresponding consumption needs, huge quantities of raw materials have to be extracted from the environment. Furthermore, after a short while, consumer goods often turn into waste that pollutes the environment. The search for sustainable solutions with the aim of preserving our environment without having to forgo prosperity is therefore one of the biggest social challenges of the 21st century. By taking a look at nature, we hope for help in this search. Biomimetic products seem to have special qualities, such as resource conservation, environmental compatibility, and sustainability. But is that really true?

What is "biomimetic"?

In the modern era, biomimetics or "learning from living nature for technical solutions" began with Leonardo da Vinci (1452–1519). In his time, he combined the knowledge of various disciplines and, in that way, met all the prerequisites for a successful specialist of biomimetics. Nowadays, a range of scientists from various disciplines, including biology, chemistry, physics, mathematics, the engineering sciences, the material sciences, architecture, and design, cooperate in the development of biomimetic products.

In recent years, two approaches have proved to be successful in biomimetics: starting from a biological issue (bottom-up process = biology push) or from a technical challenge (top-down process = technology pull), biological solutions that have been optimized through evolution are transferred to technical applications ⌈1, 2, p. 11.

⌈164 *The flowers of the bird-of-paradise plant* (Strelitzia reginae) *provided the example for joint-free facade shading devices of the Flectofin type.*

A well-known example of the bottom-up process in biomimetics is the self-cleaning facade paint Lotusan. As with the leaves of the Indian lotus flower (*Nelumbo nucifera*) ⌜**165**, droplets of water simply run off this paint, taking the dirt with them. The biomimetic Flectofin facade shading device is the result of a top-down process. In search of a joint-free shading device for buildings, biologists and engineers were inspired by the deformation principles found in the flower of the bird-of-paradise plant (*Strelitzia reginae*) ⌜**164**.

Interestingly, you cannot tell by looking at a product whether it is biomimetic or not. To come to that conclusion, it is necessary to know the product's developmental history. Only then can we find out whether all three criteria for a biomimetic product are met: (1) a biological role model exists; (2) the product is detached from the natural model (abstraction), and (3) a technical product exists ⌜**168**. The critical step between biological role model and technical product is that of abstraction. This can be a computer simulation, a mathematical formula, or a construction plan—ultimately involving a shared language that can be understood by natural scientists and engineers alike.

What is "sustainable"?

The origin of the term "sustainability" goes back more than 300 years. Hannß Carl von Carlowitz first used the term in 1713 in his work on forestry entitled *Sylvicultura oeconomica oder haußwirthliche Nachricht und Naturmäßige Anweisung zur wilden Baum-Zucht*. Since then, the term "sustainability" or "sustainable development" has been used again and again. However, it did not attract worldwide attention until the ever faster-growing economic system spread across the entire globe. The first consequences of this huge growth became evident in the middle of the 20th century.

⌜**165** *The self-cleaning leaves of the Indian lotus flower (*Nelumbo nucifera*) provided the example for facade paint with the brand name Lotusan.*

The report *The Limits to Growth* published in 1972 by the Club of Rome looks at the consequences of human interference with nature. The Brundtland Report of 1987 includes the only internationally recognized definition of sustainable development: "Sustainable development is development that meets the needs of the present without compromising the ability of future generations to meet their own needs." At the so-called Earth Summit in Rio de Janeiro, Brazil, in 1992, sustainable development was selected as the guiding principle of international environmental and development policy. Since then, large conferences have been taking place on a regular basis, and more and more companies publicly commit themselves to the guiding principle of sustainability. The key challenge is to derive a societal model from this political concept. This change is already taking place. With the so-called Sustainable Development Goals (SDGs), the United Nations adopted a catalog of objectives in 2016. It comprises seventeen development goals that are intended to protect our future. They apply to poorer countries, but also to industrial nations such as Germany. Because these goals are not a legally binding contract, the earth's nations have been asked to decide on additional national or international objectives. Managing climate change is one of the development goals, and its effects are already an acute problem for many today. For this reason, at the 2015 UN Climate

Nested model

Intersected model

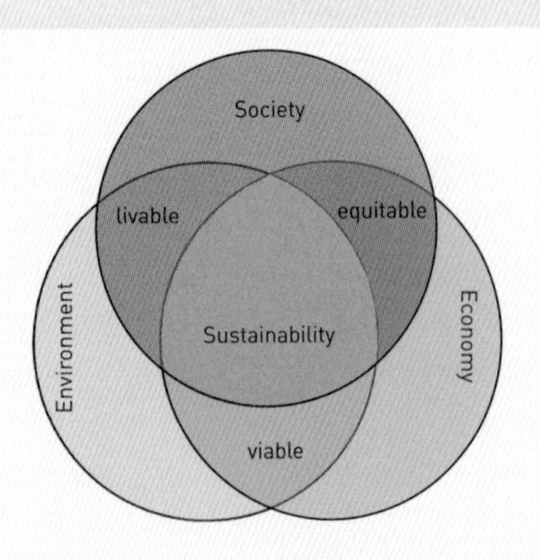

The three dimensions depend on each other and are not of equal importance. Economy is embedded in society, and this in turn in the environment. The nested model was developed by the environmental movement and makes considerable demands regarding limiting the economy and society. In the variant shown here, sustainability is shown as a linking element that extends through all dimensions.

The three dimensions are independent, each representing an area of one-dimensional sustainability. These are defined as minimum requirements (bottom line). For this reason, the model is also called "triple bottom line". Sustainable development is only possible where all three intersect. It is mostly assumed that the dimensions can influence each other and therefore can be shifted against each other.

Change Conference in Paris, worldwide goals were agreed that are binding under international law.
These big decisions are important but can only function when every individual does his or her bit to preserve our world. It is up to each individual to apply this guiding principle to his or her own concrete actions. We can all contribute to sustainable development every day by preserving resources, avoiding waste, and acting in a frugal way. To make this possible, the goals of sustainable development must be transferred from the global level to the level of everyday actions. A number of models are in existence that attempt to make this connection. In doing so, they invariably represent a certain view and interpretation of sustainability. Most models are based on a subdivision of sustainability into the dimensions of environment, society, and economy. The biggest differences lie in the way these dimensions depend on and influence each other. It is the peculiar nature of models that they only represent an image of reality. The different perspectives of the models therefore also make it possible to investigate the different interpretation options of sustainability ┌166.

┌166 *Different models emphasize the guiding principle of sustainability from different viewpoints.*

Three-pillar model

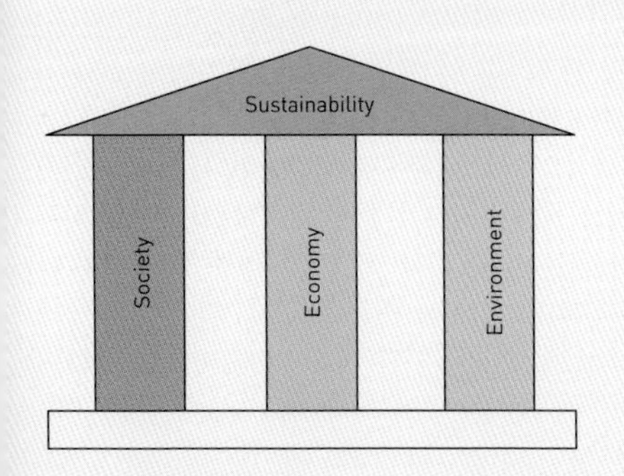

All three areas stand on their own. They are of equal importance and significance. All three pillars should contribute equally to sustainability and cannot be offset against each other.
The model represents the stability of sustainability and is particularly popular in German-speaking countries.

Bio-inspired model

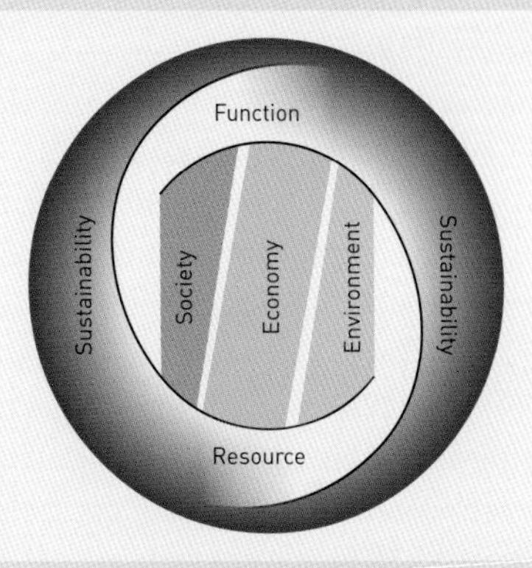

This model is inspired by the basic functionality of biological systems. It describes a system that fulfills a certain desired function with the help of resources. This system is sustainable when it can maintain itself and fulfills the function without irreversible damage to the resources. It follows that sustainability is here a time component of self-preservation. The dimensions are connecting the input (resource demand) and the output (function) of the system in question.

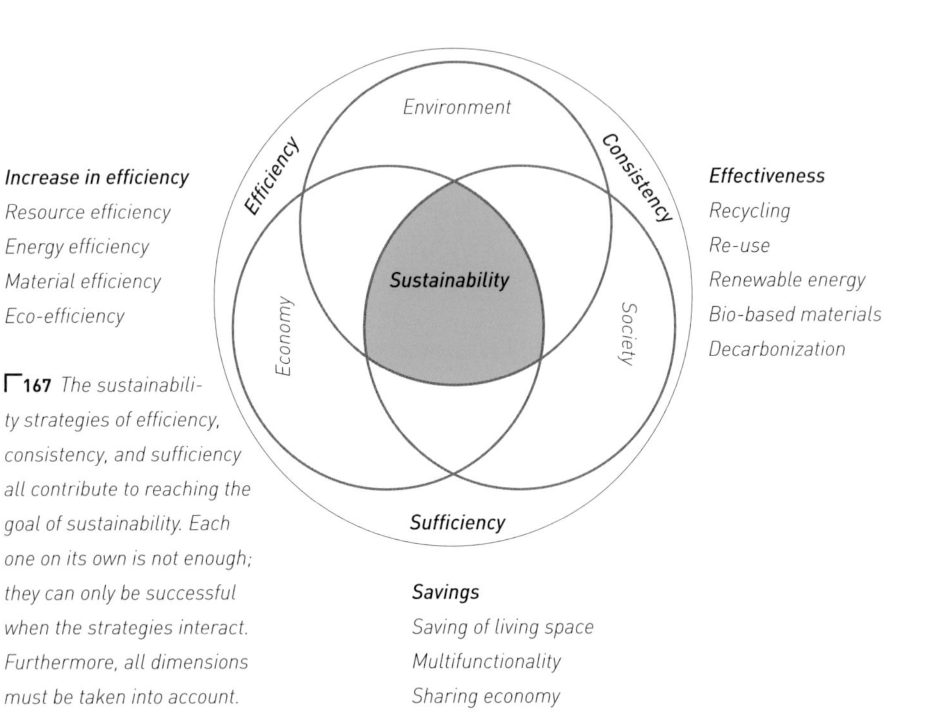

⌜167 *The sustainability strategies of efficiency, consistency, and sufficiency all contribute to reaching the goal of sustainability. Each one on its own is not enough; they can only be successful when the strategies interact. Furthermore, all dimensions must be taken into account.*

How can we contribute to sustainability?

By now, the effects of the non-sustainable industrial society are so dramatic that they threaten key functions of the global ecosystem. If we want to preserve the earth as we know it, we all have to make sure that our lifestyle is sustainable. So, what can we do? The development of our world towards a society that is fit for the future concerns all levels—from global political decisions through to the way we live our daily lives. We can take an active part in this development by participating in the social, environmental, and economic change processes. When discussing a sustainable lifestyle, three sustainability strategies are often mentioned: (1) efficiency (= better), (2) consistency (= differently), and (3) sufficiency (= less) **⌜167**. We can contribute to efficiency by making better use of resources (raw materials, energy, water, and so on). For example, in agricultural cultivation it is possible to conserve up to 80 percent of the water used by switching to droplet irrigation instead of sprinkler irrigation or open trenches. Of course, it is also possible that such savings of water will lead to an increase in the consumption of consumables. This is referred to as the rebound effect. An example of the rebound effect is when a motorist changes to a car with lower fuel consumption but then drives more or spends the money saved on a trip by air. In order to prevent this additional consumption, the two other strategies are needed, consistency and sufficiency. By means of consistency, i.e., a change from environmentally harmful to nature-compatible technologies, we can contribute to more sustainable development. Examples of consistency are solar thermal systems that cover the demand for heat by using solar energy rather than burning fossil fuels. In view of the fact that neither efficiency nor consistency are challenging to our commercial growth or our consumer model, both commerce and society as a whole, as well as each individual, accept these strategies more readily and even seek to put them into practice. However, it is a different matter when it comes to the strategy of sufficiency, which aims for a reduction in consumption and therefore demands a rethink of our behavior. But the point of the strategy is not only to forgo certain things because "sometimes less is more"; the voluntary speed limit on the highway leads to conservation of gas and to improvement in the quality of life due to more relaxed driving and improved safety.

All three strategies can contribute to sustainable development, but they are not a "free ticket." Furthermore, they unfold their greatest effect when they are applied together. We need to take into account, however, that the strategies mostly compete with each other. This means we have to find a balance between the environment, the economy, and society. For example, intensive agriculture can lead to improved commercial viability but is carried out at the expense of the environment. This complexity means that frequently there are no optimal solutions for sustainability and that the assessment of sustainability is a complicated matter. Aside from the scientific assessment, every individual can apply the strategies in everyday decisions as well as, primarily, in big decisions. People who question their actions and take into account the criteria of sustainability are taking a big step towards sustainability.

How do we measure sustainability?

Sustainable development can only take place when the criteria of sustainability play an important role in our decisions. The details of these criteria and how they are to be assessed are still a subject for scientific and social discussion. Owing to the change in the meaning of the term over its long development, and also its ubiquitous application, the term "sustainability" has come to be something of an empty shell in the public perception. On the other hand, attempts are being made to clarify and simplify the term and ultimately make it measurable. This search for meaning plays out in the realm of political boundary conditions as well as purchase decisions or choosing where to go for the annual holiday. In order to be able to compare different alternatives with a view to their sustainability, it is necessary to make the options measurable. To do that, the entire life cycle of products must be analyzed. The effects of production, use, and end-of-life disposal are investigated with respect to the dimensions of sustainability. This provides a comprehensive insight into the sustainability of a product and allows direct comparison of different products.

In all analyses of sustainability, it is essential to ensure that the items under consideration are actually comparable. Was the product selected for comparison appropriate? Is there a comparable product for a brand-new innovation available on the market? Are old products compared to current solutions? These and other questions must be carefully considered before the analysis; they must be documented in the context of the result and taken into account in the interpretation of the results. The environmental aspects can be assessed using what is known as life cycle assessment. This method is now widely accepted and standardized, which means its results can be compared reliably. Using life cycle assessment, it is possible, for example, to assess the effect of a product on climate change or to assess its impact on land use. For the economic assessment we have to consider not only negative aspects (e.g., costs) but also advantages (e.g., competitive advantage). There are a number of different approaches to assessing this dimension of sustainability. However, none of these approaches has

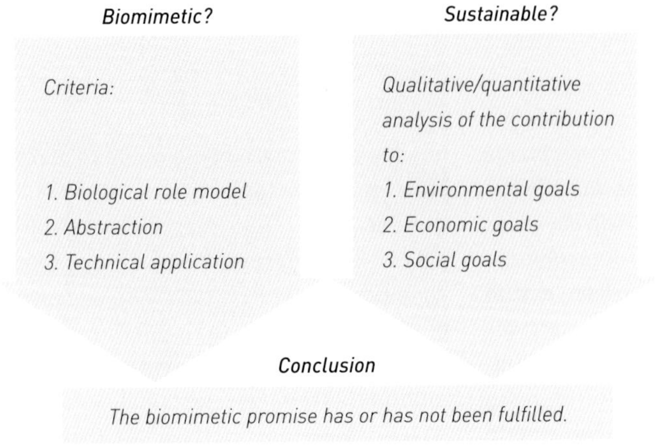

Biomimetic?

Criteria:

1. Biological role model
2. Abstraction
3. Technical application

Sustainable?

Qualitative/quantitative analysis of the contribution to:
1. Environmental goals
2. Economic goals
3. Social goals

Conclusion

The biomimetic promise has or has not been fulfilled.

168 *Schematic illustration of the procedure for defining and measuring the biomimetic promise*

yet been generally established; as a result, it is often difficult to compare products with respect to their economic sustainability. When we only consider costs, we can calculate the life cycle costs. The calculation follows a similar pattern to that of the environmental assessment, which means the two methods can both be applied consistently.

The third dimension of sustainability is the most difficult to assess. Social assessment cannot be determined via physical parameters or costs. What is socially acceptable to us depends to a large extent on our cultural background and the social environment. This means that there is no simple equation with which we can calculate social sustainability. Of the assessment approaches that have been put forward to date, none has as yet been established as standard. To respond to this challenge and find a solution is a task for future research.

Biomimetics and sustainability

Is nature sustainable?

In nature, all living beings are the result of 3.8 billion years of biological evolution. Variations in the offsprings of a particular species come about through accidental change and through combining the parental genetic information. Owing to limited resources (e.g., food), they compete with each other. The best-adapted individuals have the greatest chance of survival and the greatest success in reproduction.
Sustainability, however, is a guiding principle that has been defined and redefined by humankind over the last 300 years. It is a term that relates to the vision of human intergenerational equity in all fields, taking into account the limited availability of resources, and it provides guidance as to how this desired state can be achieved. In summary, we can say that, in contrast to sustainability, nature is not following an anthropocentric perspective and does not know teleological thinking and acting, but is characterized by biological evolution. By definition, then, nature is not sustainable and therefore cannot provide simple examples of sustainability for us to copy.

⌈169 *The lightweight ceiling structure covering the former zoology auditorium at the University of Freiburg, which was inspired by the inner structure of bones.*

Does this mean that learning from nature for sustainable development and strategies is fully precluded? No, because nature can provide inspiration for the development of solutions that enable us to achieve the environmental, economic, and social goals of sustainability. Even though nature itself is not sustainable, learning from nature for sustainable development is important, because taking natural principles (e.g., circular economy, resource conservation) into account can contribute to the development of an economy and a way of life that are compatible with nature.

Are biomimetic solutions sustainable?

If nature per se is not sustainable as defined by the guiding principle, it follows that the development and implementation of a biomimetic innovation does not automatically guarantee that it is sustainable either. However, biomimetic products are credited with the considerable potential of being able to contribute to more sustainable technological development because the idea came to technology from nature. Biomimetic solutions supply objective data, such as the identification of a biological role model and the description of the functional principle to be transferred, but also that they evoke positive emotions due to our fascination with living nature. Furthermore, biomimetic products give the impression that they have been tried and tested in evolution and therefore promise technical solutions that are more environmentally compatible. To fulfill this biomimetic promise, the product must comply with two prerequisites: firstly, it must be biomimetic, and secondly, it must fulfill relevant sustainability criteria. These two prerequisites are examined one after the other. The assessment of the contribution to sustainability can be accomplished using different sustainability assessment methods ⌈**168**. Comparative sustainability assessment of biomimetic and conventional products has already been carried out in individual case studies using this method. An example is the comparison of the lightweight building construction of a concrete ceiling based on the example of a bone ⌈**1** with two conventional solutions. In the sustainability assessment, the biomimetic ribbed slab ⌈**169** demonstrated good results in terms of life-cycle assessment and potential social aspects when compared with equivalent constructions using current technology. On the other hand, the biomimetic solution is currently 2.2 times more costly than a hollow core slab or a prestressed concrete slab. Not least for this reason, the construction covering the lecture hall at the University of Freiburg will remain unique, with a special architectural esthetic.
In another study, the biomimetic facade paint Lotusan was compared with a conventional paint. The sustainability assessment revealed that the self-cleaning paint Lotusan is cost-effective and resource-conserving, and overall preferable to conventional paint.

Appendix

Editors

Prof. Dr.-Ing. Jan Knippers, University of Stuttgart

Ulrich Schmid, State Museum of Natural History Stuttgart (SMNS)

Prof. Dr. rer. nat. Thomas Speck, University of Freiburg

Authors

Dr. rer. nat. Christoph Allgaier, University of Tübingen, Department of Geosciences, Invertebrate Paleontology and Paleoclimatology

Pouyan Asgharzadeh, University of Stuttgart, Institute of Applied Mechanics

Prof. Dr. rer. nat. Oliver Betz, University of Tübingen, Department of Biology, Evolutionary Biology of Invertebrates

Dr.-Ing. Annette Birkhold, University of Stuttgart, Institute of Applied Mechanics

Prof. Dr.-Ing. habil. Manfred Bischoff, University of Stuttgart, Institute for Structural Mechanics

Dr. rer. nat. Georg Bold, née Bauer, University of Freiburg, Plant Biomechanics Group Freiburg and Botanic Garden, Freiburg Center for Interactive Materials and Bioinspired Technologies (FIT)

Larissa Born, University of Stuttgart, Institute for Textile and Fiber Technologies (ITFT)

Gerald Buck, University of Tübingen, Department of Geosciences, Applied Mineralogy

Katharina Bunk, University of Freiburg, Plant Biomechanics Group Freiburg and Botanic Garden, Freiburg Center for Interactive Materials and Bioinspired Technologies (FIT)

Dr. rer. nat. Marco Caliaro, University of Freiburg, Plant Biomechanics Group Freiburg and Botanic Garden, Freiburg Center for Interactive Materials and Bioinspired Technologies (FIT)

Hans Christoph, University of Stuttgart, Institute for Textile and Fiber Technologies (ITFT)

Prof. Dr. phil. Gerd de Bruyn, University of Stuttgart, Institute for Principles of Modern Architecture (Design and Theory)

Dr. rer. nat. Manfred Drack, University of Tübingen, Department of Biology, Evolutionary Biology of Invertebrates

Benjamin Eggs, University of Tübingen, Department of Biology, Evolutionary Biology of Invertebrates

Prof. Dr.-Ing. Wolfgang Ehlers, University of Stuttgart, Institute of Applied Mechanics

Lukas Eurich, University of Stuttgart, Institute of Applied Mechanics

Benjamin Felbrich, University of Stuttgart, Institute for Computational Design and Construction (ICD)

Dr.-Ing. Johannes Gantner, Fraunhofer Institute for Building Physics

Florian Geiger, University of Stuttgart, Institute for Structural Mechanics

Oliver Gericke, University of Stuttgart, Institute of Lightweight Structures and Conceptual Design (ILEK)

Prof. Dr.-Ing. Götz T. Gresser, University of Stuttgart, Institute for Textile and Fiber Technologies (ITFT)

Dr. rer. nat. Tobias B. Grun, University of Tübingen, Department of Geosciences, Invertebrate Paleontology and Paleoclimatology

Dr.-Ing. Walter Haase, University of Stuttgart, Institute of Lightweight Structures and Conceptual Design (ILEK)

Fabian Henn, University of Tübingen, Department of Biology, Evolutionary Biology of Invertebrates

Dr. rer. nat. Linnea Hesse, University of Freiburg, Plant Biomechanics Group Freiburg and Botanic Garden, Freiburg Center for Interactive Materials and Bioinspired Technologies (FIT)

Rafael Horn, Fraunhofer Institute for Building Physics

Florian A. Jonas, University of Stuttgart, Institute of Building Structures and Structural Design (ITKE)

Emna Khechine, University of Freiburg, Institute of Physics, Freiburg Center for Interactive Materials and Bioinspired Technologies (FIT)

Katharina Klang, University of Tübingen, Department of Geosciences, Applied Mineralogy

Prof. Dr.-Ing. Jan Knippers, University of Stuttgart, Institute of Building Structures and Structural Design (ITKE)

Axel Körner, University of Stuttgart, Institute of Building Structures and Structural Design (ITKE)

Daria Kovaleva, University of Stuttgart, Institute of Lightweight Structures and Conceptual Design (ILEK)

Daniel Lang, University of Freiburg, Chair of Plant Biotechnology, Freiburg Center for Interactive Materials and Bioinspired Technologies (FIT)

Christoph Lauer, University of Tübingen, Department of Geosciences, Applied Mineralogy

Dr.-Ing. Armin Lechler, University of Stuttgart, Institute for Control Engineering of Machine Tools and Manufacturing Units

Dr. phil. Mirco Limpinsel, University of Stuttgart, Institute for Principles of Modern Architecture (Design and Theory)

Anja Mader, University of Stuttgart, Institute of Building Structures and Structural Design (ITKE)

Yaron Malkowsky, State Museum of Natural History Stuttgart (SMNS)

Dr. rer. nat. Tom Masselter, University of Freiburg, Plant Biomechanics Group Freiburg and Botanic Garden, Freiburg Center for Interactive Materials and Bioinspired Technologies (FIT)

Prof. AA Dipl. (Hons.) Achim Menges, University of Stuttgart, Institute for Computational Design and Construction (ICD)

Prof. Dr.-Ing. Markus Milwich, German Institutes of Textile and Fiber Research (DITF)

Pascal Mindermann, University of Stuttgart, Institute for Textile and Fiber Technologies (ITFT)

Claudia Möhl, University of Stuttgart, Institute for Textile and Fiber Technologies (ITFT)

Prof. Dr. rer. nat. James H. Nebelsick, University of Tübingen, Department of Geosciences, Invertebrate Paleontology and Paleoclimatology

Long Nguyen, University of Stuttgart, Institute for Computational Design and Construction (ICD)

Prof. Klaus G. Nickel, PhD, University of Tübingen, Department of Geosciences

Dr. rer. nat. Anna K. Ostendorf, State Museum of Natural History Stuttgart (SMNS)

Bugra Özdemir, University of Freiburg, Chair of Plant Biotechnology

Debdas Paul, University of Stuttgart, Institute for Systems Theory and Automatic Control (IST)

Dr. rer. nat. Simon Poppinga, University of Freiburg, Plant Biomechanics Group Freiburg and Botanic Garden, Freiburg Materials Research Center (FMF)

Prof. Dr. rer. nat. Nicole Radde, University of Stuttgart, Institute for Systems Theory and Automatic Control (IST)

Prof. Dr. rer. nat. Günter Reiter, University of Freiburg, Institute of Physics

Dr. rer. nat. Renate Reiter, University of Freiburg, Institute of Physics, Freiburg Center for Interactive Materials and Bioinspired Technologies (FIT)

Prof. Dr. rer. nat. Ralf Reski, University of Freiburg, Chair of Plant Biotechnology, Freiburg Center for Interactive Materials and Bioinspired Technologies (FIT)

Prof. Oliver Röhrle, PhD, University of Stuttgart, Institute of Applied Mechanics

PD Dr. rer. nat. Anita Roth-Nebelsick, State Museum of Natural History Stuttgart (SMNS)

Renate Sachse, University of Stuttgart, Institute for Structural Mechanics

Samam Saffarian, University of Stuttgart, Institute of Building Structures and Structural Design (ITKE)

Immanuel Schäfer, University of Stuttgart, Institute for Materials Testing, Materials Science and Strength of Materials (IMWF)

Dr.-Ing. Malte von Scheven, University of Stuttgart, Institute for Structural Mechanics

Prof. Dr. rer. nat. Dr. h.c. Siegfried Schmauder, University of Stuttgart, Institute for Materials Testing, Materials Science and Strength of Materials (IMWF)

Dr. rer. nat. Stefanie Schmier, University of Freiburg, Plant Biomechanics Group Freiburg and Botanic Garden, Freiburg Center for Interactive Materials and Bioinspired Technologies (FIT)

Rena T. Schott, State Museum of Natural History Stuttgart (SMNS)

Tobias Schwinn, University of Stuttgart, Institute for Computational Design and Construction (ICD)

Prof. Dr.-Ing. Klaus Sedlbauer, Fraunhofer Institute for Building Physics

Prof. Dr. Dr. e.h. Dr. h.c. Werner Sobek, University of Stuttgart, Institute of Lightweight Structures and Conceptual Design (ILEK)

Daniel Sonntag, University of Stuttgart, Institute of Building Structures and Structural Design (ITKE)

Dr. rer. nat. Olga Speck, University of Freiburg, Plant Biomechanics Group Freiburg and Botanic Garden, Freiburg Center for Interactive Materials and Bioinspired Technologies (FIT)

Prof. Dr. rer. nat. Thomas Speck, University of Freiburg, Plant Biomechanics Group Freiburg, Chair for Botany: Functional Morphology & Biomimetics and Botanic Garden, Freiburg Center for Interactive Materials and Bioinspired Technologies (FIT) and Freiburg Materials Research Center (FMF)

Nicu Toader, University of Stuttgart, Institute of Lightweight Structures and Conceptual Design (ILEK)

Nico van Gessel, University of Freiburg, Chair of Plant Biotechnology, Freiburg Center for Interactive Materials and Bioinspired Technologies (FIT)

Prof. Dr.-Ing. Alexander Verl, University of Stuttgart, Institute for Control Engineering of Machine Tools and Manufacturing Units

Dr.-Ing. Arndt Wagner, University of Stuttgart, Institute for Structural Mechanics

Anna Westermeier, University of Freiburg, Plant Biomechanics Group Freiburg and Botanic Garden, Freiburg Center for Interactive Materials and Bioinspired Technologies (FIT)

Frederik Wulle, University of Stuttgart, Institute for Control Engineering of Machine Tools and Manufacturing Units

Dr.-Ing. Karl-Heinz Wurst, University of Stuttgart, Institute for Control Engineering of Machine Tools and Manufacturing Units

Bibliography

Plants in action

Betz, O., Birkhold, A., Caliaro, M., Eggs, B., Mader, A., Knippers, J., Röhrle, O., Speck, O. (2016): *Adaptive stiffness and joint-free kinematics: actively actuated rod-shaped structures in plants and animals and their biomimetic potential in architecture and engineering*. In Knippers, J., Nickel, K., Speck, T. (eds.): *Biomimetic research for architecture and building construction: biological design and integrative structures*. Springer International Publishing Switzerland, Cham, pp. 135–167.

Caliaro, M., Flues, F., Speck, T., Speck, O. (2013): *-Novel method for measuring tissue pressure in herbaceous plants*. International Journal of Plant Sciences 174 (2):161–170.

Caliaro, M., Schmich, F., Speck, T., Speck, O. (2013): *Effect of drought stress on bending stiffness in petioles of* Caladium bicolor *(Araceae)*. American Journal of Botany 100(11):2141–2148.

Caliaro, M., Speck, T., Speck O. (2015): *Adaptive Steifigkeit bei krautigen Pflanzen – Vorbild für die Technik*. In Kesel, A. B., Zehren, D. (eds.): Bionik: Patente aus der Natur. Tagungsbeiträge zum 7. Bionik-Kongress in Bremen. Bionik-Innovations-Centrum (B-I-C), Bremen, Germany, pp. 168–173.

Kaminski, R., Speck, T., Speck, O. (2017): *Adaptive spatiotemporal changes in morphology, anatomy, and mechanics during the ontogeny of subshrubs with square-shaped stems*. American Journal of Botany 104(8):1157–1167.

Kampowski, T., Mylo, M. D., Poppinga, S., Speck, T. (2018): *How water availability influences morphological and biomechanical properties in the one-leaf plant* Monophyllaea horsfieldii. Royal Society Open Science 5(1):171076.

Kampowski, T., Mylo, M. D., Speck, T., Poppinga, S. (2017): *On the morphometry, anatomy and water stress behaviour of the anisocotyledonous* Monophyllaea horsfieldii *(Gesneriaceae) and their eco-evolutionary significance*. Botanical Journal of the Linnean Society 185(3):425–442.

Li, S., Wang, K. W. (2015): *Fluidic origami: a plant-inspired adaptive structure with shape morphing and stiffness tuning*. Smart Materials and Structures 24(10):105031.

Li, S., Wang, K. W. (2017): *Plant-inspired adaptive structures and materials for morphing and actuation: a review*. Bioinspiration and Biomimetics 12(1):011001.

Lv, J., Tang, L., Li, W., Liu, L., Zhang, H. (2016): *Topology optimization of adaptive fluid-actuated cellular structures with arbitrary polygonal motor cells*. Smart Materials and Structures 25(5):055021.

Pagitz, M., Lamacchia, E., Hol, J. (2012): *Pressure-actuated cellular structures*. Bioinspiration and Biomimetics 7(1):016007.

Vos, R., Barrett, R., Romkes, A. (2011): *Mechanics of pressure-adaptive honeycomb*. Journal of Intelligent Material Systems and Structures 22(10):1041–1055.

Movement without joints

Betz, O., Birkhold, A., Caliaro, M., Eggs, B., Mader, A., Knippers, J., Röhrle, O., Speck, O. (2016): *Adaptive stiffness and joint-free kinematics: actively actuated rod-shaped structures in plants and animals and their biomimetic potential in architecture and engineering*. In Knippers, J., Nickel, K., Speck, T. (eds.): *Biomimetic research for architecture and building construction: biological design and integrative structures*. Springer International Publishing Switzerland, Cham, pp. 135–167.

Betz, O., Wegst, U., Weide, D., Heethof, M., Helfen, L., Lee, W.-K., Cloetens, P. (2012): *Imaging applications of synchrotron X-ray phase-contrast microtomography in biological morphology and biomaterials science*. I. General aspects of the technique and its advantages in the analysis of millimetre-sized arthropods structure. Journal of Microscopy 227(1):51–71.

Blemker, S. S., Asakawa, D. S., Gold, G. E., Delp, S. L. (2007): *Image-based musculoskeletal modeling: applications, advances, and future opportunities*. Journal of Magnetic Resonance Imaging 25(2):441–451.

Cerkvenik, U., Dodou, D., van Leeuwen, J. L., Gussekloo, S. W. S. (2018): *Functional principles of steerable multi-element probes in insects*. Biological Reviews, doi:10.1111/brv.12467.

Cerkvenik, U., van de Straat, B., Gussekloo, S. W. S., van Leeuwen, J. L. (2017): *Mechanisms of ovipositor insertion and steering of a parasitic wasp*. Proceedings of the National Academy of Sciences of the United States of America 114(17), E7822:E7831.

Eggs, B., Birkhold, A. I., Röhrle, O., Betz, O. (2018): *Structure and function of the musculoskeletal ovipositor system of an ichneumonid wasp*. BMC Zoology 3:12.

Frasson, L., Ferroni, F., Young Ko, S., Dogangil, G., Rodriguez y Baena, F. (2012): *Experimental evaluation of a novel steerable probe with a programmable bevel tip inspired by nature*. Journal of Robotic Surgery 6(3):189–197.

Gorb, S. N. (2011): *Insect-inspired technologies: insects as a source for biomimetics*. In Vilcinskas, A. (ed.): *Insect biotechnology. Biologically-inspired systems*, ed. 2, Springer, Dordrecht, Netherlands, pp. 241–264.

Holdsworth, D. W., Thornton, M. M. (2002): *Micro-CT in small animal and specimen imaging*. Trends Biotechnology 20(8):34–39.

Lavoipierre, M. M. J., Dickerson, G., Gordon, R. M. (1959): *Studies on the methods of feeding of blood-sucking arthropods*: I. – The manner in which Triatomine bugs obtain their blood meal, as observed in the tissue of the living rodent, with some remarks on the effects of the bite on human volunteers. Annals of Tropical Medicine and Parasitology 53(2):235–250.

Michels, J., Gorb, S. N. (2012): *Detailed three-dimensional visualization of resilin in the exoskeleton of arthropods using confocal laser scanning microscopy*. Journal of Microscopy 245(1):1–16.

Quicke, D. L. J., Fitton, M., Harris, J. (1995): *Ovipositor steering mechanisms in braconid wasps*. Journal of Hymenoptera Research 4:110–120.

Wipfler, B., Pohl, H., Yavorskaya, M. I., Beutel, R. G. (2016): *A review of methods for analysing insect structures – the role of morphology in the age of phylogenomics*. Current Opinion in Science 18:60–68.

No joint ailments / From pure research to biomimetic products

Born, L., Körner, A., Schieber, G., Westermeier, A. S., Poppinga, S., Sachse, R., Bergmann, P., Betz, O., Bischoff, M., Speck, T., Knippers, J., Milwich, M., Gresser, G. T. (2017): *Fiber-reinforced plastics with locally adapted stiffness for bio-inspired hingeless, deployable architectural systems*. In Herrmann, A. (ed.): *21st Symposium on Composites*. Trans Tech Publications (Key Engineering Materials), 742:689–696.

Ellison, A. M., Adamec, L. (eds.) (2018): *Carnivorous plants – physiology, ecology and evolution*. Oxford University Press, Oxford, UK.

Howell, L. L. (2001): *Compliant mechanisms*. Wiley, New York, USA.

Körner, A., Born, L., Mader, A., Sachse, R., Saffarian, S., Westermeier, A. S., Poppinga, S., Bischoff, M., Gresser, G. T., Milwich, M., Speck, T., Knippers, J. (2018): *Flectofold – a biomimetic compliant shading device for complex free from facades*. In Smart Materials and Structures 27(1):017001.

Körner, A., Knippers, J. (2018): *Bioinspirierte Elastizität*. In Schumacher, M., Vogt, M.-M., Cordón Krumme, L. A. (eds.): New Move Architektur in Bewegung – Neue dynamische Komponenten und Bauteile. Birkhäuser Verlag, Basel, Switzerland.

Körner, A., Mader, A., Saffarian, S., Knipper, J. (2016): *Bio-inspired kinetic curved-line folding for architectural applications*. In ACADIA // 2016 Posthuman Frontiers: Data, Designers, and Cognitive Machines. At Ann Arbor, MI, USA, pp. 270–79.

Poppinga, S., Bauer, U., Speck, T., Volkov, A. G. (2017): Motile traps. In: Ellison, A. M., Adamec, L. (eds.): Carnivorous plants: physiology, ecology, and evolution. Oxford University Press, Oxford, pp. 180–193.

Poppinga, S., Joyeux, M. (2011): *Different mechanics of snap-trapping in the two closely related carnivorous plants* Dionaea muscipula and Aldrovanda vesiculosa. Physical Review E 84(4):41928.

Poppinga, S., Körner, A., Sachse, R., Born, L., Westermeier, A., Hesse, L., Knippers, J., Bischoff, M., Gresser, G. T., Speck, T. (2016): *Compliant mechanisms in plants and architecture*. In Knippers, J., Nickel, K., Speck, T. (eds.): Biomimetic research for architecture and building construction: biological design and integrative structures. Springer International Publishing Switzerland, Cham, pp. 169–193.

Poppinga, S., Masselter, T., Speck, T. (2013): *Faster than their prey: new insights into the rapid movements of active carnivorous plants traps*. Bioessays 35(7):649–657.

Poppinga, S., Metzger, A., Speck, O., Masselter, T., Speck, T. (2013): *Schnappen, schleudern, saugen: Die schnellen Fallenbewegungen fleischfressender Pflanzen*. Biologie in unserer Zeit / BIUZ 6 (43), pp. 2–11.

Schieber, G., Born, L., Bergmann, P., Körner, A., Mader, A., Saffarian, S., Betz, O., Milwich, M., Gresser, G. T, Knippers, J. (2017): *Hindwings of insects as concept generator for hingeless foldable shading systems*. Bioinspiration and Biomimetics 13:16012.

Schleicher, S., Lienhard, J., Poppinga, S., Speck, T., Knippers, J. (2015): *A methodology for transferring principles of plant movements to elastic systems in architecture*. Computer-Aided Design 60:105–117.

Skotheim, J. M., Mahadevan, L. (2005): *Physical limits and design principles for plant and fungal movements*. Science 308 (5726), 1308–1310.

Westermeier, A. S., Sachse, R., Poppinga, S. et al. (2018): *How the carnivorous waterwheel plant (*Aldrovanda vesiculosa*) snaps*. Proceedings of the Royal Society of London 285(1878):20180012.

Reliably withstanding high loads

Deville, S. (2010): *Freeze-casting of porous biomaterials: structure, properties and opportunities*. Materials 3:1913–1927.

Dittrich, R., Despang, F., Bernhardt, A. et al. (2006): *Mineralized scaffolds for hard tissue engineering by Ionotropic gelation of alginate*. Advances in Science and Technology 49:159–164.

Klang, K., Bauer, G., Toader, N. et al. (2016): *Plants and animals as source of inspiration for energy dissipation in load bearing systems and facades.* In Knippers, J., Nickel, K., Speck, T. (eds.): Biomimetic research for architecture and building construction: biological design and integrative structures. Springer International Publishing Switzerland, Cham, pp. 109–133.

Lauer, C., Grun, T. B., Zutterkirch, I. et al. (2017): *Morphology and porosity of the spines of the sea urchin* Heterocentrotus mammillatus *and their implications on the mechanical performance.* Zoomorphology 137:139–154.

Lauer, C., Schmier, S., Speck, T., Nickel, K. G. (2018): *Strength-size relationships in two porous biological materials.* Acta Biomaterialia 77:322–332.

Nickel, K. G., Lauer, C., Klang, K., Buck, G. (2018): *Sea urchin spines as role models for biologic design and integrative structures.* In Heuss-Aßbichler, S., Amthauer, G., John-Stadler, M. (eds.): Highlights of Applied Mineralogy. De Gruyter, Berlin, Germany, pp. 270–282.

Presser, V., Schultheiß, S., Berthold, C., Nickel, K. G. (2009): *Sea urchin spines as a model-system for permeable, light-weight ceramics with graceful failure behavior.* Part I. Mechanical behavior of sea urchin spines under compression. Journal of Bionic Engineering 6:203–213.

Schmauder, S., Schäfer, S. (eds.) (2016): *Multiscale materials modeling: approaches to full multiscaling.* De Gruyter, Berlin, Germany.

Schmier, S., Lauer, C., Schäfer, I. et al. (2016): *Developing the experimental basis for an evaluation of scaling properties of brittle and "quasi-brittle" biological materials.* In Knippers, J., Nickel, K., Speck, T. (eds.): Biomimetic research for architecture and building construction: biological design and integrative structures. Springer International Publishing Switzerland, Cham, pp. 277–294.

Speck, T., Bauer, G., Masselter, T. et al. (2018): *Biomechanics and functional morphology of plants – inspiration for biomimetic materials and structures.* In Geitmann, A., Gril, J. (eds.): Plant Biomechanics. Springer, Cham, Switzerland, pp. 399–433.

Toader, N., Sobek, W., Nickel, K. G. (2017): *Energy absorption in functionally graded concrete bioinspired by sea urchin spines.* Journal of Bionic Engineering 14:369–378.

Toader, T.-N., Haase, W., Sobek, W. (2018): *Energy absorption in functionally graded concrete under compression.* Bulletin of the Polytechnic Institute of Jassy, Construction. Architecture Section, 4. ISSN: 1224-3884, e-ISSN: 2068-4762 (accepted).

Weibull, W. (1951): *A statistical distribution function of wide applicability.* Journal of Applied Mechanics 18 (3):293–97.

Freezing – the right way

Bluhm, J., Ricken, T., Bloßfeld, M. (2011): *Ice formation in porous media.* In Advances in Extended and Multifield Theories for Continua. Springer, Berlin, Heidelberg, Germany, pp. 153–174.

Borja, R. I., Koliji, A. (2009): *On the effective stress in unsaturated porous continua with double porosity.* Journal of the Mechanics and Physics of Solids 57 (8):1182–1193.

Ehlers, W. (2002): *Foundations of multiphasic and porous materials.* In Porous media. Springer, Berlin, Heidelberg, Germany, pp. 3–86.

Ehlers, W. (2018): *Effective stresses in multiphasic porous media: a thermodynamic investigation of a fully non-linear model with compressible constituents.* Geomechanics for Energy and the Environment 15:35–46.

Ehlers, W., Häberle, K. (2016): *Interfacial mass transfer during gas–liquid phase change in deformable porous media with heat transfer.* Transport in Porous Media 114 (2):525–556.

Eurich, L., Schott, R., Wagner, A., Roth-Nebelsick, A., Ehlers, W. (2016): *Fundamentals of heat and mass transport in frost-resistant plant tissues.* In Knippers, J., Nickel, K., Speck, T. (eds.): Biomimetic research for architecture and building construction: biological design and integrative structures. Springer International Publishing Switzerland, Cham, pp. 97–108.

McCully, M. E., Canny, M. J., Huang, C. X. (2004): *The management of extracellular ice by petioles of frost-resistant herbaceous plants.* Annals of Botany 94 (5):665–674.

Prillieux, M. (ed.) (1869): *Effet de la gelée sur les plantes. Formation de glaçons dans les tissus des plantes.* Bulletin de la Société Botanique de France 16 (4):140–152.

Roth-Nebelsick, A. (2009): *Pull, push and evaporate. The role of surfaces in plant water transport.* In Gorb, S. (ed.): Functional surfaces in biology. Little structures with big effects. Springer, Berlin, Germany, pp. 141–159.

Roth-Nebelsick, A., Voigt, D., Gorb, S. (2010): *Cryo-scanning electron microscopy studies of pits in* Pinus wallichiana *and* Mallotus japonicas. IAWA Journal 31:257–267.

Schott, R. T., Roth-Nebelsick, A. (2018): *Ice nucleation in stems of trees and shrubs with different frost resistance.* IAWA Journal 39 (2):177–190.

Schott, R. T., Voigt, D., Roth-Nebelsick, A. (2017): *Extracellular ice management in the frost hardy horsetail* Equisetum hyemale L. Flora 234:207–214.

Nature as source of ideas for modern manufacturing methods

Breuninger, J., Becker, R., Wolf, A., Rommel, S., Verl, A. (2013): *Generative Fertigung mit Kunststoffen. Konzeption und Konstruktion für selektives Lasersintern*. Springer, Berlin, Heidelberg, Germany.

Christof, H., Gresser, G. T. (2017): *Räumlich gekrümmte Pultrusionsprofile durch UV-reaktive Harze*. 25. Stuttgarter Kunststoffkolloquium, Stuttgart, Germany.

Coupek, D., Kovaleva, D., Christof, H., Wurst, K.-H., Verl, A., Sobek, W., Haase, W., Gresser, G. T., Lechler, A. (2016): *Fabrication of biomimetic and biologically inspired (modular) structures for use in the construction industry*. In Knippers, J., Nickel, K., Speck, T. (eds.): Biomimetic research for architecture and building construction: biological design and integrative structures. Springer International Publishing Switzerland, Cham, pp. 319–339.

Gericke, O., Kovaleva, D., Haase, W., Sobek, W. (2016): *Fabrication of concrete parts using a frozen sand formwork*. In Kawaguchi, K., Ohsaki, M., Takeuchi, T. (eds.): Proceedings of the IASS Annual Symposium 2016. Presented at the Spatial Structures in the 21st Century, Tokyo, Japan.

Wulle, F., Coupek, D., Schäffner, F., Verl, A., Oberhofer, F., Maier, T. (2017): *Workpiece and machine design in additive manufacturing for multi-axis fused deposition modeling*. In Procedia CIRP. Volume 60, Elsevier, Amsterdam, Netherlands, pp. 229–234.

Rosenstein Pavilion

Kaijima, S., Tan, Y. Y., Lee, T. L. (2017): *Functionally graded architectural detailing using multi-material additive manufacturing*. In Janssen, P., Loh, P., Raonic, A., Schnabel, M. A. (eds.): Protocols, flows, and glitches – proceedings of the 22nd CAADRIA Conference, Xi'an Jiaotong-Liverpool University, Suzhou, China, pp. 427–436.

Kovaleva, D., Gericke, O., Kappes, J., Haase, W. (2018): *Rosenstein-Pavillon: Auf dem Weg zur Ressourceneffizienz durch Design*. In Beton- und Stahlbetonbau 113 (6):433–442.

Kovaleva, D., Gericke, O., Kappes, J., Sobek, W. (2018): *Rosenstein Pavilion: design and fabrication of a functionally graded concrete shell*. In Proceedings of the IASS Annual Symposium 2018. Boston, MA, USA.

Richards, D., Amos, M. (2014): *Designing with gradients: bio-inspired computation for digital fabrication*. In ACADIA 14: Design Agency [Proceedings of the 34th Annual Conference of the Association for Computer Aided Design in Architecture (ACADIA)]. Los Angeles, CA, USA, pp. 101–110.

Sobek, W. (2012): *Adaptive systems: new materials and new structures*. In Bell, M., Buckley, C. (eds.): Post-Ductility. Metals in Architecture and Engineering. Princeton Architectural Press, New York, USA, pp. 129–133.

Wörner, M., Schmeer, D., Schuler, B., Pfinder, J., Garrecht, H., Sawodny, O. et al. (2016): *Gradientenbetontechnologie*. In Beton- und Stahlbetonbau 111 (12):794–805.

Building principles and structural design of sea urchins / Potential applications of segmented shells in architecture

Adriaenssens, S., Block, P., Veenendaal, D., Williams, C. (eds.) (2014): *Shell structures for architecture: form finding and optimization*. Routledge, London, UK.

Bechert, S., Knippers, J., Krieg, O. D., Menges, A., Schwinn, T., Sonntag, D. (2016): *Textile fabrication techniques for timber shells*. In Adriaenssens, S., Gramazio, F., Kohler, M., Menges, A., Pauly, M. (eds.): Advances in Architectural Geometry 2016 (pp. 154–69). Zurich, Switzerland: vdf Hochschulverlag AG an der ETH Zürich. http://doi.org/10.3218/3778-4_12

Gibson, L. J., Ashby, M. F., Harley, B. A. (2010): *Cellular materials in nature and medicine*. Cambridge University Press, Cambridge, UK.

Groenewolt, A., Schwinn, T., Nguyen, L., Menges, A. (2018): *An interactive agent-based framework for materialization-informed architectural design*. Swarm Intelligence, 12(2), 155–186. http://doi.org/10.1007/s11721-017-0151-8

Grun, T. B., Mancosu, A., Belaústegui, Z., Nebelsick, J. H. (2018): *The taphonomy of Clypeaster: a paleontological tool to identify stable structures in natural shell systems*. Neues Jahrbuch für Geologie und Paläontologie 289, 189–202.

Grun, T. B., Koohi Fayegh Dehkordi, L., Schwinn, T., Sonntag, D., von Scheven, M., Bischoff, M., Knippers, J., Menges, A., Nebelsick, J. H. (2016): *The skeleton of the sand dollar as a biological role model for segmented shells in building construction: a research review*. In Knippers, J., Nickel, K., Speck, T. (eds.): Biomimetic research for architecture and building construction: biological design and integrative structures. Springer International Publishing Switzerland, Cham, pp. 217–242.

Grun, T. B., Nebelsick, J. H. (2018): *Structural design of the minute clypeasteroid echinoid* Echinocyamus pusillus. Royal Society Open Science 5(5):171323. doi:10.1098/rsos.171323

Grun, T. B., von Scheven, M., Bischoff, M., Nebelsick, J. H. (2018): *Structural stress response of segment-*

ed natural shells: a numerical case study on the clypeasteroid echinoid Echinocyamus pusillus. Journal of the Royal Society Interface 15(143):21–28. doi: 10.1098/rsif.2018.0164
Hollister, S. J., Kikuchi, N. (1994): *Homogenization theory and digital imaging: a basis for studying the mechanics and design principles of bone tissue.* Biotechnology and Bioengineering 43:586–596.
Krieg, O. D., Schwinn, T., Menges, A., Li, J.-M., Knippers, J., Schmitt, A., Schwieger, V. (2015): *Biomimetic lightweight timber plate shells: computational integration of robotic fabrication, architectural geometry and structural design.* In Ceccato, L., Hesselgren, L., Pauly, M., Pottmann, H., Wallner, J. (eds.): Advances in Architectural Geometry 2014 (Volume 1, pp. 109–125). Cham, Switzerland: Springer International Publishing. http://doi.org/10.1007/978-3-319-11418-7_8
Krieg, O. D., Schwinn, T., Menges, A. (2016): *Integrative design computation for local resource effectiveness in architecture.* In Wang, F., Prominski, M. (eds.): Urbanization and Locality (1st ed., pp. 123–143). Berlin, Heidelberg, Germany: Springer Berlin Heidelberg. http://doi.org/10.1007/978-3-662-48494-4_7
La Magna, R., Gabler, M., Reichert, S., Schwinn, T., Waimer, F., Menges, A., Knippers, J. (2013): *From nature to fabrication: biomimetic design principles for the production of complex spatial structures.* International Journal of Space Structures, 28(1), 27–40. http://doi.org/10.1260/0266-3511.28.1.27
Li, J.-M., Knippers, J. (2015): *Segmental timber plate shell for the Landesgartenschau exhibition hall in Schwäbisch Gmünd – the application of finger joints in plate structures.* International Journal of Space Structures, 30(2), 123–140. http://doi.org/10.1260/0266-3511.30.2.123
Schwinn, T., Krieg, O. D., Menges, A. (2014): *Behavioral strategies: synthesizing design computation and robotic fabrication of lightweight timber plate structures.* In Design Agency [Proceedings of the 34th Annual Conference of the Association for Computer Aided Design in Architecture (ACADIA)] (pp. 177–188). Los Angeles.
Sonntag, D., Bechert, S., Knippers, J. (2017): *Biomimetic timber shells made of bending-active segments.* International Journal of Space Structures 32, pp. 149–159.
van Berkel, B. (2012): *Pavilions: interview with Ben van Berkel.* https://www.unstudio.com/en/page/7577/interview-ben-van-berkel-pavilions (access date: 17.09.2018)
Wainwright, S. A., Biggs, W. D., Currey, J. D., Gosline, J. M. (1976): *Mechanical design in organisms.* Arnold, London, UK.

Snails as living 3-D printers

Barker, G. M. (2001): *The biology of terrestrial molluscs.* Oxon, CABI-Publishing, New York, USA.
Felbrich, B., Wulle, F., Allgaier, C., Menges, A., Wurst, K.-H., Verl, A., Nebelsick, J. H. (2018): *A novel rapid additive manufacturing concept for architectural composite shell construction inspired by the shell formation in land snails.* Bioinspiration and Biomimetics 13 (2):026010.
Frearson, A. (2014): *Foster + Partners works on "world's first commercial concrete-printing robot,"* Dezeen, http://dezeen.com/2014/11/25/foster-partners-skanska-worlds-firstcommercial-concrete-3d-printing-robot/ (access date: 26.02.2016).
Khoshnevis, B., Hwang, D. (2006): *Contour crafting.* In Kamrani, A., Abouel Nasr, E. (eds.): Rapid prototyping: theory and practice. Springer US, Boston, MA, USA, pp. 221–251.
Nebelsick, J. H., Allgaier, C., Felbrich, B., Coupek, D., Reiter, R., Reiter, G., Menges, A., Lechler, A., Wurst, K.-H. (2016): *Continuous fused deposition modelling of architectural envelopes based on the shell formation of molluscs: a research review.* In Knippers, J., Nickel, K., Speck, T. (eds.): Biomimetic research for architecture and building construction: biological design and integrative structures. Springer International Publishing Switzerland, Cham, pp. 243–260.
Reuning, A. (2018): *Komm, wir drucken uns ein Haus.* Deutschlandfunk, https://www.deutschlandfunk.de/additive-fertigung-auf-der-baustelle-komm-wir-drucken-uns.740.de.html?dram:article_id=416965 (access date: 06.05.2018).
Vermeij, G. J. (1993): *A natural history of shells.* Princeton, NJ, USA: Princeton University Press.
Wangler, T., Lloret, E., Reiter, L., Hack, N., Gramazio, F., Kohler, M., Bernhard, M., Dillenburger, B., Buchli, J., Roussel, N., Flatt, R. (2016): *Digital concrete: opportunities and challenges.* RILEM Technical Letters 1, pp. 67–75.
Wulle, F., Verl, A. (2016): *Bioinspiriertes Bauen.* X-Technik, Additive Fertigung.at. http://www.additive-fertigung.at/detail/bioinspiriertes-bauen_126503 (access date: 26.09.2018).

Evolutive approaches to explorative design methods in architecture

Bentley, P. J. (ed.) (1999): *Evolutionary design by computers.* Morgan Kaufmann Publishers, Burlington, MA, USA.
Frazer, J. (1995): *An evolutionary architecture.* Architectural Association, London, UK.

Groenewolt, A., Schwinn, T., Nguyen, L., Menges, A. (2018): *An interactive agent-based framework for materialization-informed architectural design*. Swarm Intelligence 12(2):155–186.

Holland, J. H. (1975): *Adaptation in natural and artificial systems*. MIT Press, Cambridge, MA, USA.

Lang, D., Ullrich, K. K., Murat, F. et al. (2018): *The* Physcomitrella patens *chromosome-scale assembly reveals moss genome structure and evolution*. Plant Journal 93 (3):515–533.

Lang, D., van Gessel, N., Ullrich, K. K., Reski, R. (2016): *The genome of the model moss* Physcomitrella patens. In Rensing, S. (ed.): Genomes and evolution of charophytes, bryophytes, lycophytes and ferns. Advances in Botanical Research, volume 78, Academic Press, Cambridge, MA, USA, pp. 97–140.

Menges, A. (2012): *Biomimetic design processes in architecture: morphogenetic and evolutionary computational design*. Bioinspiration and Biomimetics 7 (1):015003.

Nguyen, L., Lang, D., van Gessel, N., Beike, A. K., Menges, A., Reski, R., Roth-Nebelsick, A. (2016): *Evolutionary processes as models for exploratory design*. In Knippers, J., Nickel, K., Speck, T. (eds.): Biomimetic research for architecture and building construction: biological design and integrative structures. Springer International Publishing Switzerland, Cham, pp. 295–318.

Szövényi, P., Ullrich, K. K., Rensing, S. A., Lang, D., van Gessel, N., Stenøien, H. K., Conti, E., Reski, R. (2017): *Selfing in haploid plants and efficacy of selection: codon usage bias in the model moss* Physcomitrella patens. Genome Biology and Evolution 9 (6):1528–1546.

van Gessel, N., Lang, D., Reski, R. (2017): *Genetics and genomics of* Physcomitrella patens. In Assmann, S., Liu, B. (eds.): Plant Cell Biology. The Plant Sciences, volume 20, Springer, New York, USA, pp. 1–32.

From plant branchings to technical support structures / New branched loadbearing structures in architecture

Born, L., Jonas, F. A., Bunk, K. et al. (2016): *Branched structures in plants and architecture*. In Knippers, J., Nickel, K., Speck, T. (eds.): Biomimetic research for architecture and building construction: biological design and integrative structures. Springer International Publishing Switzerland, Cham, pp. 195–215.

Born, L., Möhl, C., Milwich, M. et al. (2018): *Textile connection technology for interfaces of fibre reinforced plastic-concrete-hybrid composites*. In Hausmann, J. M., Siebert, M., von Hehl, A. (eds.): Proceedings of Hybrid. Materials and Structures, pp. 28–33.

Bunk, K., Fink, S., Speck, T., Masselter, T. (2017): *Branching morphology, vascular bundle arrangement and ontogenetic development in leaf insertion zones and ramifications of three arborescent Araliaceae species*. Trees 31:1793–1809.

Hamm, C. (2015): *Evolution of lightweight structures: analyses and technical applications*.

Hesse, L., Leupold, J., Speck, T., Masselter, T. (2018): *A qualitative analysis of the bud ontogeny of* Dracaena marginata *using high-resolution magnetic resonance imaging*. Science Report 8:9881.

Hesse, L., Masselter, T., Leupold, J. et al. (2016): *Magnetic resonance imaging reveals functional anatomy and biomechanics of a living dragon tree*. Science Report 6:32685.

Jonas, F. A., Born, L., Möhl, C. et al. (2018): *Towards branched supporting structures out of concrete-FRP composites inspired from natural branchings*. In Mueller, C., Adriaenssens, S. (eds.): Proceedings of IASS Symposium.

Jonas, F. A., Knippers, J. (2017): *Tragverhalten von Betondruckgliedern mit Umschnürung durch geflochtene und gewickelte Carbonrohre: Tragfähigkeitssteigerung durch Aktivierung eines mehraxialen Spannungszustands im Beton*. In Beton- und Stahlbetonbau 112:517–529.

Jungnikl, K., Goebbels, J., Burgert, I., Fratz, l. P. (2009): *The role of material properties for the mechanical adaptation at branch junctions*. Trees 23:605–610.

Küppers, S., Thumm, J., Müller, L. et al. (2015): *Braiding of branches for the fibre composite technology*. In Edtmaier, C., Requena, G. (eds.): 20th Symposium on Composites. Trans Tech Publications, pp. 749–756.

Kyosev, Y. (2015): *Braiding technology for textiles*. Woodhead Publishing Series in Textiles, no. 158. Woodhead Publishing, Cambridge, UK.

Kyosev, Y. (2016): *Advances in braiding technology*. Specialized techniques and applications. Woodhead Publishing Series in Textiles. Woodhead Publishing, Oxford, UK.

Masselter, T., Hesse, L., Böhm, H. et al. (2016): *Biomimetic optimisation of branched fibre-reinforced composites in engineering by detailed analyses of biological concept generators*. Bioinspiration and Biomimetics 11:055005.

Masselter, T., Haushahn, T., Fink, S., Speck, T. (2016): *Biomechanics of selected arborescent and shrubby monocotyledons*. Beilstein Journal Nanotechnology 7:1602–19. Masselter, T., Haushahn, T., Schwager, H. et al. (2013): *From natural branchings to technical joints: branched plant stems as inspiration for biomimetic fibre-reinforced composites*. International Journal of Design and Nature and Ecodynamics 8 (2): 144–153.

Möhl, C., Born, L., Küppers, S., Jonas, F. A., Knippers, J., Milwich, M., Gresser, G.T. (2018): *Manufactur-*

ing of branched structures for fibre-reinforced plastic-concrete-hybrid composites. In: Hausmann, J. M., Siebert, M., von Hehl, A. (eds.): Proceedings of Hybrid. Materials and Structures, pp. 165–170.
Müller, L., Milwich, M., Gruhl, A. et al. (2013): *Biomimetically optimized branched fiber composites as technical components of high load capacity*. Tech. Text 56:231–235.
Müller, U., Gindl, W., Jeronimidis, G. (2006): *Biomechanics of a branch–stem junction in softwood*. Trees 20:643–648.
Niklas, K. J., Molina-Freaner, F., Tinoco-Ojanguren, C. (1999): *Biomechanics of the columnar cactus* Pachycereus pringlei. American Journal of Botany 86:767–775.
Otto, F. (1982): *Natürliche Konstruktionen*. Deutsche Verlags-Anstalt, Stuttgart, Germany.
Otto, F. (1995): *Verzweigungen*. SFB 230 (concepts SFB 230, volume 46), Stuttgart, Germany.
Rian, I. M., Sassone, M. (2014): *Tree-inspired dendriforms and fractal-like branching structures in architecture: a brief historical overview*. In Frontiers of Architectural Research 3:298–323.
Rosenbaum, J. U. (1991): *Fertigung von faserverstärkten Kunststoffbauteilen unter Einsatz der Flechttechnik*. Ingenieurwissen Kunststoffverarbeitung. Verl. TÜV Rheinland, Cologne, Germany.
Schwager, H., Haushahn, T., Neinhuis, C. et al. (2010): *Principles of branching morphology and anatomy in arborescent monocotyledons and columnar cacti as concept generators for branched fiber-reinforced composites*. Advanced Engineering Materials 12:B695–B698.
Schwager, H., Masselter, T., Speck, T., Neinhuis, C. (2013): *Functional morphology and biomechanics of branch–stem junctions in columnar cacti*. Proceedings of the Royal Society of London 280:20132244.
Schwager, H., Neinhuis, C. (2016): *Biomimetic fiber-reinforced composite structures based on natural plant ramifications serving as models*. Materialwissenschaft und Werkstofftechnik 47:1087–1098.

The plastid skeleton

Asgharzadeh, P., Özdemir, B., Müller, S. J. et al. (2016): *Analysis of* Physcomitrella *chloroplasts to reveal adaptation principles leading to structural stability at the nano-scale*. In Knippers, J., Nickel, K., Speck, T. (eds.): Biomimetic research for architecture and building construction: biological design and integrative structures. Springer International Publishing Switzerland, Cham, pp. 261–275.
Asgharzadeh, P., Özdemir, B., Müller, S. J. et al. (2016): *Analysis of confocal image data of* Physcomitrella *chloroplasts to reveal adaptation principles leading to structural stability at the nano scale*. Proceedings in Applied Mathematics and Mechanics 16:69–70.
Asgharzadeh, P., Özdemir, B., Reski, R. et al. (2018): *Computational 3D imaging to quantify structural components and assembly of protein networks*. Acta Biomaterialia 69:206–217.
Gremillon, L., Kiessling, J., Hause, B. et al. (2007): *Filamentous temperature-sensitive Z (FtsZ) isoforms specifically interact in the chloroplasts and in the cytosol of* Physcomitrella patens. New Phytologist 176:299–310.
Ingber, D. E. (2003): *Tensegrity I. Cell structure and hierarchical systems biology*. Journal of Cell Science 116:1157–1173.
Ingber, D. E. (2003): *Tensegrity II. How structural networks influence cellular information processing networks*. Journal of Cell Science 116:1397–1408.
Ingber, D. E., Wang, N., Stamenovic´, D. (2014): *Tensegrity, cellular biophysics, and the mechanics of living systems*. Reports on Progress in Physics 77:046603.
Kiessling, J., Martin, A., Gremillion, L. et al. (2004): *Dual targeting of plastid division protein FtsZ to chloroplasts and the cytoplasm*. EMBO Reports 5:889–894.
Martin, A., Lang, D., Hanke, S. et al. (2009): *Targeted gene knockouts reveal overlapping functions of the five* Physcomitrella patens *FtsZ isoforms in chloroplast division, chloroplast shaping, cell patterning, plant development, and gravity sensing*. Molecular Plant 2:1359–1372.
Özdemir, B., Asgharzadeh, P., Birkhold, A. et al. (2018): *Cytological analysis and structural quantification of FtsZ1-2 and FtsZ2-1 network characteristics in* Physcomitrella patens. Scientific Reports 8:11165.
Suppanz, I., Sarnighausen, E., Reski, R. (2007): *An integrated physiological and genetic approach to the dynamics of FtsZ targeting and organisation in a moss,* Physcomitrella patens. Protoplasma 232:1–9.
Terbush, A. D., Porzondek, C. A., Osteryoung, K. W. (2016): *Functional analysis of the chloroplast division complex using schizosaccharomyces pombe as a heterologous expression system*. Microscopy and Microanalysis 22:275–289.

Abstracting instead of copying

Alon, U. (2006): *An introduction to systems biology: design principles of biological circuits*. Chapman and Hall/CRC.
Cercignani, C. (1998): *Ludwig Boltzmann: the man who trusted atoms*. Oxford University Press, Oxford, UK.
Hentschel, K. (2011): *Analogien in Naturwissenschaften, Medizin und Technik*. In Wissenschaftliche Verlagsgesellschaft, Stuttgart, Germany.

Hodgkin, A. L., Huxley, A. F. (1952): *A quantitative description of membrane current and its application to conduction and excitation in nerve*. Journal of Physiology 117 (4):500–544.

Newton, I. (1833): *Philosophiae naturalis principia mathematica*, 1st ed., G. Brookman.

Paul, D., Dehkordi, L. K. F., von Scheven, M., Bischoff, M., Radde, N. (2016): *Structural design with biological methods: optimality, multi-functionality and robustness*. In Knippers, J., Nickel, K., Speck, T. (eds.): Biomimetic research for architecture and building construction: biological design and integrative structures. Springer International Publishing Switzerland, Cham, pp. 341–360.

Paul, D., Radde, N. (2016): *Robustness and filtering properties of ubiquitous signaling network motifs*. IFAC-PapersOnLine 49 (26):120–127.

Paul, D., Radde, N. (2018): *The role of stochastic sequestration dynamics for intrinsic noise filtering in signaling network motifs*. Journal of Theoretical Biology 455:86–96.

Poyatos, J. F. (2012): *On the search for design principles in biological systems*. In Soyer, O. (ed.): *Evolutionary systems biology*. Advances in Experimental Medicine and Biology, volume 751, Springer, New York, USA, pp. 183–193.

Zurek, W. H. (1990): *The emperor's new mind: concerning computers, minds, and the laws of physics*. Science 248 (4957):880–882.

Functionalist, organic, and biomimetic architecture

de Bruyn, G. (2001): *Fisch oder Frosch oder: Die Selbstkritik der Moderne*. Bauwelt Fundamente 124, Birkhäuser Verlag, Basel, Switzerland.

de Bruyn, G. (2008): *Paranoide Urhütten-Suite*. In Blechinger, G., Milev, Y. (eds.): Emergency design. Designstrategien im Arbeitsfeld der Krise. Springer, Vienna, Austria, pp. 89–100.

de Bruyn, G., Ludwig, F., Schwertfeger, H. (2008): *Baubotanik. Wie Technik, Natur- und Kulturwissenschaften zu einer neuen Architekturform verwachsen*. Kultur und Technik, Themenheft für Forschung, Universität Stuttgart, pp. 56–65.

de Bruyn, G. (2009): *Artefakt und Biofakt*. In Lemke Haarmann (ed.): Kultur/Natur. Kunst und Philosophie im Kontext der Stadtentwicklung. Jovis, Berlin, Germany, pp. 83–92.

de Bruyn, G. (2012): *Architektur und Natur*. In Pfeifer, G.: Zwischenräume. Bauten und Projekte 1975–2000. syntagma, Freiburg, Germany, pp. 7–15.

Drack, M., Betz, O. (2017): *The basis of theory building in biology lies in the organism concept: a historical perspective on the shoulders of three giants*. Organisms. Journal of Biological Sciences 1:69–82.

Drack, M., Limpinsel, M., de Bruyn, G., Nebelsick, J. H., Betz, O. (2017): *Towards a theoretical clarification of biomimetics using conceptual tools from engineering design*. Bioinspiration and Biomimetics 13:016007.

Maier, W., Zoglauer, T. (eds.) (1994): *Technomorphe Organismuskonzepte. Modellübertragungen zwischen Biologie und Technik*. problemata 128, frommann-holzboog, Stuttgart, Germany.

Nönnig, J. R. (2007): *Architektur. Sprache. Komplexität*. Acht Essays zur Architekturepistemologie. Bauhaus University, Weimar, Germany.

Ruskin, J. (1989): *The seven lamps of architecture*. Dover Publications 72, New York, USA.

The biomimetic promise

Antony, F., Grießhammer, R., Speck, T., Speck, O. (2014): *Sustainability assessment of a lightweight biomimetic ceiling structure*. Bioinspiration and Biomimetics 9(1):016013.

Antony, F., Grießhammer, R., Speck, T., Speck, O. (2016): *The cleaner – the greener? Product sustainability assessment of the biomimetic façade paint Lotusan® in comparison to the conventional façade paint Jumbosil®*. Beilstein Journal of Nanotechnology 7:2100-2115.

Antony, F., Mai, F., Speck, T., Speck, O. (2012): *Bionik – Vorbild Natur als Versprechen für nachhaltige Technikentwicklung?* Naturwissenschaftliche Rundschau 65 (4):175–182.

Grober, U. (2013): *Die Entdeckung der Nachhaltigkeit: Kulturgeschichte eines Begriffs*. Antje Kunstmann, Munich, Germany.

Horn, R., Dahy, H., Gantner, J., Speck, O., Leistner, P. (2018): *Bio-inspired sustainability assessment for building product development – concept and case study*. Sustainability 10 (1):130–154.

Horn, R., Gantner, J., Widmer, L., Sedlbauer, K. P., Speck, O. (2016): *Bio-inspired sustainability assessment – a conceptual framework*. In Knippers, J., Nickel, K., Speck, T. (eds.): Biomimetic research for architecture and building construction: biological design and integrative structures. Springer International Publishing Switzerland, Cham, pp. 361–377.

Mead, T., Jeanrenaud, S. (2017): *The elephant in the room: biomimetics and sustainability?* Bioinspired, Biomimetic and Nanobiomaterials 6 (2):113–121.

Speck, O., Speck, D., Horn, R., Gantner, J., Sedlbauer, K. P. (2017): *Biomimetic bio-inspired biomorph sustainable? An attempt to classify and clarify biology-derived technical developments*. Bioinspiration and Biomimetics 12(1):011004.

von Gleich, A. (2007): *Das bionische Versprechen: Ist die Bionik so gut wie ihr Ruf?* Ökologisches Wirtschaften 22 (3):21–23.

Index

Images

Cover: Revised by Harald Pridgar adapted by PBG

p. 4/5 ICD/ITKE | **p. 6/7** J. Lienhard, ITKE, T. Kulikova/Shutterstock | **p. 8/9** ITKE | **1, 2** PBG | **p. 12/13** Festo AG & Co. KG | **3** Riccardo La Magna | **4** PBG/ITKE | **5, 6** PBG | **7** PBG/ITKE | **8–10** ITKE | **11** Festo AG & Co. KG | **12** A: Klaus Eisler, Universität Tübingen, B: EvE | **13** A: adapted by Barnes et al. (2002): The invertebrates. A synthesis. 815, Blackwell Publishing, Malden, B: EvE, C: adapted by Moyes & Schulte (2008): Tierphysiologie, Pearson Studium, München | **14** A: Klaus Eisler, University of Tübingen, B: EvE | **15** CMB | **16** EvE | **17** A, B: from Collatz et al. (2006): Der Kornkäfer und sein natürlicher Feind *Lariophagus distinguendus*. Entofilm, Kiel, C: EvE | **18, 19** CMB | **20** EvE, CMB | **21–26** PBG | **27–29** ITKE | **30** ITFT | **31** adapted by Born et al. 2017 | **32, 33** ITKE | **34** adapted by Körner et al. 2018 | **35** adapted by Körner et al. 2018 | **36** ITKE | **37–39** SFB/Transregio 141/Kristína Balušíková | **40** ITKE | **p. 52/53** Ulrich Stübler | **41–45** AMIN | **46–51** PBG | **52** A: Schenk, MPA, B, C: IMWF | **53** IMWF | **54** based on S. Deville, National Center for Scientific Research (CNRS), France | **55** adapted by D. Malangré, University of Bremen | **56, 57** AMIN | **58** M. Hermann, ILEK | **59** A: N. Großmann, University of Tübingen, B: N. Toader, ILEK | **60** PBG | **61** AMIN | **62** Anita Roth-Nebelsick, SMNS | **63** from Prillieux 1869 | **64** Anita Roth-Nebelsick/Rena Schott, SMNS | **65–67** Rena Schott, SMNS | **68, 69** Lukas Eurich, MIB | **70, 71** ILEK | **72, 73** ITFT | **74** ISW | **75** ITFT | **76, 77** ILEK | **78, 79** ISW | **80** ILEK | **81** from AMIN, University of Tübingen | **82–89** ILEK | **p. 102/103** Tobias B. Grun, University of Tübingen | **90–93** Tobias B. Grun, University of Tübingen | **94** David Iliff (CC-BY-SA 3.0) | **95** Oliver Krieg, ICD | **96–98** Tobias B. Grun, University of Tübingen | **99** Malte von Scheven, IBB | **100** ICD/ITKE University of Stuttgart | **101** ICD/ITKE/IIGS University of Stuttgart | **102–110** ICD/ITKE University of Stuttgart | **111–115** Christoph Allgaier, University of Tübingen | **116, 117** Renate Reiter, EPP | **118** Frederik Wulle, ISW (below), Christoph Allgaier, University of Tübingen (above) | **119** Frederik Wulle, ISW | **120** Benjamin Felbrich, ICD | **121** Nico van Gessel, University of Freiburg | **122–126** Anna K. Ostendorf, SMNS | **127** Florian Krampe, Christopher Voss, Achim Menges, ICD | **p. 142/143** PGB | **128** PGB | **129** PBG (left), ITFT (right) | **130–134** PGB | **135, 136** ITKE | **137** ITFT | **138** Volkstanzgruppe Kürnberg | **139** ITFT | **140** A: Jan Knippers, ITKE, B: Florian Jonas, ITKE | **141** Airport Stuttgart | **142, 143** Florian Jonas, ITKE | **144** A, B: University of Stuttgart, Bildarchiv, C: Florian Jonas, ITKE | **145** Cast Connex Corporation | **146** ITKE | **147** ITKE (A,C,D), ITFT (B) | **148** Florian Jonas, ITKE | **149** ITFT | **150** Kristína Balušíková, ITKE | **151** ITKE | **152, 153** Bugra Özdemir, University of Freiburg | **154** Pouyan Asgharzadeh, University of Stuttgart | **155** Wikimedia Commons (left), Nicole Radde, Debdas Paul, IST | **156, 157** Nicole Radde, Debdas Paul, IST | **158** Wikimedia Commons (CC BY-SA 3.0) | **159** Flickr.com/pov_steve (CC BY-NC-ND 2.0) | **160** www.werkbundsiedlung-wien.at | **161** Wikimedia Commons (CC BY 3.0) | **162** Flickr/johnath (CC BY-SA 2.0) | **163** ICD/ITKE | **164, 165** PBG | **166, 167** IBP | **168, 169** PBG | **p. 206/207** Etyra-Filament Pavilion, Victoria and Albert Museum, London, 2016. Achim Menges with Moritz Dörstelmann, Jan Knippers, Thomas Auer

AMIN: Applied Mineralogy, University of Tübingen
CBM: Contiunuum Biomechanics and Mechanobiology Group, University of Stuttgart
EPP: Institute of Physics, Experimental Polymer Physics, University of Freiburg
EvE: Evolutionary Biology of Invertebrates, University of Tübingen
FIT: Freiburg Center for Interactive Materials and Bioinspired Technologies
FMF: Freiburg Materials Research Center
IBB: Institute for Structural Mechanics, University of Stuttgart
IBP: Fraunhofer Institute for Building Physics, Stuttgart
ICD: Institute for Computational Design and Construction, University of Stuttgart
ILEK: Institute for Lightweight Structures and Conceptual Design, University of Stuttgart
IMWF: Institute for Materials Testing, Materials Science and Strength of Materials, University of Stuttgart
IST: Institute for Systems Theory and Automatic Control, University of Stuttgart
ISW: Institute for Control Engineering of Machine Tools and Manufacturing Units, University of Stuttgart
ITFT: Institute for Textile and Fiber Technologies, University of Stuttgart
ITKE: Institute of Building Structures and Structural Design, University of Stuttgart
ITV: Institutes of Textile and Fiber Research Denkendorf
MIB: Institute of Applied Mechanics, University of Stuttgart
MPA: Materials Testing Institute University of Stuttgart
PBG: Plant Biomechanics Group, University of Freiburg
PBT: Plant Biotechnology, University of Freiburg
SMNS: Staatliches Museum für Naturkunde Stuttgart

Concept: Ulrich Schmid
Translation from German into English: Hartwin Busch
Copy editing: John Sweet
Project management: Regina Herr
Production: Heike Strempel
Layout: Reimund Baumann, Julia Bergener, Ulrich Stübler
Cover design: Harald Pridgar
Typesetting and revised layout: Sven Schrape

Paper: 135 g/m² Magno satin
Printing: Beltz Graphische Betriebe Bad Langensalza

Library of Congress Control Number: 2018965519

Bibliographic information published by the German National Library
The German National Library lists this publication in the Deutsche Nationalbibliografie; detailed bibliographic data are available on the Internet at http://dnb.dnb.de.

This work is subject to copyright. All rights are reserved, whether the whole or part of the material is concerned, specifically the rights of translation, reprinting, re-use of illustrations, recitation, broadcasting, reproduction on microfilms or in other ways, and storage in databases. For any kind of use, permission of the copyright owner must be obtained.

ISBN 978-3-0356-1786-3

e-ISBN (PDF) 978-3-0356-1791-7
e-ISBN (EPUB) 978-3-0356-1789-4
German Print-ISBN 978-3-0356-1785-6

© 2019 Birkhäuser Verlag GmbH, Basel
P.O. Box 44, 4009 Basel, Switzerland
Part of Walter de Gruyter GmbH, Berlin/Boston

9 8 7 6 5 4 3 2 1 www.birkhauser.com